D1370642

This book is dedicated to

Karen,
Ann, Michael and Hannah

First published 1995
Revised and reprinted 1996
Reprinted 1997
Second edition 1997

10 9 8 7 6 5 4 3 2 1
Library of Congress Cataloging-in-Publication Data is available
on file from The Lyons Press.

ISBN 1-55821-669-3

Cover design by Macintosh Red, Edinburgh

Printed by Litografia Danona S. Corp., Oiartzun, Spain

CONTENTS

Tasting notes by
John Lamond

Background and history by
Robin Tucek

INTRODUCTION

I was weaned on Scotch whisky. Of course, that was in 1953, when alcohol was not forbidden to pregnant mothers. Neither was it in 1957 when my sister was born on the 2nd January after my mother had enjoyed a very traditional Scottish Hogmanay. However, my sister, despite strenuous family efforts, does not enjoy whisky!

As I always stress, I endeavour in my tasting to be as objective as possible, but naturally any tasting note is going to contain an element of subjectivity. Each distiller produces whisky to the highest possible quality. The fact that a Speyside tastes very different to an Islay is a matter of geographical, not qualitative, fact.

Since the early 1980s, when Robin began writing the distillery histories for the first edition, the industry has moved on considerably. The malt whisky connoisseur has gained wider, and deeper, knowledge, with a realisation by the distillers that what was once a very small, niche sector of the market is now an important part of their sales. Fifteen years since first putting it down on paper, but more than 40 years of research between us!

In this, our fourth edition (the first two were published as *The Malt File*), we have included Japan and New Zealand for the first time because of the shrinking nature of the world and the raising of quality standards in Japan and New Zealand as their experience deepens. We have also included the new distilleries of Cooley at Riverstown in the Republic of Ireland and Isle of Arran at Lochranza on the Isle of Arran.

Scotland's malt distilleries are working hard at the moment, with most in full production. Spread the word, don't keep the secret of malt whisky to yourself. If we can reopen one or two of the distilleries which were mothballed in the 1980s, then it will help to maintain the patchwork of flavours which is so essential for a truly healthy industry.

I am frequently asked, "What is your favourite malt?", or "What is the best malt?" There is no single answer to either question. Taste is very much a personal sense and mine is not necessarily yours. In any case, I do not have any one favourite, I enjoy (almost) all whiskies, depending on the mood. As to which is best – the whisky which you enjoy is the best.

And what we most want you to do is to continue to enjoy them in *all* their different and distinct styles.

Slainte!

JOHN LAMOND
MASTER OF MALT

No two single malt whiskies are alike. Even malts produced by sister distilleries using the same source of water have their own distinct individuality. But, although single malt whiskies cannot be neatly packaged and parcelled, certain whiskies do have shared characteristics which can, broadly defined, help to identify a malt's original provenance. For example, some, but not all, Islay malts share similarities, as do some Speyside whiskies, particularly those in that elastic glen, Glenlivet.

Traditional Regions
The traditional regions are Highland, Lowland, Islay and Campbeltown, although the latter's once numerous distilleries have now dwindled to just two. The Highland region may also be subdivided into Speyside, Northern Highland, Eastern Highland, Perthshire and Island (not to be confused with Islay) malts.

Islay Malts
Islay malts are the weightiest, most pungent and most heavily peated and are therefore generally the easiest to identify. These malts take their characteristics both from the peat used to dry the barley and their closeness to the sea. These factors give them what is often described as a seaweedy, medicinal taste and a distinct peaty flavour.

Lowland Malts
Lowland malts are dry, when compared with their Highland counterparts, and, although often quite spirity, are light whiskies with generally fewer individual differences than those of other regions.

Northern Highland Malts
Northern Highland malts are sweeter and have more body and character than their Lowland relations. They can have very distinctive and subtle characters, with a rich mellowness and fullness of flavour, but, equally, they can show a dry peatiness or a delicate fragrance.

Speyside Malts
The Speyside malts are the sweetest whiskies. Although they do not have as much body as some Highland malts, their flavours are richer and more complex with fruity, leafy and honeyed notes and a subtle delicacy of aroma which, once recognised, should be easy to identify.

Eastern Highland Malts
Eastern Highland malts come from the area between the North Sea coast and Speyside. Often full-bodied, they tend to have a dry, fragrant, fruity-sweet flavour, together with a touch of smokiness.

Perthshire Malts

The Perthshire malts, although Highland by definition, come from the area bordering the Lowland region. They tend to be medium-sweet, clean-tasting whiskies which are both light and fruity. Their identity may be best considered as falling somewhere between that of Lowland and Speyside whiskies.

The Island Malts

The Island malts from Skye, Jura, Mull and Orkney are characterised by a peaty, smoky nose and flavour. Some could be said to more closely resemble Islay malts while others are more like Northern Highland whiskies.

Campbeltown

If it is possible to categorise Campbeltown nowadays, then it must fall between the Lowlands and the Highlands in dryness, but shows a distinct smoky character with good body and a salty tang.

Irish Malt Whiskey

Irish malt whiskey (note the "e" in whiskey) is much lighter, smoother and fresher than its Scottish counterpart. This is, in part, due to the fact that it is mostly triple distilled, although there are a couple of Scottish single malts also produced in this way. Irish whiskey has traditionally usesd unpeated barley, unlike most Scotch whisky. The new Cooley Distillery company produces some peated whisky, however.

Although it is possible to map out generalised characteristics for single malts, each distillery produces a malt which has its own unique personality. It has its own micro-climate, wild yeasts, source of water and specific malting requirements. All of these factors (and even the shape of the still used) will have an effect on the individual character and flavour of a malt.

THE ART OF NOSING

It seems somewhat perverse that those who most appreciate the finest spirit in the world spend a great deal of their time not drinking it. They do not even go so far as serious-minded wine connoisseurs who swill it round their mouths before ejecting it. No, the master blender will use nothing other than his nose – and his experience – to assess and evaluate malt whisky. He noses rather than sips to preserve his ability to "taste" after the first sample. The reasoning behind this is simple: unlike wine or other less alcoholic substances, a distilled spirit will anaesthetise the taste buds, the very taste mechanisms which need to be used time and time again.

Aromatics
Our sense of aromatics (or "volatiles" as they are sometimes called) is derived from an organ known as the olfactory epithelium, located at the back of the nasal passage, which is directly linked to the brain. This helps to explain why we cannot taste so well when we have a cold.

Using the nose to detect aromatic ingredients provides a more immediate route to this area than via the back of the throat. The palate can detect only four taste elements: salt, sweet, sour and bitter. All other flavour characters are created when the palate warms the contents of your mouth and causes aromas to rise through your nasal passages to the olfactory epithelium. The palate should merely confirm the aromas detected by the nose, although there will be slight differences and the strength of individual flavours may vary.

Our sense of smell is one of the most under-used of the human senses, being relegated in most cases by sight and taste to a subordinate role and only called into use for rather crude analysis of whether something smells "good" or "bad". In fact, it is one of the most subtle of the senses, capable of detecting even faint changes in style or balance, and having a large "vocabulary" of its own. The tasting vocabulary used throughout this book has evolved over the years and, we hope, is easily comprehended by the reader.

The Master Blender
A master blender has an "educated" nose and can detect more than 150 separate flavours or characters in a whisky. Some of these will tell him that the product has been adversely affected in some way during maturation; others will indicate the type or style of wood in which it has matured. But although your senses are not as highly tuned as the blender's, each whisky has a sufficient number of different characteristics to enable you to distinguish one from another.

THE ART OF NOSING

The Nosing

In general, the nosing of malt whiskies is carried out in a small, tulip-shaped or similar glass which, being bulbous at the base and reducing to a relatively narrow rim, releases the aromatics and concentrates them at the rim, where the nose can pick up aromas. The sample is always diluted, or cut, with water; this releases the esters and aldehydes and thus makes the aroma more pronounced, the amount of water to be added depends on the alcoholic strength of the spirit which is being nosed. As a rough guide, malt whisky in the strength band 40% to 43% alcohol by volume (abv) should be cut with one third water, preferably a soft water - Scottish spring water - or clean tap water. Avoid waters with high mineral contents.

Higher Strength Whiskies

Other, higher strength whiskies should be cut with a greater quantity of water to reduce the sample to approximately the same strength. A high strength whisky of, for example 60% abv, should be diluted with twice its volume of water for sampling. There is a very good reason for this. The olfactory senses are adversely affected by the high alcohol level, even to the extent of feeling pain. Dilution removes the likelihood of this pain being inflicted. The quantity used for sampling should be fairly small, to allow plenty of room for the aromatics to collect in the glass. There is enough spirit for an adequate assessment in a 25ml measure of whisky diluted with water.

You will find that different elements in the sample become dominant at different periods of the nosing. You may become confused by concentrating too hard and, very often, your first opinion will be the correct one. As you become more expert, you will discover a greater range of aromas in the glass. For example, one person may detect a hint of rubber in a whisky, while that same characteristic may come over to another as something else - liquorice, for example. The difficulty with either tasting or nosing is in the descriptions used by individuals to describe sensation or flavour. Attempts have been made to categorise these flavours and John Lamond produced a *Malt Whisky Wheel* for *Aberlour*. This helped identify the principal flavour characteristics, and their taste relationships, using taste bands rather like spokes on a bicycle wheel.

While it is possible to create a common language to describe the aromas, the sense of smell is very subjective. Malt whisky is a gregarious spirit, so that the next time you are with friends discussing flavour, let your nose lead your opinions. You can still have as much fun trying to describe the aromas in your own words as you will get from finally drinking the whiskies. This is the fascination of single malts.

FILE NOTES

The pages in this book are arranged in alphabetical order by distillery name. In cases where two distinct styles of whisky are still produced at the same distillery, eg Longrow and Springbank, each whisky has its own alphabetical entry. Where the whisky is from an independent bottling source, this has been noted in the tasting notes.

There are three types of Scotch whisky: **Malt** whisky, **Grain** whisky and **Blended** whisky. **Malt** whisky is produced only from 100% malted barley. **Grain** whisky is produced from a variety of cereals which may, or may not, include a proportion of malted barley. **Blended** whisky is a combination of **Malt** whisky and **Grain** whisky, mixed together in the same bottle.

Single Malts

Most of the whiskies covered in this book are **Single Malt** whiskies. These are the products of individual malt whisky distilleries. For example, *Aberlour, Edradour, Laphroaig* or *Macallan*. However, the actual distillery name does not have to be identified on the label for a whisky to be called a single malt. Single malt may come from different casks of various ages, but they must all be from the same distillery. Not all distillery owners bottle their single malts under the name of the distillery. For example, the single malt from Macduff distillery is bottled as *Glen Deveron* by its owners.

Vatted Malts

Vatted malts are whiskies from more than one malt distillery which have been blended together, according to the specifications of the blender, to produce a fine, consistent product with a personality of its own. This whisky may well be given an individual name, such as *Sheep Dip* or *Poit Dhubh*. A **vatted malt** may not contain any **grain whisky**, otherwise it is **blended whisky**. Some **vatted malts** have been included in a section at the end of this book, as have some **single malts** bottled under "brand names" of independent bottlers.

Pure Malt

All Scotch malt whiskies, whether single or vatted, are **pure malt**. They are produced only from malted barley. If a whisky contains even one millilitre of **grain** whisky, then it is a **blended** whisky.

Grain Whisky

Grain whisky is produced from a mash of various cereal grains usually, but not exclusively, made from wheat, maize and barley. Both **malted barley** (barley which has started to germinate and then been dried to arrest its germination) and **unmalted barley** (barley which remains dormant) are used in the production of **grain whisky**.

FILE NOTES

Scotch Whisky

All **Scotch** (and **Irish**) whisk(e)y is produced by first grinding the particular cereal grain(s) to a coarse flour and then steeping this in hot water in a **mash tun**. The resultant liquid, called **wort**, is then cooled to between 22° and 24°C and run into a **wash back**. Yeast is then added. Once the yeast has been fermented out, a strong ale called **wash** remains, which is about 9% alcohol by volume. This pot ale is then distilled by heating it in **copper stills**, either in a continuous still, called a **Coffey** still, for **Grain** whisky, or twice in the case of **Malt** whisky using a pair of **Pot** stills. Three stills are used for **Irish** whiskey and the Scottish malts Auchentoshan, Benrinnes and Rosebank, these all being **triple distilled.** Pot stills are usually onion-shaped, with tall, tapering swan necks designed to help the alcohols condense, after which they are collected, cooled and put into casks.

A whisky, however produced, may only be legally described as **Scotch** whisky if it has matured in oak cask in Scotland for a minimum of three years. It must also have been bottled at a minimum strength of 40% alcohol by volume. There is no legal requirement for Scotch whisky to be bottled in Scotland. The same legal restrictions also apply to **Irish** whiskey (note the addition of an "e") in Ireland.

Whisky casks are made of oak, from the genus *Quercus*. The species *Q. cerris* (French oak), *Q. falcata* (Spanish oak), or *Q. alba* (American white oak) are used. Oak is a natural substance and therefore variations in density, quality and porosity are inherent. To further complicate and confuse the issue, the wood is split by hand and the casks are constructed by hand. Thus each cask is unique in that it is larger or smaller than its neighbours, its staves vary in thickness and no two pores are the same size. Its influence on the maturing spirit which it holds is therefore going to be different from that of any of its neighbours.

That is why the recipe for each blended whisky is different. A blender cannot state categorically that the blend for his "Hamish's Choice" Blended Whisky is, for example:

    23 casks of Glenardle, 10-year-old
    2 casks of Harport, 18-year-old
    15 casks of Royal Lochmaben, 7-year-old
    13 casks of Leith grain, 5-year-old etc.

because the proportions of each constituent whisky will vary with each blend. When you enjoy a bottle from a single cask bottling, you are drinking a very finite resource, you are consuming our heritage.

Continued on page 12

SCOTLAND'S MALT DISTILLERIES

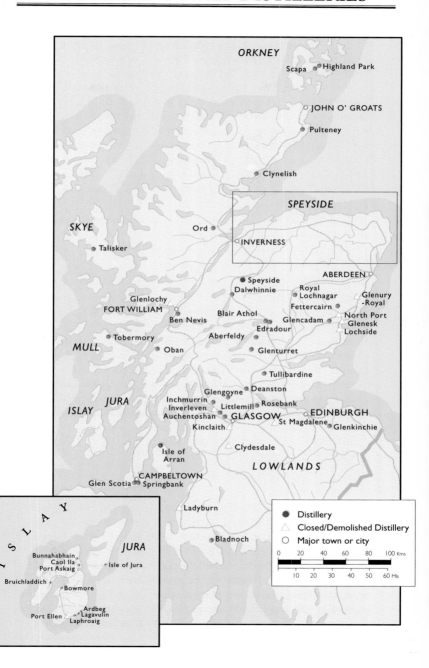

ORKNEY
Scapa • Highland Park

○ JOHN O' GROATS

• Pulteney

• Clynelish

SPEYSIDE

SKYE
Ord •

○ INVERNESS

• Talisker

ABERDEEN ○

• Speyside
Dalwhinnie

Royal
Lochnagar   △ Glenury
                      -Royal
Fettercairn
                   North Port
Glencadam •   △ Glenesk
                   Lochside

Glenlochy
FORT WILLIAM   △
Ben Nevis   Blair Athol
               •   Edradour
• Tobermory   Aberfeldy

MULL   • Oban

               • Glenturret

               • Tullibardine

               • Deanston
         Glengoyne
Inchmurrin △ Littlemill • Rosebank
Inverleven •
Auchentoshan △ • GLASGOW
         Kinclaith △   St Magdalene • • Glenkinchie
                              • EDINBURGH

JURA
ISLAY

         Isle of
         Arran

         △ Clydesdale

                   LOWLANDS

CAMPBELTOWN
Glen Scotia • Springbank

         Ladyburn

         • Bladnoch

Legend:
● Distillery
△ Closed/Demolished Distillery
○ Major town or city

0   20   40   60   80   100 Kms
10   20   30   40   50   60 Mls

Islay inset:
I S L A Y

JURA

Bunnahabhain •
Caol Ila •   • Isle of Jura
Port Askaig •
Bruichladdich •
         • Bowmore

               • Ardbeg
Port Ellen △ • Lagavulin
         Laphroaig

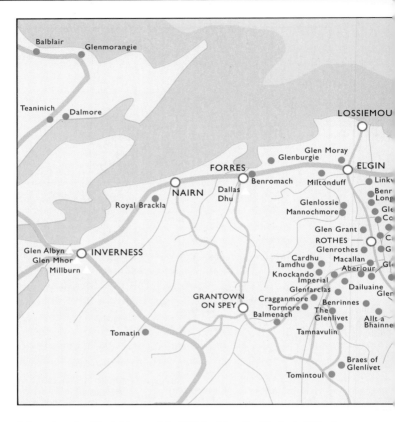

A **hogshead** will yield roughly 300 bottles (bottled at 40% abv strength) after 10 to 12 years, a **butt** 500, a **barrel** 200. The variations in the oak cask mean that the distiller cannot deliberately repeat exactly this magic of creation.

Generally the whisky drunk pre-1900 was young, only the landed gentry being able to afford to mature their spirit. The ageing cask could be new or previously have held wine, or rum, or butter, or herring, or anything which a cask could hold. Until the 1850s, whisky was sold by the distiller in cask and the publican or whisky merchant bottled it as required. From 1916, the government insisted whisky be aged in cask for a minimum of three years. The industry was then obliged to find supplies of casks in which to age their product. At this time, all Sherry imported into the United Kingdom was shipped in cask, to be bottled in the UK by the British merchants. Once emptied, the casks were surplus to the importers' requirements.

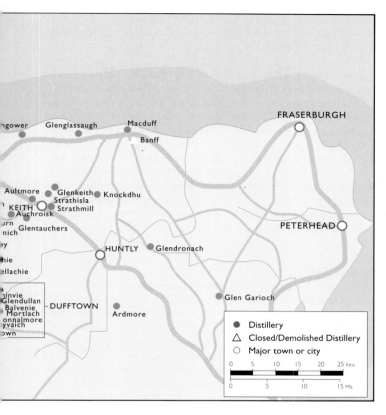

Ever keen to save a few pennies, the canny Scots were thus able to pick them up very cheaply. Likewise, because of the strength of the coopers' union in the USA at the time the laws governing Bourbon production were being created by Congress, it was written into American law that a Bourbon barrel could be used only once. When empty, they were worth only their value as firewood. Once again the thrifty Scots stepped in and established another economic source of cask. The situation has now changed in that, since 1983, the Spanish government has decreed that all Sherry must be bottled in Jerez and Sherry butts are now reusable by the Jerezanos. New Sherry casks are now a considerable cost to the whisky distiller.

With casks being used as many as four or five times over, the most usual type of cask used for filling Scotch whisky and Irish whiskey is known as a **Refill** cask. The casks are carefully checked by coopers between each fill to ensure that there will be no leakage of precious spirit. **First fill** Sherry casks are nowadays very rarely used to fill new grain whisky, second, third and fourth refill casks being the usual choice for such whiskies.

One element which has developed in importance in the past 20-25 years is the distiller's awareness of the origins of the cask. So much so that some now have them made to order by Spanish or French coopers and loan them to a Sherry bodega. *Glenmorangie*, preferring Bourbon casks, has even gone to the length of buying an oak forest in the Ozark mountains in Missouri to ensure continuity of supply of a particular quality of oak. The cask has moved a very long way from being a vehicle for transporting whisky or a container of a handy size for sale, and companies are now experimenting with whiskies aged in oak casks that have previously held Port, Brandy and Rum. Sometimes whiskies are filled in one type of cask, e.g. Bourbon, and then "finished" for their last few months or so of maturation in another, e.g. Sherry.

The respect of age
Much is made of the age of a whisky, and great respect and often considerable prices are given to whiskies of more senior years. The age of a whisky, if given on a bottle, must be that of the youngest whisky contained in that particular bottling. If all of the whisky used except for one centilitre is 21 years old and that centilitre is 11 years old then the whisky may only carry an age statement that it is not more than 11 years, although it could be described as being of a younger age, e.g. 10 years. The date of distillation of a particular cask, as well as the date of bottling, may be given on a label, but the age of the whisky itself, unless given in days, may be given only as not more than the number of complete years that the whisky has remained in cask. For example, if a whisky was distilled in May 1960 and bottled in April 1973, then the whisky is 12 years old, although it could be sold as an 11- or 10-year-old or less, or even not be given an age statement.

Whisky is usually about 70% alcohol by volume when distilled, slightly higher in the case of triple distilled whisky. The remainder of volume is water from steam condensed with the distillation. It is a clear, colourless spirit, with few subtleties of flavour, and the actual volume of alcohol will vary slightly from batch to batch. With the exception of a few selected casks, it is now industry practice to reduce all casks by the addition of water to a standard 11 degrees over proof, 63.4% by volume. While in cask, a whisky loses about 2% a year in evaporation. This is known as the **Angel's Share**. A whisky matures and changes in cask, the spirit leaching out

FILE NOTES

tannins and other flavours from the oak cask, and absorbing notes from the air passing through the porous wood while it lies slumbering in the warehouse. Just as the type of cask can make quite a difference to the whisky, so can the location at which it lies. A cask of Islay malt, maturing in a warehouse next to the Atlantic Ocean, for example, will give a very different whisky to a similar cask maturing in a warehouse at Broxburn or Leith. Most whisky is reduced further in volume in the bottling hall, being reduced to 40% by volume for the standard European strength and 43% by volume for the general Export strength. A few selected casks may be bottled at a higher strength. **Cask Strength** whisky is whisky that is bottled straight from cask without the further addition of any water.

The longer a whisky remains in cask, the more flavour it will acquire and the less spirit will remain. A 21-year-old whisky, for example, will therefore usually have more complex flavours than a 12-year-old whisky, although the degree of change is greatly dependent on the quality and type of cask used for filling. It will certainly be more expensive. Some whiskies are known to mature more quickly than others, Lowland whiskies generally being the quickest maturing, while others age particularly well, as is the case with many of the Speyside malts. However, although greater age means a more expensive whisky, it does not necessarily mean a better one. It is all a matter of personal taste. Some will not care much for a very woody, tannic 25-year-old malt, preferring a soft, honeyed 18-year-old and yet others may choose a sherried 12-year-old. As with most things in life, it is a matter of personal preference.

The following are some of the independent bottlers, starting with the two most important and influencial, Gordon & MacPhail and William Cadenhead:

Gordon & MacPhail

Established as licensed grocers in Elgin, Moray, in 1895, Gordon & MacPhail has just celebrated its centenary. Scotland's leading independent bottler, and largely responsible for the availability of so many bottled single malts, Gordon & MacPhail were shipping single malt whiskies round the world when many of today's best-selling single malt whiskies were unheard of away from the distillery. The company is now also a distiller, being the new owner of Benromach distillery. A very independently minded and spirited company and justly proud of what they have achieved in bringing single malt whisky to the world's attention.

FILE NOTES

William Cadenhead
Established in Aberdeen in 1842 and now based in Campbeltown, William Cadenhead are Scotland's oldest established firm of independent bottlers. The business is owned by J. & A. Mitchell of Springbank. Cadenhead believes in bottling whiskies that are uncoloured and without chill-filtration. The company has for several years now run a malt whisky shop at 172 Canongate, Edinburgh. In 1995, a second franchised Cadenhead shop opened in Covent Garden, London.

The Adelphi Distillery Ltd
Established in 1993 by the great-grandson of the former owner of the Adelphi distillery, Glasgow, which closed in 1902, the company specialises in cask strength, non chill-filtered, non coloured single malts.

Blackadder International
Blackadder International bottles non chill-filtered, non coloured single malt whiskies under the *Blackadder* and other labels.

Glenhaven
Marketed mainly in the USA, these whiskies are the selections of Bill Thomson, a former Managing Director of Cadenhead's.

Hart Brothers
The Glasgow-based company offers a selection of single malt whiskies, bottled from casks selected by Donald and Alistair Hart.

James MacArthur
Established in Edinburgh in 1982 and specialising in rarely=available malts from closed distilleries.

The Master of Malt
Based in Tunbridge Wells, Kent, The Master of Malt offers a selection of malt whiskies bottled under its own label.

The Scotch Malt Whisky Society
The Edinburgh based Society bottles cask strength whiskies for members. Each cask is bottled under a numerical code, so as not to identify the source distillery on the label.

Signatory
The Signatory Vintage Malt Whisky Company, to give it its full name, was established in Leith in 1988. Signatory bottles an extensive selection of single malt whiskies.

The Vintage Malt Company
Another young company, based in Bearsden, Glasgow, they specialise in vatted and single malts under their own brand names.

FILE NOTES

Judging and understanding the differences

Each of our tasting notes contains its own numerical rating system. This system, developed by John Lamond and Robin Tucek, is designed to give you an approximate idea of **Sweetness, Peatiness** and **Availability** for each whisky. It is intended as a helpful guide only and is not meant to be used as a qualitative or quantitative rating system for malt whiskies. In our opinion, malt whisky is too much of a personal preference to justify any attempt to give rating scores to individual whiskies. After all, one man's *Macallan* is another woman's *Laphroaig*. Some will choose *Bowmore* and others *The Balvenie*. We would not wish to position any malt before any other – all are to be respected and enjoyed for their relative qualities, all are made to similar quality levels and *all* are aged in oak casks. Only *you* can decide the whiskies which are your favourites.

The Malt Whisky File Tasting Codes

The scale runs from **0** to **10**, with **0** being the driest and least peated end of the scale, **10** the sweetest and most pungent. The ratings are a statement of fact; a guide to help you find those malt whiskies which are most akin to your own taste. If, for example, you like a malt with a **Sweetness** factor of 7 and a **Peatiness** factor of 4, then those other malts which have a similar rating should be of interest to your palate.

Most bottlings from the independents are of limited availability. We have given such bottlings a maximum **Availability** rating of 4. If the vintage listed is finished, then they normally follow up with the next vintage which, making allowances for individual cask influences, will usually be very similar to its predecessor. The **Availability** factor **0** means that this whisky is no longer available, **1** to **3** mean that these whiskies are difficult to obtain; **4** to **6** are available from the more specialist shop, **7** to **10** are increasingly more widely available. The **Availability** rating is based on the UK market, including Duty Free. We have not shown availability for Japanese whiskies.

Following the success of the independent companies in marketing single cask and cask strength whiskies, several of the major brand owners have now followed suit, making some very interesting whiskies available. These whiskies are often bottled with little or minimum filtration and it is increasingly frowned on to add caramel colouring to them. Such limited edition bottlings are an important and growing market but, because of the extra production costs involved, these whiskies are very much a specialist interest. Because each single cask of whisky can be such an individual product, they cannot possibly have the same consistency of style and taste as the more widely available malt whisky brands, each of which is bottled after blending together several carefully selected casks from the owner's warehouses of maturing whiskies.

The popularity of single malt whisky today owes much to the efforts of the specialist bottler in making such whiskies available when, with one or two notable exceptions, the brand owners showed little interest in producing malt whisky for anything other than blending. With the growth in interest and availability of single malt whisky, certain brand owners have let it be known that they do not like the independents bottling casks filled at their distilleries as single malts. This is a pity, as distilleries' own bottlings are always clearly identified for what they are, while the independents recognisably make their own name a clear endorsement of quality as part of their own label design. Some independent bottlings can be quite superb, with each cask bottled having its own differing and interesting personality. However, the better and rarer of these bottlings usually carry a price premium. With today's consumer increasingly wanting to know exactly what it is he is drinking, it is clearly neither realistic not fair to the consumer to expect such whiskies to be bottled without their origin being disclosed. Some distillery owners keep all of their cask fillings for their own use and this would seem to be the sensible approach for those distillers not happy about other companies bottling their own distillery's product.

Vocabulary

We feel that, as any tasting note is necessarily a very personal and subjective thing, some of our descriptions may need explanation, in particular for readers outwith Scotland. **Tablet** is a Scottish confection, similar to a firm fudge, very sweet and sugary. We have "created" some words which pedants might object to – for this we apologise. Some of these are: **toffeeyed**, meaning having the character of toffee; **cerealy**, having the aromas of the grain from which the malt is produced; **mashy**, retaining the aromas of malt and sugars from the mash tun. We hope that our manipulation of the language does not upset too many of you and that our reasons for this are understood!

Labels

In some cases, the labels depicted above the tasting notes are not the vintage tasted. This is usually because of the bottler "following" on with the next vintage — which has not yet been tasted. The current vintage should be very similar to the previous vintage when the whisky is bottled at a similar age. It is only where there are much greater older, or younger, age differences that these nuances become more noticeable.

Water

Although water from a kitchen tap is safe to drink in many parts of the world, it can often be far from ideal as an accompaniment to malt whisky. In some areas, the water is naturally quite chalky or has a high mineral content. In others, for reasons of public health, various additives are put into water supplies. In Britain, for example, varying amounts of chlorine are added to drinking water and this can affect the nose of a whisky.

Water filters can be an answer, but even they cannot refresh the water. In a perfect world, the water which we would add would come from the distillery's own water supply. As an alternative, clear, pure soft spring water with a low mineral content, such as one of the bottled Scottish waters, is eminently suitable.

Choose a still water rather than a sparkling one and avoid the more strongly flavoured waters. These may be excellent as a drink in their own right, but they adversely affect the delightful aromas of malt whiskies. Finally, don't be put off adding water. The belief that nothing but more malt whisky should be added to malt whisky is a misconception. Try it for yourself; one glass with one third water and one without. Your enjoyment will be enhanced.

FILE NOTES

Whiskies by post:
The following offer a mail order whisky service, as do many of the specialists listed on page 237:

Blackadder International, Logie Green, Glen View, Larkhall, ML9 1DA

Gordon & MacPhail, 58-60 South St, Elgin, Moray, IV30 1JY

The Scotch Malt Whisky Society, The Vaults, 87 Giles St, Leith, EH6 6BZ

The Whisky Connoisseur, Thistle Mill, Biggar, ML12 6LP

William Cadenhead, 172 Canongate, Edinburgh, EH8 8DF

Loch Fyne Whiskies, Inverary, Argyll, PA32 8UD

Abbreviations

Certain companies are mentioned throughout the text in abbreviated form. These include:

DCL   The Distillers Company Limited, now United Distillers (UD), a part of Guinness plc

Note: At the time of writing a merger is planned between Guinness and Grand Metropolitan

IDG   The Irish Distillers Group

IDV   International Distillers and Vintners, part of Grand Metropolitan

SMD   Scottish Malt Distillers. The malt distilling operational arm of DCL. Merged with SGD, Scottish Grain Distillers, to form SMGD, Scottish Malt and Grain Distillers. Now UMGD, United Malt and Grain Distillers. Part of Guinness plc.

How to use this book
The pages are arranged in alphabetical order by distillery name. In cases where two distinct styles of whisky are still produced at the same distillery, eg Longrow and Springbank, each whisky has its own alphabetical entry.

Visitors **indicates that the distillery welcomes visitors.**

Key to Symbols
The following symbols are used at the head of each entry to denote the geographical area of production.

A Arran		**IR** Irish
C Campbeltown		**S** Speyside
H Highland		**L** Lowland
I Islay		

HINTS ON PRONUNCIATION

Unless you are an expert Gaelic speaker, you may have difficulty in pronouncing some of the names of the malts in this book or of the areas in which they are produced. The following list contains those names that may cause a problem, with their phonetic alternatives:

Aberlour	Aber-lower
Allt-a'Bhainne	Olt-a vane
Auchentoshan	Ochentoshen
Auchroisk	Othrusk
Balmenach	Bal-MAY-nach
Bruichladdich	Brew-ich-laddie
Bunnahabhain	Boon-a-havun
Caol Ila	Kaal-eela
Cardhu	Kar-doo
Clynelish	Klyn-leesh
Craigellachie	Krai-GELLachy
Dailuaine	Dall-YEWan
Dallas Dhu	Dallas Doo
Drumguish	Drum-oo-ish
Edradour	Edra-dower
Glen Garioch	Glen Gee-ree
Glenglassaugh	Glen Glass-och
Glen Mhor	Glen Voar
Glenmorangie	Glen-MORanjee
Glentauchers	Glen-tochers
Glenury-Royal	Glen-you-ree
Islay	Eye-la
Knockdhu	Nock-doo
Laphroaig	La-froyg
Ledaig	Led-chig
Old Pulteney	Pult-nay
Pittyvaich	Pit-ee-vay-ich
St Magdalene	Magdaleen
Strathisla	Strath-eye-la
Tamdhu	Tam-DOO
Tamnavulin	Tamna-VOO-lin
Teaninich	Tee-an-inich
Tomintoul	Tomin-towel
Tullibardine	Tully-bard-eye-n

and finally...

Slainte (Cheers!)	Schlan-jer

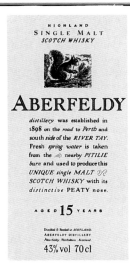

HIGHLAND
SINGLE MALT
SCOTCH WHISKY

ABERFELDY

distillery was established in
1898 on the *road* to *Perth* and
south *side* of the *RIVER TAY.*
Fresh *spring water* is taken
from the nearby *PITILIE
burn* and used to produce this
UNIQUE single MALT
SCOTCH WHISKY with its
distinctive PEATY nose.

A G E D **15** Y E A R S

Distilled & Bottled in *SCOTLAND.*
ABERFELDY DISTILLERY
Aberfeldy, Perthshire : Scotland.
43% vol 70 cl

ABERFELDY, PERTHSHIRE EST. 1896

Built between 1896-8 by Perth-based blenders, John Dewar & Sons Ltd. Run by SMD since 1930, Dewar's having joined DCL in 1925. The distillery building is most impressive. The still house and tun-room were rebuilt in 1972/3 using the original stonework. Four stills. Now part of United Distillers plc, Aberfeldy remains at the heart of the world famous Dewar's blend.

LOCATION   Immediately to the east of the village of the same name; next to the former railway line and the main A827 road and overlooking the River Tay.

NOTES   Previously about a dozen distilleries had been opened in the Aberfeldy neighbourhood by men who had been smugglers in earlier times. The distillery lies in a beautiful setting, with close by woodland housing a rare colony of red squirrels, hence the label above. Tommy Dewar set off on a two year world tour in 1892. He returned with 32 new agents in 26 different countries.

WATER   The Pitilie Burn.

Age 15 years   **Strength** 43% abv

Sweetness   7   Peatiness   7   Availability   6

Colour Straw/amber with gold highlights **Nose** Quite full and ripe with rich oaky vanilla, a creamy lanolin oiliness with a slight nuttiness **Flavour** Full, smooth, round and medium-sweet with layers of oak at the back **Finish** Full, round and rich, smooth and almost luscious **Notes** United Distillers bottling

Age 13 years   **Strength** 43% abv

Sweetness 5 Peatiness 7 Availability 2

Colour Very pale straw with lemon tinges **Nose** Fresh, medium-bodied with a fruity character and an earthy smokiness **Flavour** Fresh, medium-dry and smooth with an orangey fruitiness **Finish** Fresh, rich and quite long **Notes** Master of Malt bottling, cask nos. 7786-7

Distillation 1974   **Strength** 40% abv

Sweetness 6 Peatiness 7 Availability 4

Colour Straw/amber, gold highlights with a hint of green **Nose** Quite full, earthy, medium-sweet, quite peaty for the region with hints of hazelnuts **Flavour** Medium-dry, quite full and rich with a slight oily smoothness **Finish** Rich, slightly spicy with a touch of bitter chocolate and a smokiness on the tail **Notes** Gordon & MacPhail bottling

Distillation 1982   **Strength** 43% abv

Sweetness 6 Peatiness 6 Availability 1

Colour Straw with pale yellow highlights **Nose** Medium-sweet, frsh, malty and quite delicately peated with a rich lemon peel character **Flavour** Smooth, round, medium-sweet and fruity with a good, soft peat character **Finish** Long, clean and fresh with a soft shortbread sweetness on the tail **Notes** *Cooper's Choice* bottling from the Vintage Malt Whisky Company

The Cooper's Choice
Single Malt Scotch Whisky
DISTILLED AT
ABERFELDY DISTILLERY
DISTILLED
1982   AGED 14 YEARS   BOTTLED 1997
THE VINTAGE MALT WHISKY CO. LTD. GLASGOW G61 3RW
DISTILLED AND BOTTLED IN SCOTLAND
750 ml   PRODUCT OF SCOTLAND   43%Alc./Vol.

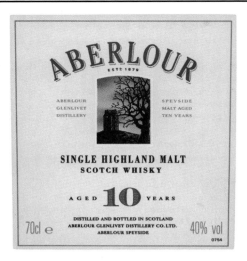

ABERLOUR, BANFFSHIRE EST. 1826

Founded in 1826 by James Gordon & Peter Weir. Rebuilt in 1879 after a fire. This is the date which appears on the label. Re-equipped with four stills in 1973. The Aberlour Glenlivet Distillery Company is a subsidiary of Campbell Distillers, itself a part of Pernod-Ricard.

LOCATION Aberlour is situated about a quarter of a mile below the Linn of Ruthrie, a 30 foot cascade on Ben Rinnes which falls into the pool which gives rise to the Lour Burn. The distillery is about 300 yards from the Lour's confluence with the River Spey.

NOTES Aberlour is a delightful village by the Lour at the foot of Ben Rinnes, from the summit of which, ten counties (from Caithness in the north, to Perthshire in the south) are visible. The early Christian missionary, St Dunstan (or St Drostan as he was known in Scotland), used the waters of the Lour for baptisms.

WATER A spring on Ben Rinnes.

Age 10 years **Strength** 40% abv

Sweetness 7 Peatiness 4 Availability 10

Colour Deep amber/golden **Nose** Full, rich, sweet and slightly toffee-like **Flavour** Quite full-bodied and sweet with a well-balanced richness **Finish** Good, full and long **Notes** Campbell Distillers bottling

Age 21years **Distillation** 1970 **Strength** 43% abv

Sweetness 7 Peatiness 6 Availability 5

Colour Deep, bright amber with rich old gold highlights **Nose** Quite fresh, lanolin, oily character, ripe, almost walnut character with a touch of hedgerow greenness at the back, full-bodied and delicately peated **Flavour** Medium-dry, full, fresh, walnuts, creamily smooth with a touch of spice and a hint of citrus **Finish** Long, clean and creamy with a gentle smokiness on the tail **Notes** Campbell Distillers bottling

Age No age statement **Strength** 57.1% abv

Sweetness 8 Peatiness 3 Availability 3

Colour Quite deep amber with old gold/bronze highlights **Nose** Quite full-bodied, almost stickily sweet, rich and honeyed with a slight green apple character **Flavour** Sweet, soft and round, with good body, a slight green edge and a touch of spice **Finish** Long, slightly chewy, sweet and lingering **Notes** Campbell Distillers bottling as *Aberlour 100*

Age No age statement **Strength** 43% abv

Sweetness 8 Peatiness 3 Availability 3

Colour Quite deep amber with bronze highlights **Nose** Full-bodied, medium-sweet with a slightly green apple perfumed hedgerow character, rich and softly oaky **Flavour** Rich, sweet, quite full-bodied and with a touch of spice **Finish** Long, sweet and lingering **Notes** Campbell Distillers bottling as *Aberlour Anique*

Age 15 years **Strength** 43% abv

Sweetness 7 Peatiness 3 Availability 4

Colour Deep amber with old gold highlights **Nose** Medium-sweet, fresh and clean with a slight green fruity note and a delicate peatiness **Flavour** Medium-sweet, medium-bodied, round and smooth with a very gentle peatiness **Finish** Long, very delicately peated, elegant and complex **Notes** Campbell Distillers bottling as *Cuvee Marie d'Ecosse*

Distillation 1990 **Strength** 43% abv

Sweetness 8 Peatiness 3 Availability 2

Colour Very pale straw with pale lemon highlights **Nose** Fresh, clean, medium-sweet, quite mashy and honeyed, it has a slightly green edge, a touch of a floral note and a hint of liquorice **Flavour** Sweet, fresh, spicy, round and quite full with a slight tannic note and a hint of liquorice **Finish** Long, sweet and full **Notes** Clydesdale Original bottling

ALLT-A-BHAINNE

NEAR DUFFTOWN, BANFFSHIRE EST. 1975

A modern building of contemporary architecture, built in 1975 by Chivas Brothers Ltd, a subsidiary of the Seagram Company of Canada. As a reminder of the traditional distillery, four small pagoda roofs are set on the main roof.

LOCATION   Sited on the southern slopes of Ben Rinnes to the north of the B9009, some eight miles south-west of Dufftown.

NOTES   Allt-a' Bhainne is the Gaelic for Burn of Milk.

WATER   A spring on Ben Rinnes.

Age 13 years   **Distillation** 1979   **Strength** 43% abv
Sweetness 9 Peatiness 4 Availability 1

Colour Pale straw with lemon highlights **Nose** Quite soft and sweet with a rich, ripe fruitiness - dried apricots, lightly smoky with a floral note at the back **Flavour** Soft, quite sweet, smooth and round with a fruity character and gently peated **Finish** Long, smooth, soft and almost stickily sweet **Notes** Cask no 026329, distilled 10/79 and bottled 2/93 for The Whisky Castle of Tomintoul

Distillation 1980   **Strength** 60.5% abv
Sweetness 8 Peatiness 6 Availability 1

Colour Deep amber with old gold highlights **Nose** Full, rich, unctuous, almost rancid, over-ripe character, toffee, vanilla, tablet and coffee **Flavour** Medium-sweet, ripe, rich, toffee, tablet with a tang of smokiness **Finish** Smoky and rich **Notes** Wm Cadenhead bottling - cask no 100027

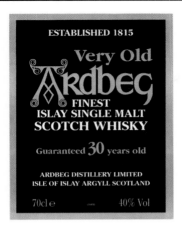

ESTABLISHED 1815

Very Old

Ardbeg

FINEST
ISLAY SINGLE MALT
SCOTCH WHISKY

Guaranteed **30** years old

ARDBEG DISTILLERY LIMITED
ISLE OF ISLAY ARGYLL SCOTLAND

70cl e   40% Vol

NEAR PORT ELLEN, ISLAY, ARGYLL EST. 1794

The original distillery was run by a notorious band of smugglers, before excisemen overran the place, destroying the buildings. John McDougall established the present distillery in 1815. Owned from 1979 by Hiram Walker and operated by Allied Domecq, Ardbeg had been closed before being purchased in early 1997 by the Glenmorangie Distillery Co. Ltd.

LOCATION A very romantic, lonely site at the water's edge on the south coast of Islay.

WATER Supply from Lochs Arinambeast and Uigidale.

Age 10 years   **Strength** 40% abv

Sweetness	1	Peatiness	10	Availability	1

Colour Pale straw with golden reflections **Nose** Big and peaty with an unexpected unusual sweet edge **Flavour** Full-bodied, peaty and rich with no hint of the sweetness indicated on the nose **Finish** Long and smoky **Notes** This was an Allied Distillers bottling

Distillation 1974   **Strength** 40% abv

Sweetness	1	Peatiness	10	Availability	2

Colour Amber with gold highlights **Nose** Big-bodied, dark and pungent with a burnt peaty character and hints of ozone **Flavour** Big, powerful and slightly salty with a burnt mahogany peatiness and quite firm tannins **Finish** Big, long, chewy and pungent with a salty touch on the tail **Notes** Gordon & MacPhail bottling

ARDBEG

Age 30 years **Strength** 40% abv

Sweetness 1 Peatiness 9 Availability 1

Colour Amber with gold highlights **Nose** Big, dry, pungent, dark and tarry; quite elegant, full- bodied, a relatively slight sea character with hints of creosote and cocoa **Flavour** Big, dry, pungent and tarry, not overwhelmingly peaty and gently chewy **Finish** Long with just a hint of richness, quite elegant and almost delicate **Notes** Allied Domecq bottling

Distillation 1967 **Strength** 52% abv

Sweetness 1 Peatiness 10 Availability 1

Colour Quite deep amber with bronze highlights **Nose** Big-bodied and pungent with a dark nuttiness, rich and full with a medicinal note - iodine/creosote/tarry rope **Flavour** Big, powerful and gently chewy with a burnt smokiness **Finish** Long, medicinal and smoky with a note of burnt Christmas cake richness on the tail **Notes** Signatory bottling

Age 21 years **Distillation** 1976 **Strength** 49.2% abv

Sweetness 1 Peatiness 10 Availability 1

Colour Pale amber with pale gold highlights **Nose** Full-bodied, pungent, dark and earthy with a dry, medicinal peatiness and a sweet vanilla touch **Flavour** Dry, powerful, dark, smoky and gently chewy with an edge of richness **Finish** Long, dry and finishes relatively delicately after the initial explosion **Notes** Adelphi bottling from cask no. 453

FROM ARDBEG, 21 YEARS OLD

ADELPHI
Distillery
LIMITED
EDINBURGH SCOTLAND

PURVEYORS OF RARE MALT WHISKIES AGED IN WOOD AND BOTTLED DIRECT FROM THE CASK

AGED IN WOOD AND BOTTLED DIRECT FROM THE CASK PURVEYORS OF RARE MALT WHISKIES

1826

KENNETHMONT, ABERDEENSHIRE EST. 1898

Built by Wm. Teacher with two stills and doubled in size twice - four stills in 1955 and eight stills in 1974. The distillery was built as part of a major expansion programme for the company's popular blended whiskies. Now operated by Allied Distillers Ltd, a part of Allied Domecq.

LOCATION   Situated alongside the Aberdeen to Inverness railway line, below the 1,425 ft Knockandy Hill. Close by is Leith Hall.

NOTES   Wm. Teacher use the make in blending "Teacher's Highland Cream". The stills are still coal fired and the steam engine, boiler front and other relics of the original distillery are preserved. One of the largest malt whisky distilleries in Scotland, Ardmore also houses extensive research laboratories.

WATER   A spring on Knockandy Hill.

Distillation 1977   **Strength** 40% abv

Sweetness 6   Peatiness 6   Availability 4

Colour Pale amber with pale gold highlights **Nose** Quite full and smoky with a slight green touch, medium-dry with a touch of richness **Flavour** Medium-bodied, quite smoky and medium-dry with good richness **Finish** Sweet with a good underpinning of smokiness a touch of spice and quite chewy **Notes** Gordon & MacPhail bottling

Age 18 years   **Strength** 46% abv

Sweetness 8   Peatiness 6   Availability 4

Colour Full amber with golden highlights **Nose** Light, slightly sweet and oaky **Flavour** Malty, richly sweet and full **Finish** Creamy and oaky **Notes** Wm Cadenhead bottling

DALMUIR, DUMBARTONSHIRE EST. CIRCA 1800

The name Auchentoshan is believed to derive from the Gaelic words "achad oisnin" possibly meaning "corner of the field". Not much is known of the distillery's early years, but a Mr Thorne has been recorded as owning it in 1825. It is now one of three distilleries owned by Morrison Bowmore Distillers, itself owned by Suntory of Japan. Although not the only distillery to experience war damage (see Banff) it had the misfortune to suffer heavily when Clydebank's shipyards were the target of enemy bombing, an event which caused extensive damage and great loss of spirit!

LOCATION The distillery is situated close to the Erskine Bridge on the A82, between Duntocher and the River Clyde.

NOTES Although geographically situated south of the Highland Line, the source of Auchentoshan's water supply is north of the line. Thus the distillery is a Lowland one, but its water supply is Highland. The make is triple distilled and very lightly peated. The first distillation takes an hour, the second five, the third nine hours.

WATER Near Cochna Loch in the Kilpatrick Hills.

AUCHENTOSHAN SELECT
Age No statement   **Strength** 40% abv

Sweetness 2   Peatiness 7   Availability 7

Colour Straw with lemon/gold highlights **Nose** Fresh and dry with a touch of green cereals and quite good body **Flavour** Dry and smooth with a slight richness and a touch of perfume **Finish** Quite perfumed with a touch of richness **Notes** Bottled as *Auchentoshan Select*. Carries no age statement. Morrison Bowmore bottling

Age 10 years **Strength** 40% abv

Sweetness 4 Peatiness 4 Availability 5

Colour Very pale straw with a slight green edge **Nose** Fresh, clean and floral **Flavour** Light, soft, quite sweet and slightly fruity **Finish** Finishes quite well, although light **Notes** Morrison Bowmore bottling

Age 21 years **Strength** 43% abv

Sweetness 2 Peatiness 4 Availability 3

Colour Mid-amber with old gold highlights **Nose** Soft, round, nutty and quite full-bodied with an almost buttery character **Flavour** Dry, soft and smooth with a hint of richness, gentle tannins and medium bodied **Finish** A hint of sweetness at first, nutty, long, quite delicate and complex **Notes** Morrison Bowmore bottling

MULBEN, BANFFSHIRE EST. 1974

The Singleton of Auchroisk, to give the whisky its full name, is produced at the Auchroisk distillery. That name being rather a mouthful, the company's own bottlings are marketed as "The Singleton". Independent bottlings are under the name Auchroisk. The distillery is managed by Justerini & Brooks (Scotland) Ltd, a subsidiary of IDV, which is itself part of Grand Metropolitan. Eight stills.

LOCATION On the north side of the A95 between Keith and Aberlour.

NOTES A new distillery producing its first make in 1975. Despite being a modern complex, the buildings are in the Scots vernacular style and the distillery received a Saltire Award (for outstanding architectural achievement in a traditional Scottish style). Sherry casks are used predominantly. Auchroisk is a showpiece distillery and has an old steam engine from Strathmill preserved in its entrance hall.

WATER Dorie's Well.

Age 10 years **Strength** 40% abv

Sweetness 7	Peatiness 5	Availability 8

Colour Mid-amber with old gold highlights **Nose** Quite full-bodied and medium-sweet with a dark peaty note, good nutty richness and a dark fruity character **Flavour** Medium-bodied and quite sweet, round with a touch of greenness to the peatiness and a definite toffee character to the richness **Finish** Long and smooth with a vanilla tablet sweetness **Notes** IDV bottling as *The Singleton of Auchroisk*

Distillation 1981 **Strength** 43% abv

Sweetness 7 Peatiness 5 Availability 4

Colour Amber with gold highlights **Nose** Full-bodied, clean, medium-sweet and fresh with a slightly green unripe peachy fruitiness and a delicately perfumed smokiness at the back **Flavour** Medium-sweet, quite smoky, creamily smooth with an almost chocolatey flavour **Finish** Long and round with a hint of coffee **Notes** IDV bottling as *The Singleton of Auchroisk*

Distillation 1983 **Strength** 40% abv

Sweetness 4 Peatiness 3 Availability 2

Colour Full amber with old gold highlights **Nose** Quite rich and medium-sweet with a dark nuttiness and reasonable weight **Flavour** Medium-bodied, round, dark, nutty and medium-dry **Finish** Almost dry, slightly bitter and with a toffee-like tail **Notes** IDV bottling as *The Singleton of Auchroisk*

Distillation 1976 **Strength** 40% abv

Sweetness 7 Peatiness 4 Availability 1

Colour Amber with gold highlights **Nose** Rich, quite full-bodied and minty with a peachy sweetness and good weight **Flavour** Quite full-bodied and smooth with a sherried nuttiness, a vanilla oaky-oiliness and quite delicately peated **Finish** Quite long, nutty and dark with a smokiness on the tail **Notes** IDV bottling as *The Singleton of Auchroisk*

Age 12 years **Distillation** 1978 **Strength** 59.3% abv

Sweetness 8 Peatiness 3 Availability 1

Colour Pale straw with lemon/yellow highlights **Nose** Fresh, fruity-citrus and cherries, quite full-bodied with a touch of raisins at the back **Flavour** Sweet, fruity, smooth and round with good oaky tannins and quite spirity **Finish** Smooth and spirity with a hint of cloves and quite long **Notes** Wm Cadenhead bottling as *Auchroisk*

Distillation 1989 **Strength** Natural

Sweetness 6 Peatiness 3 Availability 1

Colour Water-white with silver/white highlights **Nose** Very young, mashy and medium-sweet, floral with a slight fruity note and very light peat. **Flavour** Young, mashy, vegetal and medium-sweet **Finish** Long and spirity. **Notes** Clydesdale Original bottling as *Auchroisk*

SPEYSIDE
SINGLE MALT *SCOTCH WHISKY*

AULTMORE

distillery located between *KEITH* and *BUCKIE* began production in
1897. The name, derived from the *Gaelic*, means *"big burn"*.
Ideal supplies of *water* and *peat* from the *Foggie Moss* made this area
a haunt of *illicit distillers* in the past. *Water* from the *Burn* of
AUCHINDERRAN is now used to produce this *smooth, well balanced
single MALT ℈ SCOTCH WHISKY* with a *mellow* finish.

AGED **12** YEARS

43% vol Distilled & Bottled in *SCOTLAND.* AULTMORE DISTILLERY Keith, Banffshire, *Scotland.* 70 cl

KEITH, BANFFSHIRE EST. 1895

Built by Alexander Edward of Sanquhar, Forres, with two stills. The first of the make was produced in early 1897. It became a part of DCL in 1925 and was transferred to SMD's management in 1930. Rebuilt in 1970/71 and doubled to four stills. Now part of United Distillers plc.

LOCATION An isolated building standing on the A96 Keith to Elgin road close to the turning to Buckie.

NOTES Until 1969 a steam engine had been providing power, operating 24 hours a day, seven days a week since 1898. The old engine is still kept for show.

WATER The burn of Auchinderran.

Age 12 years **Strength** 43% abv

Sweetness 5 Peatiness 4 Availability 6

Colour Pale straw with lemon highlights **Nose** Rich, round, medium-bodied, a cooked mash character, appley and spirity **Flavour** Medium-bodied, lightly peated and medium-dry **Finish** Smooth, malty and quite long **Notes** United Distillers bottling

Age 13 years **Distillation** 1983 **Strength** 43% abv

Sweetness 6 Peatiness 5 Availability 2

Colour Very pale straw with pale lemon highlights **Nose** Fresh, clean and medium-bodied, medium-sweet with a slight apples and cloves aroma **Flavour** Medium-sweet, quite round and spicy, gently smoky and with good body **Finish** Long, sweet and smoothly peaty **Notes** A *Cooper's Choice* bottling from The Vintage Malt Whisky Co

EDDERTON, ROSS-SHIRE EST. 1790

The present distillery was built in 1872 when the then owner, Andrew Ross, decided to extend the business, the new buildings being higher up the slope of the hill. The older buildings were converted into a bonded warehouse. Extended from two to three stills in the 1970s by owners Hiram Walker and operated by Allied Domecq. Sold to Inver House Distillers in 1996. The fermenting of ale on the site is said to have taken place as long ago as 1749.

LOCATION Less than a quarter of a mile from the Dornoch Firth, about six miles from Tain on the A9.

NOTES Distilling in the area predates Balblair by a considerable number of years, there being many suitable sources of water and peat in abundance. Indeed, the Edderton area is known as "the Parish of the Peats" and once abounded in smuggling bothies. One of the malts associated with *Ballantine's* blended Scotch Whisky.

WATER The Allt Dearg, a burn four miles from the distillery.

Age 5 years	Strength 40% abv		
Sweetness 6	Peatiness 4	Availability 1	

Colour Very pale straw **Nose** Peaty, aromatic, quite light and spirity **Flavour** Slightly sweet, faintly peaty, spirity and quite light **Finish** Shortish and light **Notes** Sold on German market

Age 10 years	Strength 40% abv		
Sweetness 8	Peatiness 3	Availability 4	

Colour Mid-amber with gold highlights **Nose** Quite full-bodied, dark and sweet and lightly nutty with a toffee/aniseed character **Flavour** Sweet, nutty, quite round and smooth with quite good body and lightly peated **Finish** Clean and quite sweet **Notes** Gordon & MacPhail bottling

BALMENACH

SPEYSIDE
SINGLE MALT
SCOTCH WHISKY

Sometime in the early (19th, after *walking*
in the *CROMDALE* hills *with*
his 2 *BROTHERS*, *James McGregor* settled
and established

BALMENACH

distillery. Spring water from beneath those
same HILLS is still used to produce
this *RICH flavoured single MALT SCOTCH*
WHISKY of *exemplary* quality.

AGED 12 YEARS

43% vol   Distilled & Bottled in *SCOTLAND.*
BALMENACH DISTILLERY, Cromdale, Moray, Scotland.   70 cl

BALMENACH, CROMDALE, MORAY EST. 1824

The distillery was established in 1824 by James McGregor. At the time, it was at the centre of an area which was full of smugglers' bothies and illicit distilling was a way of life. Bought by SMD in 1930 and extended from four stills to six stills in 1962. A Saladin Box malting system was installed in 1964 and used until the mid-1980s. It is now part of United Distillers plc, but was closed and mothballed at the end of May, 1993.

LOCATION   The distillery lies in a bowl in the hills off the A95 main road heading towards Bridge of Avon from Grantown-on-Spey. The distillery stands about a mile from the former Cromdale station on the Spey Valley railway line.

NOTES   A branch line was built to the distillery in the late 1880s and the steam engine which worked the line is preserved on the Strathspey railway at Aviemore. Local lore tells that farmer James McGregor was visited by an excise officer just after the 1823 Excise Act had been passed. He was shown round the farm and experienced typical hospitality with a bottle of fine whisky. The officer then pointed out an outbuilding and asked what it was used for. "That's just the peat shed," came the reply. The officer said nothing, and continued to enjoy his whisky. After a few more drams, the officer made to leave. "If I were you, Mr McGregor," he said, "I'd take out a licence for that peat shed." McGregor took the hint and took out the necessary licence. In 1690 the Jacobites were defeated by William of Orange in a battle on the hills above the village of Cromdale.

WATER   The Cromdale Burn.

Age 12 years   **Strength** 43% abv

Sweetness 7   Peatiness 5   Availability 6

Colour Quite deep amber with bronze highlights **Nose** Quite full-bodied, heather floral characters, medium-sweet, rich and sherried with a light honeyed nuttiness **Flavour** Full-bodied, sherried and nutty with a touch of oily vanilla **Finish** Long, nutty and medium-sweet with a touch of tannin **Notes** United Distillers bottling

Distillation 1981   **Strength** 62.6% abv

Sweetness 6   Peatiness 5   Availability 4

Colour Very pale, watery straw with pale lemon highlights **Nose** Very mashy, youthful character, lightly spirity with a sweetness at the back **Flavour** Medium-sweet, rich and unctuous with gentle tannins, a hint of austerity at the front of the palate and lightly peated **Finish** Quite short, but smooth with a light chewiness **Notes** Wm Cadenhead bottling

Distillation 1972   **Strength** 40% abv

Sweetness 6   Peatiness 7   Availability 2

Colour Mid-amber with light bronze highlights **Nose** Medium-sweet, quite full-bodied, dark, rich, brazil nutty and smoky, oaky with a good unctuous richness **Flavour** Medium-dry, nutty, of good body with a soft richness and smoky oak **Finish** Long and slightly chewy with a slight perfumed smokiness **Notes** Gordon & MacPhail bottling

Distillation 1971   **Strength** 40% abv

Sweetness 5   Peatiness 7   Availability 2

Colour Amber/straw with yellow/gold highlights **Nose** Quite smoky & peaty, medium-bodied with a slight green nuttiness **Flavour** Dryish, smoky, quite full and delicately peaty with an edge of sweetness **Finish** Dry with oaky tannin and reasonable length **Notes** Gordon & MacPhail bottling

Age 18 years   **Distillation** 1977   **Strength** 43% abv

Sweetness 5   Peatiness 7   Availability 1

Colour Very pale straw with pale yellow highlights **Nose** Medium-dry and quite full-bodied with a slightly earthy peat character and a slight burnt vegetal note **Flavour** Medium-dry, smooth and creamy with good body and an earthy peatiness **Finish** Long and quite elegant with a slight edge of richness **Notes** Blackadder bottling; distilled 18 November 1977

EST? 1892

SINGLE MALT

Distilled at

THE BALVENIE

Distillery, Banffshire

SCOTLAND

FOUNDER'S RESERVE

MALT SCOTCH WHISKY

AGED **10** YEARS

The Balvenie Distillery has been owned

AND MANAGED BY OUR INDEPENDENT

family company for five generations.

AT BALVENIE

there are four maltmen, three mashmen, three tun room men, and three stillmen

AND BETWEEN THEM

they make all The Balvenie we bottle.

THE BALVENIE MALTMASTER

THE BALVENIE DISTILLERY COMPANY, BALVENIE MALTINGS, DUFFTOWN, BANFFSHIRE, SCOTLAND AB55 4BB

70 cle   PRODUCT OF SCOTLAND   40% vol

DUFFTOWN, BANFFSHIRE EST. 1892

Built next to William Grant's Glenfiddich distillery in 1892. The stills came second-hand from Lagavulin and Glen Albyn. Three further stills were added to make eight in all (two in 1965 and one in 1971). Floor malting is still carried out at Balvenie, this supplying about 15% of the distillery's malt requirement. The peat used is hand-cut locally, being dried and seasoned before being used to fire the malt kiln. The stills at Balvenie are heated using the heat waste from Glenfiddich to produce steam heat to boil them.

LOCATION Situated just below Glenfiddich on the lower slopes of the Convals, the hills which dominate Dufftown.

NOTES The Balvenie is an excellent example of just how different single malts can be. Standing next door to its more famous sister, Glenfiddich, it draws its water from the same source and shares the same supply of malt - even the distiller is the same person - and yet the two whiskies are very different in character. In 1992, 100 years after Balvenie was built, the Grants opened another new distillery, Kininvie, next door.

WATER The Robbie Dhu (pronounced "doo") springs.

THE BALVENIE FOUNDER'S RESERVE

Age 10 years   **Strength** 40% abv

Sweetness 8   Peatiness 3   Availability 8

Colour Straw with good golden highlights **Nose** Full and rich with a green edge, medium-sweet with an appley aroma **Flavour** Medium-dry, smooth, oaky and malty **Finish** Of reasonable length, quite rich **Notes** William Grant bottling

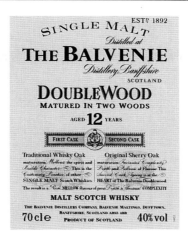

THE BALVENIE DOUBLEWOOD
Age 12 years   **Strength** 40% abv

Sweetness 7   Peatiness 3   Availability 7

Colour Quite full amber with old gold highlights and a hint of lemon **Nose** Quite full mashy/spirity and ripe with a slightly walnutty character and a fresh, almost Riesling-like diesel touch. **Flavour** Medium-sweet, slightly spicy, smooth and round with a dark nuttiness, a chocolatey/malty character and delicately peated **Finish** Fresh, warm, rich, quite tangy, long and with the walnut character of the nose. **Notes** Partly aged in a Bourbon cask, its maturation is finished off in a Sherry cask, hence its name *Balvenie DoubleWood*. William Grant bottling

The maltings floor at Balvenie

BALVENIE

THE BALVENIE SINGLE BARREL
Age 15 years **Distillation** 1978 **Strength** 50.4% abv
Sweetness 7 Peatiness 3 Availability 4

Colour Bright, pale mid-amber with yellow-gold highlights
Nose Quite full-bodied, ripe, rich and medium-sweet with an
unctuous oily honeyed vanilla-oak character, delicately peated
with hints of green apples **Flavour** Medium-sweet, quite full-
bodied, smooth and round with a backbone of oaky tannin, an
oily-vanilla texture and a slight green edge to the peatiness
Finish Very long and complex with hints of bitter chocolate,
hazelnuts, toffee, honey and a nice green coffee tang **Notes**
William Grant bottling. Bottle no 134 from cask no 199. This
cask was filled on 17.1.1978 and bottled on 13.10.1993. Sold
as *The Balvenie Single Barrel*

THE BALVENIE PORT WOOD
Age 21 years **Strength** 43% abv
Sweetness 5 Peatiness 4 Availability 2

Colour Mid-amber with bronze highlights and a slight ruby hue
Nose Soft, round, quite full- bodied and sweet with a rich toffee and vanilla oak character, a touch of beeswax and a note of
soft, ripe peach **Flavour** Quite dry with chewy tannins, good
body and richness and quite delicately peated **Finish** Long and
gently chewy with a touch of beeswax **Notes** Wm Grant bottling, finished in a Port pipe.

CONNOISSEURS CHOICE

Connoisseurs Choice, a range of single malts from various districts of Scotland.

In the Highlands are situated the greatest number of malt whisky distilleries.

SINGLE HIGHLAND
MALT SCOTCH WHISKY
DISTILLED AT
BANFF
DISTILLERY
Proprietors: Slater, Rodger Ltd

DISTILLED 1974 DISTILLED

SPECIALLY SELECTED, PRODUCED AND BOTTLED BY

70cl   GORDON & MACPHAIL   40%vol
ELGIN · SCOTLAND
PRODUCT OF SCOTLAND

BANFF, BANFFSHIRE EST. 1863

Built by James Simpson junior to replace an earlier distillery of the same name built in 1824. Rebuilt after a fire in 1877. Owned by SMD since 1932. Two stills. Closed and dismantled in 1983.

LOCATION Half a mile west of Banff on the B9139.

NOTES One of the first distilleries located to take advantage of the railways. On Saturday, 16 August 1941 a single German plane machine-gunned and bombed No 12 Warehouse. Exploding casks flew through the air and a local newspaper reported, ". . . thousands of gallons of whisky were lost, either burning or running to waste over the land . . . even farm animals became intoxicated". Cows were not milked because they could not be got to their feet. Banff was known locally as "Inverboyndie distillery".

WATER Springs on Fiskaidly Farm.

Distillation 1974 **Strength** 40 % abv
Sweetness 10 Peatiness 6 Availability 2

Colour Medium-peaty gold **Nose** Quite peaty, slightly oily with a slight hint of ozone **Flavour** Round, mellow and slightly spicy **Finish** Good, long, slightly sugar-sweet, perhaps a little overpoweringly so **Notes** Gordon & MacPhail bottling

Distillation 1976 **Age** 17 years **Strength** 60.5 % abv
Sweetness 6 Peatiness 6 Availability 1

Colour Mid-amber with yellow/gold highlights **Nose** Fresh and clean with a soft green fruitiness, hints of perfume and a cedar note **Flavour** Fresh, smooth, medium-dry and quite round with good body and gentle tannins **Finish** Of reasonable length, it has a light earthy smokiness with a green edge **Notes** Wm Cadenhead bottling

DISTILLED AND BOTTLED IN SCOTLAND

BEN NEVIS

SINGLE HIGHLAND MALT
SCOTCH WHISKY

BEN NEVIS DISTILLERY (FORT WILLIAM) LIMITED
DISTILLED IN 1972

75cl   55.6% vol

LOCHY BRIDGE, FORT WILLIAM   EST. 1825

Founded by "Long John" Macdonald in 1825. Owned by various Macdonalds until taken over by Ben Nevis Distillery (Fort William) Ltd in 1955, which installed a Coffey still. Later sold to Long John International Ltd (a part of Whitbread) in 1981, when the Coffey still was removed. Four pot stills. Sold by the Whitbread group to the Japanese company, Nikka, early in 1989.

LOCATION Situated two miles north of Fort William on the A82.

NOTES A cask of Ben Nevis was presented to Queen Victoria on her visit to Fort William on 21 April 1848. The cask was not to be opened until the Prince of Wales reached his majority 15 years later.

WATER Allt a' Mhuilinn (The Mill Burn), which flows from two small lochans, Coire Leis and Coire na' Ciste, situated at over 3,000 ft up Ben Nevis.

Age 21 years   **Strength** 55.6% abv

Sweetness 5   Peatiness 6   Availability 2

Colour Quite deep amber with bronze highlights **Nose** Full-bodied, rich, oaky and medium-sweet with a firm peatiness **Flavour** Full-bodied, dark and nutty with a rich peatiness, medium-sweet with quite gentle oaky tannins **Finish** Long, powerful and delicately smoky with a tangy touch of spice and just an edge of sweetness on the tail **Notes** Ben Nevis bottling

Age 22 years   **Strength** 46% abv

Sweetness 3   Peatiness 6   Availability 2

Colour Deep, peaty amber with good gold highlights **Nose** Spirity, malty, dryish, lightly peated and slightly leafy **Flavour** Dry, lightly peaty, spirity and slightly spicy **Finish** Smooth, clean and enjoyably long **Notes** Wm Cadenhead bottling

Distillation 1967 **Age** 26 years **Strength** 58% abv

Sweetness 4 Peatiness 5 Availability 3

Colour Mid-amber with old gold highlights **Nose** Medium-sweet, quite rich and fresh with a touch of oily oaky vanilla, a green character and medium-bodied **Flavour** Medium-dry, quite full and rich with a slight oily smoothness **Finish** Long and gently smoky with good rich sweetness and a tail of bitter toffee **Notes** Ben Nevis bottling

Distillation 1972 **Strength** 60.5% abv

Sweetness 5 Peatiness 6 Availability 2

Colour Pale amber with gold highlights **Nose** Quite full, earthy, medium-sweet, quite peaty for the region with hints of hazelnuts **Flavour** Medium-sweet, smoky and smooth with a little tannin and a green freshness **Finish** Long and gently smoky with a touch of spice **Notes** Ben Nevis bottling from cask no 619

Distillation 1977 **Age** 15 years **Strength** 60.9% abv

Sweetness 6 Peatiness 5 Availability 1

Colour Straw with yellow/pale gold highlights **Nose** Full-bodied with a dark peatiness and a rich, medium-dry tang of orange peel **Flavour** Soft, medium-sweet, rich and velvety smooth with a gentle peatiness **Finish** Long, fresh, clean and rich with a lightly toffeeed tail **Notes** Wm Cadenhead bottling

BEN NEVIS DISTILLERY.

BENRIACH DISTILLERY
EST. 1898
A SINGLE
PURE HIGHLAND MALT
Scotch Whisky
Benriach Distillery, in the heart of the Highlands,
still malts its own barley. The resulting whisky has
a unique and attractive delicacy
PRODUCED AND BOTTLED BY THE
BENRIACH
DISTILLERY CO
ELGIN, MORAYSHIRE, SCOTLAND, IV30 3SJ
Distilled and Bottled in Scotland
AGED 10 YEARS
70 cl ℮ 43%vol

LONGMORN, NR ELGIN, MORAY EST. 1898

Founded in 1898 as the whisky market moved suddenly into recession. It was then closed in 1900 and did not open again until 1965, when it was rebuilt by The Glenlivet Distillers Ltd. Owned by The Seagram Company of Canada since 1977. Four stills.

LOCATION Situated three miles south of Elgin to the east of the A941.

NOTES The floor maltings are still in use. Previously only available from independent bottlers, Seagram introduced their own bottling in 1994. The sister distillery to the much prized Longmorn next door, both distilleries were built within four years of each other in the boom years of the 1890s. Like Longmorn, it is an important constituent of the flagship Seagram blend, Chivas Regal.

WATER Local springs.

Age 10 years **Strength** 43% abv

Sweetness 6 Peatiness 3 Availability 7

Colour Quite pale straw with lemon highlights **Nose** Fresh, green appley bubble-gum character, lightly malty and lightly peated, medium-sweet **Flavour** Medium-dry, soft, quite full-bodied with a chocolatey richness and touches of spice and coffee **Finish** Rich with a tang of coffee, quite long and lingering **Notes** Seagram bottling

Distillation 1969 **Strength** 40% abv

Sweetness 6 Peatiness 3 Availability 4

Colour Pale straw with gold highlights **Nose** Sweet, distinctive fruitiness, fresh and appley **Flavour** Sweet, appley, distinctive, reminiscent of Calvados **Finish** Spicy and good with the apple flavour lingering **Notes** Gordon & MacPhail bottling

SPEYSIDE
SINGLE MALT
SCOTCH WHISKY

BENRINNES

distillery stands on the
northern shoulder of BEN RINNES
700 feet above *sea level*.
It is ideally located to exploit
the *natural advantages* of the
area-pure *air*, *peat* and
barley and the *finest* of *hill* water,
which rises through *granite*
from *springs* on the *summit*
of the *mountain*. The resulting
single MALT SCOTCH WHISKY,
is *rounded* and *mellow*.

AGED **15** YEARS

Distilled & Bottled in *SCOTLAND*
BENRINNES DISTILLERY
Aberlour, Banffshire, Scotland.

43% vol 70 cl

ABERLOUR, BANFFSHIRE EST. 1835

The original distillery was located at Whitehouse Farm, three quarters of a mile to the south east and was washed away in the great flood of 1829. The present building was founded in 1835 by William Smith & Co. as an extension of the farm steading. Acquired by Dewar's in 1922, and thereby becoming a part of DCL in 1925. Run by SMD since 1930, the licensees were A. & A. Crawford Ltd. Major reconstruction took place between 1955 and 1956. Doubled from three to six stills in 1966. Now part of United Distillers plc.

LOCATION Situated one and a half miles south of the A95 on a loop of an unclassified road which runs between the A95 at Daugh of Kinermony and the B9009 at Succoth in Glen Rinnes.

NOTES A form of triple distillation is practised.

WATER The Scurran and Rowantree Burns.

Age 15 years **Strength** 43% abv

Sweetness 8 Peatiness 4 Availability 4

Colour Amber with old gold highlights **Nose** Medium-bodied, biscuity-yeasty, fresh, vanilla and medium-sweet with a slight floral note **Flavour** Medium-sweet, round, smooth, biscuity and honeyed **Finish** Nice, sweet, round, biscuity and honeyed **Notes** United Distillers bottling

Age 14 years **Distillation** 1982 **Strength** 43% abv

Sweetness 7 Peatiness 5 Availability 1

Colour Pale amber with bright gold highlights **Nose** Quite full-bodied, medium-sweet and rich with a slight hint of green apples and a rubbery peatiness **Flavour** Quite big-bodied, medium-dry and slightly smoky **Finish** Dry, long and gently chewy **Notes** Signatory bottling from cask nos. 95/1171/4 distilled 25 November 1982

Age 16years **Distillation** 1980 **Strength** 43% abv

Sweetness 6 Peatiness 6 Availability 2

Colour Pale straw with pale yellow highlights **Nose** Quite a mashy cereal note, soft and medium-dry with quite gentle peatiness **Flavour** Medium-sweet with an almost fragrant peatiness, smooth round and of good body **Finish** Long, fragrant & clean **Notes** Blackadder International bottling from cask no 1350 distilled 19 March 1980

Distillation 1968 **Strength** 40% abv

Sweetness 6 Peatiness 6 Availability 2

Colour Straw/gold with good bright highlights **Nose** Sweet, nutty and slightly fatty in an unctuous way **Flavour** Medium-sweet, smoky, spicy and oaky **Finish** Good, smoky and dry, smooth and creamy **Notes** Gordon & MacPhail bottling

SINGLE SPEYSIDE MALT WHISKY
from
Benrinnes
distillery
16 years old
Distilled 19th March. 1980
Cask no. 1350 Bottled September 1996

Benrinnes distillery, which is named after a dominant mountain peak overlooking the Spey Valley, is notable for the use of a form of triple distillation in its production process. This bottling gives a medium-dry whisky with good body, an almost fragrant peatiness and a long, clean finish.

70cl Blackadder International 43%vol
Larkhall ML9 1DA
Product of Scotland

Product of Scotland

FORRES, MORAY EST. 1898

Built by the Benromach Distillery Company. Bought by Associated Scottish Distilleries Ltd in 1937, who sold it to DCL in 1953. It was managed by SMD and licensed to J. & W. Hardie. The still house was rebuilt in 1966 and the mash house was rebuilt and the tun-room modernised in 1974. Two stills. Bought by Gordon & MacPhail in 1992, who reopened it in 1996

LOCATION North of Forres on the north side of the railway line.

NOTES In 1925 the mash tun was wooden. Benromach was designed by Elgin architect Charles Doig and has high pitched gables and narrow mullioned windows in the Scots vernacular style of the 17th century.

WATER Chapeltown springs near Forres.

Age 12 yo **Strength** 40% abv

Sweetness 7 Peatiness 4 Availability 5

Colour Amber with yellow highlights **Nose** Medium-bodied and medium-sweet with a rich, almost bubble-gum fruitiness and a touch of apple with good background peat **Flavour** Medium-sweet, round and smooth with good, quite chunk peat flavours **Finish** Long, very gently smoky and quite complex **Notes** Gordon & MacPhail bottling

Distillation 1969 **Strength** 40% abv

Sweetness 7 Peatiness 4 Availability 2

Colour Mid-amber with yellow/gold highlights **Nose** Fresh and medium-dry with an oily-oaky aroma, soft and smooth with a touch of green apples **Flavour** Medium-dry, quite rich and soft, sweetness develops in the palate, gently peated **Finish** Quite long and lightly smoky with a touch of spice in the tail **Notes** Gordon & MacPhail bottling

LOWLAND
SINGLE MALT
SCOTCH WHISKY

The Broad Leaved Helleborine,
a rare species of *wild orchid*, can be found growing
in the *ancient oak woodland* behind the

BLADNOCH

distillery. The most southerly in *SCOTLAND*,
founded in the *early 1800's,* ✍ the
distillery stands by the *RIVER BLADNOCH*
near *Wigtown.* It produces a *distinctive*
LOWLAND single MALT WHISKY – delicate and
fruity with a *lemony* aroma and *taste.*

A G E D **10** Y E A R S

43% vol   Distilled & Bottled in SCOTLAND   70 cl
                 BLADNOCH DISTILLERY, Bladnoch, Wigtownshire, Scotland

BLADNOCH, WIGTOWN   EST. 1817

Founded in 1817 by John & Thomas McClelland. Sold by Dunvilles, the Irish whisky distillers, in 1936 for £3,500, this "representing a considerable loss for the premises and plant". Closed in 1938 and reopened in 1956. Run by United Distillers plc which closed it in 1993.

L O C A T I O N   The southernmost distillery in Scotland. Situated on the river of the same name, just a mile outside Wigtown.

N O T E S   Close to the distillery is Baldoon Farm, where stands the ruined castle to which Janet Dalrymple, the "Bride of Lammermoor", came to die after her marriage to David Dunbar of Baldoon.

W A T E R   The River Bladnoch.

Age 10 years   **Strength** 43% abv

Sweetness 4 Peatiness 4 Availability 6

Colour Straw/amber with yellow highlights and green tinge **Nose** Fresh, quite full, fruity and floral, medium-dry with an attractive grape spirit-like aroma **Flavour** Fresh with good weight, a sweet edge and a touch of spice **Finish** Fresh with nice sweetness and quite light **Notes** United Distillers bottling

Age 11 years   **Distillation** 1984   **Strength** 43% abv

Sweetness 2 Peatiness 5 Availability 1

Colour Straw with yellow highlights **Nose** Quite fresh, with good body, fruity, rich and quite delicately peated with a tarry note to the peat and a hint of quinine on the end **Flavour** Almost dry, of good weight with a fruity touch of richness and good peatiness **Finish** Long and quite delicate with a hint of perfume to the peaty tail **Notes** James MacArthur bottling

HIGHLAND
SINGLE MALT
SCOTCH WHISKY

BLAIR ATHOL

distillery, established in 1798, stands
on *peaty moorland* in the *foothills* of the
GRAMPIAN MOUNTAINS. An ancient
source of *water* for the *distillery, ALLT*
DOUR BURN ~ 'The Burn of the Otter',
flows close by. This *single MALT*
SCOTCH WHISKY has a *mellow deep*
toned aroma, a *strong fruity*
flavour and a *smooth* finish.

43% vol   Distilled & Bottled in SCOTLAND   70 cl
BLAIR ATHOL DISTILLERY, Pitlochry, Perthshire, Scotland.

PITLOCHRY, PERTHSHIRE EST. 1798

Although originally founded almost 30 years earlier, the present distillery was established in 1826, when revived by John Robertson. It passed into the hands of John Conacher & Company in 1827. It closed in 1932 and, although purchased by Arthur Bell & Sons the following year, it did not come into production again until 1949 after rebuilding. Extended from two to four stills in 1973. Now part of United Distillers plc.

LOCATION Not at Blair Atholl, as its name suggests, the distillery is to be found on the southern approach road to Pitlochry, just off the main A9.

NOTES The Conacher family, who owned the distillery for a time in the 1800s, are said to be descended from the chivalrous young Conacher who so admired Catherine Glover, the Fair Maid of Perth. The distillery has a large modern visitor centre. Blair Athol is well worth a visit, having an excellent audio-visual presentation as part of a tour of the distillery. Blair Athol malt (note the difference in spelling from the town) plays an important part in the Bell's blend.

WATER From a spring on the nearby 2,760 ft. high Ben Vrackie.

Age 12 years   **Strength** 43% abv

Sweetness 7   Peatiness 6   Availability 6

Colour Pale, mid-amber with gold highlights **Nose** Quite full with touches of nuttiness and greenness, medium-sweet with a fresh smokiness **Flavour** Medium-sweet and quite full-bodied, spicy and round with a definite smoky tang **Finish** Fresh, quite long and smoky with a sweetness on the tail **Notes** United Distillers bottling

Age 8 years   **Strength** 40% abv

Sweetness 5   Peatiness 5   Availability 0

Colour Straw/golden **Nose** Fresh, clean and lightly peated **Flavour** Sweet, almost almondy **Finish** Quite good and distinctive **Notes** Arthur Bell Distillers bottling

Age 23 years   **Distillation** 1966   **Strength** 57.1% abv

Sweetness 6   Peatiness 5   Availability 1

Colour Mid-amber with yellow/gold highlights **Nose** Medium-sweet, quite good body and round with nice vanilla-oak and a citrus oil tang **Flavour** Soft, smooth, medium-sweet with a dry oakiness, quite gentle tannins and good body **Finish** Long with a distinctive perfumed sweetness and a gentle smokiness **Notes** Wm Cadenhead bottling distilled October 1966

Age 18 years   **Distillation** 1977   **Strength** 50.4% abv

Sweetness 5   Peatiness 5   Availability 1

Colour Straw with yellow highlights **Nose** Light-bodied, sweet and malty with a hint of darkness to the peat character and a touch of liquorice and apple **Flavour** Medium-sweet, quite lightly peated and gently chewy with an appley flavour **Finish** Long and chewy with a touch of spiciness **Notes** James MacArthur bottling

The workforce at Blair Athol, 1895

BOWMORE

BOWMORE, ISLE OF ISLAY, ARGYLL EST. 1779

In 1776, an Islay merchant, David Simpson, obtained permission from the local laird to build dwellings and "other buildings". The "other buildings" were soon converted into a distillery. Bought by Stanley P. Morrison in 1963, the distillery is now owned by Morrison Bowmore Distillers, who were themselves purchased outright by Suntory of Japan in 1994. The company had been part owned by Suntory for some years previously, having had a long-term trading relationship with the Japanese company.

LOCATION Bowmore stands, almost fortress-like, on the shores of Loch Indaal.

NOTES Bowmore uses a revolutionary waste heat recovery system to reduce energy costs. The distillery donated a warehouse to the village of Bowmore which has been converted to a swimming pool. The waste heat from the distillery is used to heat the swimming pool. The distillery was built early in the village's history, at the foot of Hill Street, and has proved important to its economic survival. It is said to be the oldest legal distillery on the island.

WATER Laggan River.

BOWMORE LEGEND
Age No age statement **Strength** 40% abv

Sweetness 1 Peatiness 8 Availability 9

Colour Light amber with gold highlights and a touch of green **Nose** Full, pungent, a touch perfumed and a phenol character with a little greenness **Flavour** Dry with an edge of richness, perfumed and quite pungent **Finish** Long, gently smoky and perfumed **Notes** Morrison Bowmore bottling. Sold as *Bowmore Legend*

Age 10 years **Strength** 40% abv

Sweetness 0 Peatiness 8 Availability 8

Colour Mid-amber with gold highlights **Nose** Full, dry, pungent with a touch of burnt heather and perfumed **Flavour** Dry, heather-perfumed, fresh and smoky, quite full-bodied with whiffs of ozone **Finish** Long, characterful and smoky **Notes** Morrison Bowmore bottling

Age 12 years **Strength** 40% abv

Sweetness 0 Peatiness 8 Availability 7

Colour Full, amber, very bright **Nose** Lightish, peaty, burnt heather with a characteristic tang of ozone/iodine and even a whiff of chocolate! **Flavour** Smooth, refined flavour with a pronounced smoky peatiness **Finish** Good, long and dry **Notes** Morrison Bowmore bottling

Age 17 years **Strength** 43% abv

Sweetness 2 Peatiness 8 Availability 6

Colour Quite full, deep amber with old gold highlights **Nose** Rich, medium bodied with a pungency, but delicate, and aromas of violets **Flavour** Round, quite full-bodied, smoky and rich with gentle tannins **Finish** Soft, gently smoky, quite elegant and slightly salty **Notes** Morrison Bowmore bottling

Age 21 years **Strength** 43% abv

Sweetness 2 Peatiness 8 Availability 5

Colour Mid-amber with old gold highlights **Nose** Quite big-bodied, dark and smoky, rounded and quite dry with just a hint of ozone **Flavour** Big, round, burnt heather roots, quite pungent with a delicate floral note at the back **Finish** Long with a hint of sweetness/richness and finely smoky with a touch of bitter chocolate on the tail **Notes** Morrison Bowmore bottling

Age 25 years **Strength** 43% abv

Sweetness 3 Peatiness 7 Availability 3

Colour Quite deep amber with pale bronze highlights **Nose** Quite full-bodied, rich with a slightly green hedgerow freshness, a floral smokiness and burnt vanilla notes **Flavour** Full-bodied, fresh and round, medium-dry but rich, a slightly perfumed dark peaty smokiness and a touch of oaky tannin **Finish** Long, gently chewy, almost floral, quite delicately smoky with a hint of seaweed and bitter chocolate - very complex **Notes** Morrison Bowmore bottling

BLACK BOWMORE
Distillation 1964 **Strength** 50% abv

Sweetness 2 Peatiness 7 Availability 1

Colour Very deep, dark mahogany/teak with deep bronze highlights **Nose** Big-bodied, full, dark, nutty and rich, quite delicately peated, dry with slight notes of burnt mahogany **Flavour** Big, powerful, full-bodied, quite tannic with dark nutty flavours, smooth, although chewy **Finish** Long, full-flavoured, quite chewy with a smoky/nutty character, a good perfumed peatiness and a rich salty tang on the tail **Notes** Morrison Bowmore bottling. Known as **Black Bowmore**, this is from a very rare old sherry cask bottling. There were three issues of Black Bowmore, the first and the last being the most rare

BOWMORE MARINER
Age 15 years **Strength** 43% abv

Sweetness 2 Peatiness 8 Availability 5

Colour Amber with gold/bronze highlights **Nose** Rich, gloriously chocolatey and with good body; a delicate note of burnt heather roots and a peatiness at the back **Flavour** Quite full-bodied, smoky, clean and round with a richness at the back **Finish** Long, fresh and smoky with an appealing green edge **Notes** Morrison Bowmore bottling

Vintage 1979
Single Highland Malt Scotch Whisky
Matured in sherry casks for 15 years
Distilled at the Braes of Glenlivet Distillery
on 06.06.79 *Bottled 3.95*
Butt no. 16040 *Bottle no. 57e of 570*
This whisky has been selected, produced and bottled in Scotland for and under the sole responsibility of Signatory Vintage Scotch Whisky Co. Ltd. Edinburgh EH6 Scotland
70cl 60%vol

NEAR TOMINTOUL, BANFFSHIRE EST. 1973

Originally called Braes of Glenlivet, Braeval was built between 1973-4 by Chivas Bros Ltd, a subsidiary of the Seagram Co Ltd of Canada. Originally three stills, with two more being added in 1975 and a sixth in 1978. Although a very modern distillery, it is nevertheless of a most attractive design, with a decorative, albeit non-functional pagoda-style roof.

LOCATION High up above the remote hamlet of Chapeltown off the B9008, it is one of the most isolated distilleries in Scotland.

NOTES This whisky is at last becoming available through independent bottlers. The distillery's name was changed to *Braeval* to avoid confusion with its illustrious sister, *The Glenlivet*.

WATER The Pitilie Burn.

Age 15 years **Strength** 43% abv

Sweetness 7 Peatiness 5 Availability 2

Colour Quite deep amber with bronze highlights **Nose** Quite full-bodied, round and gently peaty; rich and creamy with a slightly perfumed character **Flavour** Round, smooth, full-bodied, medium-sweet with a not unpleasant, slightly perfumed, green edge **Finish** Long, smooth, medium-dry and slightly nutty **Notes** Signatory bottling distilled on 6 June 1979

Age 8 years **Distillation** 1987 **Strength** 60% abv

Sweetness 7 Peatiness 4 Availability 2

Colour Pale straw with pale, watery lemon highlights **Nose** Medium-dry, of quite good body, a young mashy character with a slight touch of citrus, a hedgerow greenness and a soft maltiness **Flavour** Soft, medium-sweet, quite good body and round with a touch of peat at the back **Finish** Clean, of reasonable length, with good sweetness **Notes** Wm Cadenhead bottling

BRORA, SUTHERLAND EST. 1819

Brora was known as Clynelish until 1969. Established by the Duke of Sutherland, who had cleared his tenant-farmers off the land to make way for sheep. Having moved some of the inland farmers to the coastal strip, the distillery was established to create a market for the farmers' grain. Owned by SMD, now UMGD, since 1930.

LOCATION Just off the A9 at Brora.

NOTES After the modern distillery had been built in 1967-8, the old "Clynelish" reopened in April 1969, housed in the former mash house, which had been rebuilt. It subsequently ceased distillation in May 1983. The old buildings are now used as warehouses and the visitor centre for the "new" Clynelish. Brora had two stills.

WATER The Clynemilton Burn.

Distillation 1972 **Strength** 40% abv

Sweetness 3	**Peatiness** 9	**Availability** 1

Colour Mid-amber with gold highlights **Nose** Full and heavily peated with a sooty character **Flavour** Big, and smooth with smoky characters of burnt oak **Finish** Nutty, chewy and smoky with a hint of sweetness **Notes** Gordon & MacPhail bottling

Age 22 years **Strength** 58.7% abv

Sweetness 4	**Peatiness** 8	**Availability** 1

Colour Amber with gold highlights **Nose** Big bodied, quite pungent, a dark, smoky - almost sooty, burnt tang with richness at the back **Flavour** Quite big with a soft peatiness, but a burnt character, medium-sweet, quite rich and with big tannins **Finish** Long, with an almost burnt character, spicy with chewy tannins. **Notes** United Distillers bottling

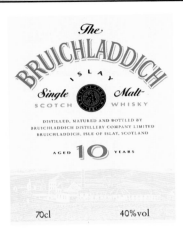

BRUICHLADDICH, ISLAY, ARGYLL EST. 1881

Built by Robert, William & John Gourlay Harvey (of the Dundashill & Yoker Harveys). Became the Bruichladdich Distillery Company (Islay) Ltd in 1886. Doubled from two to four stills in 1975. Owned in recent years by Invergordon Distillers, who were taken over by JBB (Greater Europe) plc in late 1993. A lot of very old machinery and distillation techniques were employed in the distillery, making it an exciting distillery to visit. Sadly it was closed abruptly at the end of January 1995, its new owners having decided to mothball Bruichladdich and two other distilleries in the newly enlarged JBB group, Tamnavulin and Tullibardine.

LOCATION   Sited on the western shore of Loch Indaal on the A847 to Port Charlotte and the picturesque village of Portnahaven.

NOTES   The distillery is the most westerly in Scotland and, despite this, it has a lighter, more delicate character than the other Islay Malts. It is thought that this is because it is sheltered from the prevailing winds - and weather - by the Rhinns of Islay, a range of hills which lie between Bruichladdich and the open sea.

WATER   A reservoir in the local hills.

Age 10 years   **Strength** 40% abv
Sweetness 2   **Peatiness** 7   **Availability** 7

Colour Pale golden with slight green tinges **Nose** A delicate peatiness, fairly light and with no great pungency **Flavour** Full and flavoursome, smoky and dry without the heavier notes of other Islays **Finish** Of good length and with a well-defined finish **Notes** Invergordon Distillers bottling

Age 15 years **Strength** 40% abv

Sweetness 3 Peatiness 6 Availability 4

Colour Straw with amber/gold highlights **Nose** Rich, delicately peated, but with an underlying sweetness **Flavour** Slightly sweet with hints of nuttiness and very little of Islay's heavier characteristics **Finish** Spicy, warm, long, with sweet oak, but finally dry **Notes** Invergordon Distillers bottling

Age 21 years **Strength** 43% abv

Sweetness 3 Peatiness 6 Availability 4

Colour Light amber with yellow/gold highlights **Nose** Quite light, fresh and rich with a faint touch of ozone **Flavour** Medium-bodied, fresh, almost dry, but with an edge of richness - an intriguing mixture of sweetness and dryness **Finish** Tangy, fresh, rich and clean and gently smoky **Notes** Invergordon Distillers bottling

Age 32 years **Distillation** 1964 **Strength** 49% abv

Sweetness 4 Peatiness 5 Availability 0

Colour Very dark, deep amber with bronze highlights and a ruby hue **Nose** Dark, Slightly sweet, nutty (sweet hazelnuts) and full-bodied with an edge of burnt heather roots, and a soft, vanilla-oaky character **Flavour** Wonderfully soft and mature, very delicately peated, gently chewy with a sweetly dark edge **Finish** Long, elegant, complex and very gently smoky with a slight hint of fruitcake sweetness **Notes** *Piper's Preferred* bottling from an oloroso cask. Sold in Germany

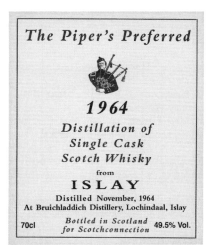

The Piper's Preferred

1964

Distillation of
Single Cask
Scotch Whisky

from

ISLAY

Distilled November, 1964
At Bruichladdich Distillery, Lochindaal, Islay

70cl | *Bottled in Scotland* *for Scotchconnection* | 49.5% Vol.

"Westering Home..."

Bunnahabhain
SINGLE ISLAY MALT SCOTCH WHISKY
PRODUCT OF SCOTLAND
THE BUNNAHABHAIN DISTILLERY COMPANY,
BUNNAHABHAIN, ISLE OF ISLAY, SCOTLAND. BOTTLED IN SCOTLAND.
40% vol.   70 cl

NEAR PORT ASKAIG, ISLAY, ARGYLL EST. 1880

Became part of Highland Distilleries Ltd in 1887 when amalgamated with William Grant and Company of Glenrothes. Extended from two to four stills in 1963.

LOCATION Situated towards the north east tip of Islay on the bay from which it takes its name.

NOTES Bunnahabhain means "mouth of the river". Prior to the building of this distillery which is the island's most northerly, the adjacent area was inhospitable and uninhabited. Now a small hamlet has built up around the distillery.

WATER River Margadale.

Age 12 years   **Strength** 40% abv

Sweetness 3 Peatiness 6 Availability 9

Colour Straw with golden highlights **Nose** Distinctive, quite light and flowery **Flavour** Smoother, softer and less pungent than other Islays **Finish** Smooth, round, lovely and long **Notes** Highland Distilleries bottling

Age 25 years   **Distillation** 1964   **Strength** 46% abv

Sweetness 5 Peatiness 6 Availability 0

Colour Straw with yellow highlights **Nose** Medium-sweet, rich, ripe and fruity with a dark tarriness at the back and a floral note **Flavour** Medium-sweet and rich with oaky tannins, quite smooth and creamy **Finish** Rich, full-bodied and quite long with an earthy smokiness on tail **Notes** Master of Malt bottling

Age 17 years **Distillation** 1979 **Strength** 43% abv

Sweetness 4 Peatiness 6 Availability 2

Colour Pale amber with yellow/gold highlights. **Nose** Quite soft, rich, medium-dry with good body and menthol and floral notes, **Colour** Pale amber with yellow highlights **Nose** Fresh, medium-dry, rich, fruity with notes of lemon, apple and sweet vanilla and quite gently peated **Flavour** Medium-dry with an edge of richness, a soft fruity touch and gentle peat **Finish** Long, malty and softly smoky **Notes** Blackadder International bottling from cask no. 8770 distilled 5 September1979

SINGLE ISLAY MALT WHISKY
from
Bunnahabhain Distillery
Distilled 5th September 1979
Cask no. 8770   Bottled May 1997
Matured in Oak Cask

17 years old

Islay's most gentle malt. Built in 1880 on the north-east coast of the island, it is protected from the prevailing south-westerlies by the bulk of the island. With a soft, delicate peatiness and floral and menthol notes, the whisky has good richness and a gentle, malty, cereal touch.

Blackadder International
Larkhall Ml9 1DA
Product of Scotland 43%vol
70cl

Product of Scotland

Age 17 years **Distillation** 1979 **Strength** 58.4% abv

Sweetness 3 Peatiness 5 Availability 2

Colour Full amber with old gold highlights **Nose** Full, ripe and nutty with a fine, delicate peatiness, medium-dry with a slight hint of liquorice/trout fishing basket **Flavour** Smooth, medium-dry and nutty with good body and a very gentle peatiness **Finish** Nuttily soft, lingeringly complex and round **Notes** Signatory bottling from butt no. 5110, distilled 18 April 1979

Age 17 years **Distillation** 1979 **Strength** 56.3% abv

Sweetness 3 Peatiness 6 Availability 1

Colour Mid-amber with yellow highlights **Nose** Medium-bodied, rich and slightly nutty with a sweet vanilla, sherried note and delicately peated **Flavour** Medium-dry, creamy and smooth with a vanilla note and good peatiness **Finish** Long, gently chewy and almost dry **Notes** Limited Edition bottling from cask no. 8771 distilled 5 September 1979

COUNTY ANTRIM, N. IRELAND EST. 1608

Bushmills was granted a licence to distil in 1608, making it by far the earliest legal distillery of all. Operated by Irish Distillers which, in 1988, was the target of a hard-fought takeover battle between British giant Grand Metropolitan and French rival Pernod-Ricard, which the latter won.

LOCATION   Near the Giant's Causeway on the north coast of Ulster.

NOTES   Bushmills is triple distilled, although it is not alone in this respect. Auchentoshan, Rosebank and Benrinnes also use forms of triple distillation. Bushmills is also available in duty-free markets at 43% abv. Irish whiskey is unpeated, unlike most Scotch whisky. Irish Distillers own two distilleries: Bushmills and the modern Midleton complex near Cork. Irish blends such as Jameson, Original Bushmills, Black Bush, Powers, Paddy and Tullamore Dew are produced from whiskies distilled at these two distilleries. In 1920, there were 23 distilleries in Ireland and 134 in Scotland.

WATER   Saint Columb's Rill.

Age 10 years   **Strength** 40% abv

Sweetness	7	Peatiness	0	Availability	9

Colour Amber with yellow-gold highlights **Nose** Fresh, clean and grassy with a bubble-gummy sweetness (medium-sweet) and a slight grassy character **Flavour** Medium-sweet with quite good body and round with a nice vanilla wood note **Finish** Clean, long and fresh **Notes** Irish Distillers bottling

Age 16 years   **Strength** 40% abv

Sweetness	5	Peatiness	0	Availability	6

Colour Mid-amber with old gold highlights and an edge of ruby **Nose** Full-bodied, fresh and slightly green with a goose-berry character, it has a rich, woody nuttiness and is medium-sweet with a nutty toffee character **Flavour** Almost dry with good body, smooth, dark and nutty; round with a slight goose-berry ripeness and a touch of toffee **Finish** Long, with a good, nutty richness, a dark complexity and an almost mahogany-flavoured chewiness **Notes** Irish Distillers bottling; aged in a mixture of Bourbon barrels and Sherry butts, then finished off for six months in Port pipes.

ISLAY
SINGLE MALT *SCOTCH WHISKY*

CAOL ILA

distillery, built in 1846 is situated near *Port Askaig* on the *Isle of Islay.*
Steamers used to call twice a week to collect *whisky* from this remote
site in a cove facing the *Isle of Jura.* Water supplies for mashing
come from *Loch nam Ban* although the sea provides *water* for
condensing. Unusual for an *Islay* this *single MALT SCOTCH
WHISKY* has a *fresh aroma* and a *light* yet *well rounded* flavour.

AGED **15** YEARS

43% vol Distilled & Bottled in *SCOTLAND.* CAOL ILA DISTILLERY Port Askaig, Isle of Islay, *Scotland.* 70 cl

PORT ASKAIG, ISLAY, ARGYLL EST. 1846

Built by Hector Henderson on what, when you are standing at the distillery, seems a very isolated spot. The distillery was taken over in 1863 by Bulloch Lade & Co., who extended and rebuilt it in 1879. It came under DCL's control in 1927 and management has been by SMD, now UMGD, since 1930. It was completely rebuilt, apart from warehouses between April 1972 and January 1974, when it was extended from two stills to six.

LOCATION Another distillery which is literally at the end of the road, in this case, the northern end of the A846.

NOTES Caol Ila's still house has arguably the finest view in the Scotch Whisky industry. It overlooks Caol Ila (the Gaelic name for the Sound of Islay) to the Paps of Jura. Hot water from the condensers is pumped through a sea water condenser, cooled and returned for reuse in the still house condensers. Never one of United Distillers' mainstream malts and thus mainly available as a single from independent bottlers, it is nevertheless an important and extensive building block for blended whisky. It is now one of the key malts in *Bell's* 8-year-old blend.

WATER Loch Nam Ban (Torrabolls Loch).

Age 15 years **Strength** 43% abv

Sweetness 2 Peatiness 9 Availability 5

Colour Straw/pale amber with lemon-yellow highlights **Nose** Full, quite pungent and peaty, smoky, burnt heather roots with a touch of unripe greenness **Flavour** Big, full, smoky and pungent with an edge of sweetness **Finish** Long, rich and smoky with a touch of bitter chocolate and spice **Notes** United Distillers bottling

Age 12 years **Strength** 63% abv

Sweetness 5 Peatiness 9 Availability 2

Colour Amber-peaty with good gold highlights **Nose** Peaty, burnt heather, quite earthy and medicinal **Flavour** Medium-sweet, rich, smoky, spicy, full with burnt heather predominating **Finish** Smooth, smoky, spicy and very long **Notes** Sherry cask bottling from James MacArthur & Company. The richness derives from the Sherry casks used for maturation

Age 13 years **Distillation** 1980 **Strength** 62.6% abv

Sweetness 1 Peatiness 9 Availability 3

Colour Pale amber with pale gold highlights **Nose** Medium to full-bodied and almost dry with an earthy peatiness and a hint of ozone **Flavour** Dry, gently tannic, round and smooth with an earthy smokiness and a slight edge of richness **Finish** Long, smoky and tangy **Notes** Gordon & MacPhail bottling

Age 17 years **Strength** 43% abv

Sweetness 1 Peatiness 9 Availability 0

Colour Pale amber with a tinge of lemony gold **Nose** Full-bodied, rich, round and nutty, medium pungency, soft peatiness and quite dry **Flavour** Dry, smoky, pungent and full-bodied **Finish** Long and smoky **Notes** Master of Malt bottling

Age 19 years **Strength** 43% abv

Sweetness 1 Peatiness 9 Availability 2

Colour Very pale straw with lemon highlights **Nose** Full-bodied, pungent and dry with the aroma of burnt heather roots **Flavour** Full, pungent, smoky and dry with just a hint of sweetness on the edge **Finish** Long, characterful and smoky with oaky tannins **Notes** Blackadder International bottling

Distillation 1972 **Strength** 40% abv

Sweetness 2 Peatiness 9 Availability 2

Colour Palish gold with green tinges **Nose** Peaty, almost medicinal with a strange touch of sweetness **Flavour** Heavy, clean, peaty, burnt heather with more than a tang of ozone **Finish** Long, distinguished, peaty **Notes** Gordon & MacPhail bottling

Distillation 1974 **Strength** 40% abv

Sweetness 2 Peatiness 9 Availability 2

Colour Bright gold/amber with gold highlights **Nose** Peaty, malty, earthy, more than a hint of the sea, but with a rich, almost perfumed fruitiness to it **Flavour** Dry, round, quite full-bodied and peaty **Finish** Smoky and dry, but rich **Notes** Gordon & MacPhail bottling

ROTHES, MORAY EST. 1897

Following the industry slump at the end of the 19th century, Caperdonich was closed in 1902 and did not produce again until 1965 following rebuilding. Extended from two to four stills in 1967. Now owned by the Seagram Company of Canada.

LOCATION Situated at one end of the small town of Rothes, across the road from its sister distillery, Glen Grant.

NOTES The distillery was built to supplement the output of Glen Grant and was known as Glen Grant No. 2. The whisky, using the same water, is lighter and fruitier than Glen Grant. The two distilleries were originally joined by a pipe which carried spirit from Caperdonich to Glen Grant across the town's main street. Rothes supports five distilleries, with Caperdonich being the last to be built. Glen Grant, established in 1840, was the first.

WATER The Caperdonich Well, adjacent to the Glen Grant Burn.

Distillation 1979 **Strength** 40% abv

Sweetness 8 Peatiness 3 Availability 3

Colour Pale straw, almost yellow **Nose** Sweet, ripe, grapey with a hint of cloves and apples **Flavour** Sweet and spirity with a slight flavour of cloves **Finish** Quite good for its youth, but shortish **Notes** Gordon & MacPhail bottling

Age 16 years **Distillation** 1972 **Strength** 40% abv

Sweetness 7 Peatiness 3 Availability 0

Colour Honey-amber with old gold highlights **Nose** Full, fruity, almost raisin-like, nutty and delicately peated with hints of demerara sugar **Flavour** Quite full and oaky with good peatiness, smooth and medium-sweet **Finish** Long, creamy and spicy with oaky tannins **Notes** Master of Malt bottling

KNOCKANDO, MORAY EST. 1824

Built on Cardow farm, the distillery was also known by that name until recently. The original licensee was John Cumming, who had previously gained a string of convictions as a whisky smuggler. Acquired by John Walker & Son in 1893, becoming part of DCL in 1925. Managed by SMD since 1930. Rebuilt in 1960 and extended from four to six stills. Now part of United Distillers plc.

LOCATION   Situated high up above the River Spey on its north bank, on the B9102 between Knockando and Craigellachie.

NOTES   A "flagship" of the United Distillers Group, the malt has long played an important role in the success of Johnnie Walker's famous Red and Black Label brands. Cardhu means "black rock". A large reception centre was opened in 1988. John Cumming took a lease on Cardow farm in 1811 and made whisky from the very outset. His wife, Helen, played no small part in the business and would always manage to disguise mashing and fermenting as bread-making when Excise officers came calling. She lived to be 85 and villagers still tell colourful stories of her passed on by their grandparents.

WATER   Springs on the Mannoch Hill or the Lyne Burn.

Age 12 years   **Strength** 40% abv

Sweetness 8   Peatiness 7   Availability 9

Colour Pale mid-amber with a definite green tinge **Nose** Quite full-bodied, rich, medium-sweet and smoky with a green apple character **Flavour** Round and mellow, sweet with a delicate peatiness **Finish** Long, peaty and sweet **Notes** United Distillers bottling

GLASGOW ROAD, WISHAW, LANARKSHIRE EST. 1825

Clydesdale distillery was said to have been built by Lord Belhaven and his first tenant was Patrick Chalmers. Lord Belhaven pulled out in 1848. Clydesdale Distillery Co. Ltd was founded in 1894 and this was one of the founding members of Scottish Malt Distillers Ltd in 1914.

LOCATION On the south east side of Glasgow Road, Wishaw, where the local Glasgow - Lanark railway crosses the road.

NOTES Production ceased in 1919, although the premises were used by DCL as bonded warehouses until 1988 when the buildings were demolished.

WATER A burn rising in the Cambusnethan peat moss.

Age Unknown - circa1900   **Strength** 45% abv

Sweetness 7   Peatiness 3   Availability 0

Colour Quite dark amber with bronze highlights **Nose** Quite full-bodied, rich and sherried, dark nuttiness (Brazil nuts), quite soft vanilla with a dryness at the back **Flavour** Round, quite full, sherried, rich, soft, medium-sweet, nuttiness and a greenness **Finish** Long, rich, a touch of oakiness, creamy and nutty with a nice spicy tang. **Notes** One of two bottles taken from the distillery in 1917 and kept by the Campbell family of Wishaw for use at funerals. This sample was also tasted by one of Scotland's master blenders who was of the opinion that it had been aged in a liqueur cask, a common practice at the turn of the century when casks for aging were at a premium

HIGHLAND
SINGLE MALT
SCOTCH WHISKY

One of the most *northerly* in *Scotland,*

CLYNELISH

distillery, was established in *Brora*
by the *Marquess* of *STAFFORD*
in 1819. Its building *signalled* the
end of illicit *distilling*
in the area and provided a
ready market for locally grown
barley. Water is piped from the
CLYNEMILTON burn to produce this
fruity, // slightly smoky single
MALT SCOTCH WHISKY much
appreciated by *connoisseurs*

YEARS 14 OLD

Distilled & Bottled in *SCOTLAND*
CLYNELISH DISTILLERY
Brora, Sutherland, Scotland

43% vol   70 cl

BRORA, SUTHERLAND EST. 1967

The original Clynelish distillery was the old, now closed, Brora distillery next door. It was founded by the Marquess of Stafford, later the first Duke of Sutherland. It was intended as a ready market for barley produced by crofters who had been evicted from inland farms and moved down to the coastal plain. Established as a brewery in 1817, it was turned into a distillery two years later. Operated by UMGD and now part of United Distillers. Six stills.

LOCATION Just off the A9 north of Brora on the north side of the extensive plain which forms the mouth of Strath Brora.

NOTES Brora was known as Clynelish until 1969. After the modern distillery had been built in 1967-8, the old "Clynelish" reopened in April 1975, housed in the rebuilt mash house. It subsequently ceased distillation in May 1983. There is no little confusion as Brora is often called "Clynelish". The whisky from the old distillery was only bottled as Clynelish prior to 1967. Between 1967 and 1983, production from the old distillery was stencilled as "Brora" on casks.

WATER The Clynemilton Burn.

Age 14 years   **Strength** 43% abv

Sweetness 4   Peatiness 6   Availability 6

Colour Pale amber with good green/gold highlights **Nose** Rich, medium-dry, a citrus fruitiness, quite full and round with good smokiness at the back **Flavour** Smoky with a soft sweetness, quite full-bodied and almost luscious - very complex **Finish** Long and elegant with a touch of bitter chocolate **Notes** United Distillers bottling

CLYNELISH

H

Age 12 years **Strength** 40% abv
Sweetness 6 Peatiness 5 Availability 4

Colour Mid-amber with yellow/gold highlights **Nose** Clean with good body and a richness at the back, gently peated and medium-dry with a light apple touch **Flavour** Good body, medium-sweet, smooth, creamy and gently peated with an apple character at the back **Finish** Quite long with good sweetness and a creamy peatiness **Notes** Gordon & MacPhail bottling

Age 14 years **Distillation** 1982 **Strength** 43% abv
Sweetness 3 Peatiness 7 Availability 2

Colour Pale straw with pale lemon highlights **Nose** Quite full-bodied, fresh and medium-dry with a nice oaky vanilla note and a chunky peatiness **Flavour** Unctuously smooth and medium-dry, but with a slight edge of sweetness, fresh and well-peated **Finish** Long, ethereally soft and slightly tangy **Notes** A "Cooper's Choice" bottling from The Vintage Malt Whisky Co.

Age 15 years **Distillation** 1980 **Strength** 64% abv
Sweetness 3 Peatiness 7 Availability 1

Colour Pale Amber with pale lemon highlights **Nose** Big, powerful and medium-dry with a sooty peatiness and just a hint of richness at the back **Flavour** Big, medium-dry with a nice hidden sweetness, good, gently chewy tannins and a sooty peatiness **Finish** Long-lasting, lingering, spicy and tangy with a toffee-like sweetness **Notes** Blackadder International bottling

Age 23 years **Distillation** 1965 **Strength** 57.1% abv
Sweetness 4 Peatiness 6 Availability 1

Colour Pale amber with a touch of green, good yellow highlights **Nose** Full, fruity, herby, medium-dry with a touch of woodiness and high spiritiness **Flavour** Dry, but with a touch of sweetness, round, full, a slight unctuous oiliness and good fruit character **Finish** Long, nutty, spicy and very full - something of a blockbuster **Notes** Wm. Cadenhead bottling

Age 28 years **Distillation** 1965 **Strength** 50.7% abv
Sweetness 3 Peatiness 6 Availability 2

Colour Mid-amber with yellow/gold highlights **Nose** Quite full-bodied, fresh, round and medium-sweet with an unctuous sweet-oak character **Flavour** Dry, but with a nice edge of sweetness, rich, round, good dry oaky tannins, nutty and softly unctuous **Finish** Long, elegant and gently smoky with just a touch of sweetness at the front **Notes** Signatory bottling

CONNOISSEURS
CHOICE

*Connoisseurs Choice, a
range of single malts from
various districts of
Scotland*

*The distilleries situated in
the area of the valley of the
River Spey produce some of
the finest malt whiskies.*

GRAMPIANS

SINGLE SPEYSIDE
MALT SCOTCH WHISKY
DISTILLED AT

COLEBURN
DISTILLERY
Proprietors: J. & G. Stewart Ltd

DISTILLED **1972** DISTILLED

SPECIALLY SELECTED, PRODUCED AND BOTTLED BY

70cl   GORDON & MACPHAIL   40%vol
ELGIN - SCOTLAND
PRODUCT OF SCOTLAND

LONGMORN, ELGIN, MORAY EST. 1897

Built by John Robertson & Son. Became part of DCL in 1925 and managed by SMD from 1930. Two stills.

LOCATION Situated to the east of the A491, four miles south of Elgin. It is "faced on one side by a plantation of Scotch firs and birches, and swept by the cool mountain breezes of Brown Muir" according to Robertson's original announcement in 1896.

NOTES The distillery was built from warm-coloured Moray sandstone and roofed with blue Welsh slates. A problem which faced the architect was the provision of a lavatory to the Excise Office - it took 18 months to resolve! The Excise Officer's house took even longer to be completed. Closed in 1985 and unlikely to reopen.

WATER A spring in the Glen of Rothes.

Distillation 1965 **Strength** 40% abv

Sweetness 8 Peatiness 5 Availability 2

Colour Warm peaty/gold with amber highlights **Nose** Sweet, nutty-almondy oily rich **Flavour** Medium-sweet, delicate, slightly spirity, rich **Finish** Smooth and creamy with good length **Notes** Gordon & MacPhail bottling

Distillation 1972 **Strength** 40% abv

Sweetness 7 Peatiness 6 Availability 3

Colour Straw/amber with yellow/gold highlights **Nose** Medium-bodied, quite heavily peated, fresh and nutty with a touch of greenness **Flavour** Medium-dry, smoky, quite heavy with a richness and an unripe green character **Finish** Smoky with richness at the back and light touches of oaky tannins **Notes** Gordon & MacPhail bottling

SINGLE SPEYSIDE
MALT SCOTCH WHISKY
DISTILLED AT
CONVALMORE
DISTILLERY
Proprietors: W.P. Lowrie & Co. Ltd
DISTILLED **1969** DISTILLED
SPECIALLY SELECTED, PRODUCED AND BOTTLED BY
70cl   **GORDON & MACPHAIL**   40%vol
ELGIN · SCOTLAND
PRODUCT OF SCOTLAND

DUFFTOWN, BANFFSHIRE EST. 1894

Founded 2 June 1893 by the Convalmore-Glenlivet Distillery Co. Ltd. Purchased from the liquidator in March 1905 for £6,000 plus stock at 2s 6d (12.5p) per gallon by W. P. Lowrie & Co. Ltd, who were controlled by James Buchanan & Co. Ltd from 1906. Fire broke out on 29 October 1909 and the malt barn, kiln, malt mill, mash house and tun-room were destroyed. After the distillery had been rebuilt, it was used for experiments into the continuous distillation of malt. W.P. Lowrie & Co. joined DCL in 1925 and production was carried out by SMD from 1930. Doubled from two to four stills in 1964. Closed in 1985 and the site sold to Wm. Grant & Sons in 1990.

LOCATION Just north of Dufftown on the A941.

NOTES The distillery accommodated a signals detachment of the 51st (Highland) Division from 1940 to 1942 and then gunners of the 52nd (Lowland) Division until 1944.

WATER Springs in the Conval Hills.

Distillation 1969   **Strength** 40% abv

Sweetness 8 Peatiness 5 Availability 4

Colour Very pale straw, almost watery **Nose** Sweet, with the smell of a field of grain after rain in summer **Flavour** Medium-sweet, nutty, spicy **Finish** Spicy and of reasonable length **Notes** Gordon & MacPhail bottling

Age 31 years **Distillation** 1962   **Strength** 48.9% abv

Sweetness 6 Peatiness 5 Availability 2

Colour Mid-amber with old gold highlights **Nose** Gently smoky with a slight burnt oak character **Flavour** Quite big-bodied, medium-sweet with an appley malic character **Finish** Quite fresh with a touch of liquorice and good length with a delicate smoky edge **Notes** Wm Cadenhead bottling

PURE POT STILL
Connemara

PEATED SINGLE MALT
40% vol.   **IRISH WHISKEY**   70 cl e
Distilled, Matured & Bottled in Ireland. Cooley Distillery Plc, Riverstown, Dundalk, Co. Louth.

• PRODUCT OF IRELAND •

RIVERSTOWN, DUNDALK, CO. LOUTH, EIRE EST. 1987

The Cooley Distillery Plc was established in 1987. The company took over the site of an old industrial distillery at Riverstown, Dundalk and installed Coffey and pot stills. The first whiskey was distilled in 1989.

LOCATION   At Riverstown, Dundalk, not far from the border of the Irish Republic and Northern Ireland.

NOTES   The Cooley Distillery produces two different styles of Irish malt whiskey, a traditional unpeated malt and the peated malt the company markets under its Connemara brand.

WATER   A spring on Slieve Na gCloc in the Cooley Mountains.

CONNEMARA
Age no age statement   **Strength** 40% abv

Sweetness 5	Peatiness 6	Availability 4

Colour Mid-amber with old gold highlights **Nose** Quite full-bodied, fresh ad medium-dry with a round fruitiness and a good measure of slightly green peatiness **Flavour** Medium-sweet, with good body, a nice weight of peat and a round dark nuttiness **Finish** Long and clean with a good background smokiness **Notes** Peated Irish single malt from Cooley

THE TYRCONNELL
Age No age statement **Strength** 40% abv

Sweetness 7	Peatiness 0	Availability 4

Colour Straw with yellow highlights **Nose** Fresh and clean with a touch of liquorice, a good ripe richness, medium-sweet and quite round with a slight unctuous character **Flavour** Medium-sweet, fresh, round and smooth with quite good body **Finish** Long and clean with an almost barley-sugar sweetness and a slight citrus note **Notes** Unpeated Irish single malt from Cooley

SINGLE *Highland* MALT

SPEYSIDE

CRAGGANMORE

Scotch Whisky

DISTILLERY CRAGGANMORE BALLINDALLOCH

YEARS *12* OLD

SPECIALLY BOTTLED IN SCOTLAND FOR THE
CRAGGANMORE DISTILLERY, BALLINDALLOCH, BANFFSHIRE

BALLINDALLOCH, BANFFSHIRE EST. 1869

Built by John Smith, the lessee of Glenfarclas from 1865 to 1869, manager of Macallan in the early 1850s, Glenlivet from 1858 and Clydesdale in the early 1860s. The distillery never closed for even a fortnight in any year up until the summer of 1901, when reconstruction began. The Cragganmore Distillery Company did not become a wholly owned subsidiary of DCL until 1965-6. Extended from two to four stills in 1964.

LOCATION Cragganmore occupies a site north of the A95 between Grantown-on-Spey and Ballindalloch, close to the River Spey. It was the first Speyside distillery to be sited to take advantage of railway transport, the former railway line (now the *Speyside Way* footpath) passing the distillery's doors.

NOTES Originally available only at the distillery or through independent bottlers, the make is now widely available as one of United Distillers' Classic Malts portfolio. An interesting feature is that the spirit stills have flat-topped, T-shaped lyne pipes instead of the usual swan necks. The stills have cooling worms rather than condensers.

WATER The Craggan Burn - a spring on the Craggan More Hill.

Age 12 years **Strength** 40% abv

Sweetness 6 Peatiness 7 Availability 9

Colour Amber with pale gold highlights **Nose** Clean with quite good body, medium-dry, smokily peaty, slightly creamy with a light green touch **Flavour** Quite full-bodied, round with a hint of spice, smoky and creamy **Finish** Quite long, clean and fresh **Notes** United Distillers bottling, one of the *Classic Malts*

Distillation 1978 **Strength** 40% abv

Sweetness 7 Peatiness 7 Availability 3

Colour Amber with good yellow highlights **Nose** Quite full-bodied and medium-sweet with a quite chunky peatiness, a touch of citrus and an almost jammy note **Flavour** Rich and medium-sweet with quite solid peat and of good weight **Finish** Long and sweet with a note of cocoa to the peat **Notes** Gordon & MacPhail bottling

Distillation 1976 **Strength** 40% abv

Sweetness 4 Peatiness 7 Availability 3

Colour Quite full amber with bronze highlights **Nose** Quite full and sweet with an oily nutty unctuousness and a slight green edge to the peatiness **Flavour** Big-bodied, medium-dry with firm tannins, a dry smokiness and a light touch of richness **Finish** Long and smooth with a touch of perfume to the smokiness **Notes** Gordon & MacPhail bottling

Age 17 years **Distillation** 1976 **Strength** 53.8% abv

Sweetness 6 Peatiness 7 Availability 2

Colour Pale to mid-amber with yellow/gold highlights **Nose** Quite full-bodied and medium-sweet with a dark nutty peatiness **Flavour** Medium-dry, round and quite smooth with good body, a rich oakiness and a firm smokiness **Finish** Long, clean and gently smoky with richness on the tail **Notes** Gordon & MacPhail bottling; cask nos. 3588-91 distilled 21 July 1976

DISTILLED

≋ *1976* ≋

CASK

≋ 53.8% ≋
VOL

NATURAL HIGH STRENGTH

SINGLE MALT
SCOTCH WHISKY
CRAGGANMORE

PROPRIETORS D & J McCALLUM LTD
SPECIALLY SELECTED, PRODUCED AND BOTTLED BY
GORDON & MACPHAIL
ELGIN SCOTLAND
PRODUCT OF SCOTLAND

NATURAL
CASK
STRENGTH

1976

53.8%
VOL

70cl

CASK No.
3588, 3589,
3590, 3591
DISTILLED

21/7/76

BOTTLED

October 1993

CRAIGELLACHIE, BANFFSHIRE EST. 1891

Built by the Craigellachie Distillery Co. Ltd, a partnership formed by a group of blenders and whisky merchants. Rebuilt in 1964-5 and doubled to four stills. Now a part of United Distillers plc.

LOCATION The distillery stands on the spur of a hill, overlooking the village of Craigellachie, the precipitous Rock of Craigellachie, the River Spey and Thomas Telford's elegant single-span iron bridge of 1815.

NOTES Sir Peter Mackie, founder of *White Horse* blended whisky, was one of its original owners. The workers in 1923 lived in tied cottages and tended their gardens carefully. The owners of the best-kept gardens received prizes annually from the White Horse directors.

WATER A spring on Little Conval hill.

Age 14 years **Strength** 43% abv

Sweetness 8 Peatiness 3 Availability 6

Colour Straw with lemon highlights **Nose** Fresh and cerealy with a touch of greenness, a sherbert character, medium-sweet with good body **Flavour** Fresh, round, smooth, sweet and cerealy **Finish** Long and sweet with a touch of spice and a hint of smokiness at the back **Notes** United Distillers bottling

Age 15 years **Strength** 46% abv

Sweetness 7 Peatiness 6 Availability 2

Colour Very pale, almost crystal clear, watery coloured **Nose** Pungent, peaty, burnt heather with a slight orange/citrus tang to the edge **Flavour** Heavy, pungent, peaty , but with an edge of sweetness **Finish** Good, spicy and long - reminiscent of Islay **Notes** Wm Cadenhead bottling

SPEYSIDE

SINGLE MALT *SCOTCH WHISKY*

DAILUAINE

is the GAELIC for "the green vale". The *distillery*, established
in 1852, lies in a hollow by the *CARRON BURN* in *BANFFSHIRE*. This
single Malt Scotch Whisky has a *full bodied fruity* nose and a *smoky* finish.
For more than a *hundred years* all *distillery supplies* were despatched by
rail. The *steam locomotive* "DAILUAINE NO.1" was in use
from 1939 ~ 1967 and is *preserved* on the *STRATHSPEY RAILWAY*.

A G E D **16** Y E A R S

43% vol   Distilled & Bottled in *SCOTLAND*. DAILUAINE DISTILLERY, Carron, Aberlour, Banffshire, Scotland.   70 cl

CARRON, BY ABERLOUR, BANFFSHIRE   EST. 1852

Founded by William Mackenzie, a farmer at Carron and Rinnachat, the business was amalgamated with Talisker on Skye and nearby Imperial in 1898 to form Dailuaine-Talisker Distilleries Ltd. Became part of DCL in 1925 and run by SMD since 1930. Rebuilt after a fire in 1917 and again in 1959-60 when it was increased from four to six stills. Now part of United Distillers plc and licensed to UMGD. The old floor maltings were converted to a Saladin Box system, the use of which was discontinued in 1983.

LOCATION Situated in a natural hollow by the Carron Burn with river meadows all round it on an unclassified road between the A95 and B9102 at Archiestown. It is to the south of the River Spey.

NOTES The name "Dailuaine" comes from the Gaelic words "Dail Uaine", meaning "green valley", an apt description of its location. Although electricity reached the Carron area in 1938, it was not introduced to Dailuaine until 1950. For some years from the late 1880s the distillery operated a rail link to the Spey Valley line at Carron Station, a few hundred yards away. The steam locomotive which once worked the line is preserved on the Strathspey Railway which runs from Aviemore to Boat of Garten. The Spey Valley line itself fell to the Beeching axe in 1967, but much of it is now given over to walkers as *The Speyside Way*. Like its near neighbour, Cardhu, Dailuaine is one of the principal malts used in the Johnnie Walker blends.

WATER The Bailliemullich Burn.

DAILUAINE

Age 16 years **Strength** 43% abv

Sweetness 5 Peatiness 7 Availability 6

Colour Deep, full amber with bronze highlights **Nose** Quite full and sherried, a nutty, rubbery and damp oak character, medium-dry, slightly spirity **Flavour** Full-bodied, nutty, rubbery, medium-dry with a touch of tannin and a hint of richness **Finish** Long, dark and quite smooth with a touch of peat **Notes** United Distillers bottling

Age 23 years **Strength** 46% abv

Sweetness 4 Peatiness 6 Availability 2

Colour Very pale straw with a slight green tinge **Nose** Slightly medicinal, sweet with a gentle smokiness **Flavour** Very sweet, rich, peppery , fruity and spicy **Finish** Fine, smooth and with a nice sweetness **Notes** Wm Cadenhead bottling

Distillation 1971 **Strength** 40% abv

Sweetness 3 Peatiness 6 Availability 3

Colour Straw/amber with lemon/gold highlights **Nose** Quite dry with a rich fruitiness at the back **Flavour** Not quite dry, softly smoky and quite big-bodied with an oaky fullness **Finish** Smooth with good smoky length, but no real pungency **Notes** Gordon & MacPhail bottling

Distillation 1974 **Strength** 40% abv

Sweetness 5 Peatiness 6 Availability 3

Colour Amber with good yellow highlights **Nose** Soft, round, medium-bodied, medium-sweet and quite delicately peated with a slight note of toffee **Flavour** Quite soft and rich with good body, delicate peat and medium-sweet **Finish** Long, quite fresh and clean **Notes** Gordon & MacPhail bottling

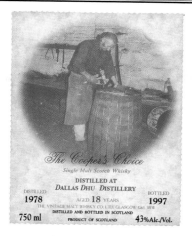

The Cooper's Choice

Single Malt Scotch Whisky

DISTILLED AT
DALLAS DHU DISTILLERY

DISTILLED
1978

AGED **18** YEARS

BOTTLED
1997

THE VINTAGE MALT WHISKY CO. LTD. GLASGOW G61 3RW

DISTILLED AND BOTTLED IN SCOTLAND

750 ml

PRODUCT OF SCOTLAND

43%Alc./Vol.

FORRES, MORAY EST. 1899

Originally to be called Dallasmore in 1898, the plans for the new distillery, designed by local Elgin architect Charles Doig, caused much correspondence in the local paper, the *Forres Gazette*. This included some verses from a local councillor. The fillings were eventually advertised as Dallas Dhu in November 1899, when it came on stream. One of several distilleries on the estate of the local laird, Alexander Edward, who in 1900 sold the distillery to the proprietors of Roderick Dhu, a whisky brand popular at the turn of the last century. The still house was burned down on 9 April 1939 and it did not reopen until 1947. It closed in 1983 and the licence was cancelled in 1992.

LOCATION Built in a hollow to the east of an unclassified road which forks south of the A940 on the southern outskirts of Forres.

NOTES The distillery buildings were handed over by Scottish Malt Distillers to the Historic Buildings and Monuments department of the Scottish Office who now run them as a model example of a distillery on the tourist trail. It is still possible to obtain special bottlings from old casks, although supplies of the whisky are now dwindling all the time. Dallas Dhu is a perfectly preserved example of what a small Highland distillery would have been like at the turn of the century. Had its water supply been more plentiful, it is most likely that the distillery would have been one of the ones chosen for expansion in recent years. As it is, its single pair of old stills has been preserved, as have all the old plant and machinery and the fine old distillery buildings.

WATER The Altyre Burn (known locally as the Scourie Burn).

Age 18 years   **Distillation** 1978   **Strength** 43% abv

Sweetness 4   Peatiness 6   Availability 2

Colour Amber with yellow highlights **Nose** Quite full-bodied, slightly spirity and medium-dry with a dark, burnt stick peaty character **Flavour** Smooth, slightly chewy and medium-dry with good body **Finish** Long, smoky and gently chewy **Notes** A "Cooper's Choice" bottling from The Vintage Malt Whisky Co.

Age 18 years   **Distillation** 1974   **Strength** 60.8% abv

Sweetness 4   Peatiness 3   Availability 1

Colour Mid-amber with gold highlights **Nose** Medium-bodied, nutty and malty, medium-dry with an edge of richness and a touch of lanolin **Flavour** Medium-dry, gently peaty, oaky tannins and a woody character **Finish** Quite dry, almost astringently tannic and spirity **Notes** Signatory bottling

Age 24 years   **Strength** 60.6% abv

Sweetness 4   Peatiness 4   Availability 2

Colour Pale amber with pale gold/lemon highlights **Nose** Medium-dry, slightly peppery with oaky vanilla **Flavour** Oaky, quite full, round and medium-dry **Finish** Chewy, spirity and gently oaky **Notes** United Distillers bottling

Distillation 1974   **Strength** 40% abv

Sweetness 6   Peatiness 4   Availability 2

Colour Straw/amber with yellow/gold highlights **Nose** Quite full, gently peated, oaky vanilla and a slight greenness **Flavour** Round, smooth, medium-sweet with a touch of nuttiness **Finish** Almost dry, oaky **Notes** Gordon & MacPhail bottling

Distillation 1971   **Strength** 40% abv

Sweetness 3   Peatiness 6   Availability 2

Colour Amber with old gold highlights **Nose** Quite rich, medium-sweet and appley with a smokiness at back **Flavour** Medium-dry, rich, quite fresh, clean and peaty with an appley richness **Finish** Clean, gently smoky, of medium length with a richness on the tail **Notes** Gordon & MacPhail bottling

Distillation 1969   **Strength** 40% abv

Sweetness 7   Peatiness 4   Availability 2

Colour Peaty/gold with good yellow highlights **Nose** Sweet, oaky and malty **Flavour** Medium-sweet, peppery with good body **Finish** Woody and dry with a good vanilla note on the finish **Notes** Gordon & MacPhail bottling

ALNESS, ROSS-SHIRE EST. 1839

Alexander Matheson was a partner in the Hong Kong trading firm Jardine Matheson & Co., traders in everything from tea to opium and, of course, whisky. In 1839, the very year of the first Opium War between China and Britain, Matheson purchased Ardross farm, on the shore of Cromarty Firth and opened a distillery. Whisky production at Dalmore was taken over by the Mackenzie family, who were able to buy the distillery and land as a result of the 1886 Crofters Act. Much of the whisky went to supply long-standing customers and friends, James Whyte and Charles Mackay, who owned the popular blend of Whyte & Mackay. The two businesses eventually merged in 1960. Whyte & Mackay is now owned by JBB (Greater Europe) plc, which is itself owned by Jim Beam Bourbon.

LOCATION Situated just off the A9, the distillery is in a beautiful position overlooking the Cromarty Firth to the Black Isle.

NOTES The distillery was well sited by its founders in the middle of a fine barley growing district. Its handsome offices are panelled with carved oak taken from a nearby shooting lodge. During the First World War, it was used by the US Navy as a base for manufacturing deep-sea mines and was burned down as the result of a fire. Production resumed again in 1922. Doubled from four to eight stills in 1966. Two of the stills in use today date from 1874.

WATER The River Alness which flows from Loch Morie.

DALMORE

Age 12 years   **Strength** 40% abv

Sweetness 6   Peatiness 6   Availability 8

Colour Full deep amber with good gold highlights **Nose** Slightly sweet, lightly oaky, with a fruitiness that is almost grape-like **Flavour** Full, medium-sweet, quite round and spicy with a slight smokiness **Finish** Lightly malty, smooth and almost dry - quite distinguished **Notes** Whyte & Mackay bottling

Age 30 years   **Distillation** 1963   **Strength** 54.5% abv

Sweetness 6   Peatiness 5   Availability 2

Colour Straw with pale yellow highlights **Nose** Quite full-bodied, round, medium-sweet and smooth with a rich liquorice/aniseed aroma **Flavour** Big-bodied, medium-sweet and round with a tangy touch of spice, pleasantly chewy tannins and gently peated **Finish** Long and gently chewy with a tang of aniseed **Notes** Wm Cadenhead bottling

Age 52 years   **Distillation** 1939   **Strength** 51.5% abv

Sweetness 6   Peatiness 3   Availability 0

Colour Full, rich amber **Nose** Enormous! Soft, gentle and smooth, a dark nuttiness, a slight delicate smokiness, very complex and with a liquorice character at the back **Flavour** Very full, still quite a fresh, green flavour, reminiscent of hedgerows **Finish** Long, powerful and very distinguished **Notes** A cask sample supplied by Whyte & Mackay for a tasting at Christie's in Glasgow

Distillation 1978   **Strength** 60.5% abv

Sweetness 6   Peatiness 5   Availability 2

Colour Quite pale straw with pale lemon highlights **Nose** Medium-bodied, fresh, clean and slightly green with an aroma of fennel, medium-dry with a slight mashy/malty character **Flavour** Medium-bodied, fresh, medium-dry with a ripe ripe greenness, slightly chewy with a delicate peatiness **Finish** Long, fresh and clean with a slight hedgerow character **Notes** Scotch Malt Whisky Society bottling: Cask no.13.14; bottled January,1994

DALWHINNIE, INVERNESS-SHIRE EST. 1897

Originally called Strathspey distillery, the company went into voluntary liquidation the year after it opened. Its name was changed c.1900, when it was purchased from the liquidator by the Dalwhinnie Distillery Co. The distillery was then sold at auction for £1,250 in 1905 to Cook & Bernheimer of New York and Baltimore, who, in turn, sold it to Macdonald Greenlees of Edinburgh in 1919. Macdonald Greenlees joined DCL in 1926 and SMD took over its management in 1930. Badly damaged by fire in 1934, it reopened in 1938. The distillery is now owned by United Distillers and licensed to James Buchanan & Co. Ltd. Two stills.

LOCATION   The distillery is situated next to the main railway line at the junction of the A9 (Inverness to the north, Perth to the south) and the A889 to Fort William.

NOTES   "Dalwhinnie" derives from the Gaelic word meaning "meeting place". At 326 m (1,073 ft) above sea-level, Dalwhinnie is Scotland's highest distillery. The distillery was located to take advantage of plentiful supplies of local peat, access to the railway line and its close access to the abundant supply of pure Highland water from the Lochan an Doire-Uaine. The distillery is Station 0582 of the Meteorological Office and it is the manager's duty to take daily readings of maximum and minimum temperatures, the number of hours of sunshine, wind speed and snow depth. Now readily available as one of United Distillers' *Classic Malts*, Dalwhinnie was previously better known for its role as one of the main building blocks of the Buchanan blends.

WATER   Lochan an Doire-Uaine.

Age 15 years   **Strength** 43% abv

Sweetness 7   Peatiness 5   Availability 8

Colour Straw/golden, honey-like **Nose** Quite aromatic, with a light peatiness and medium-sweet **Flavour** Round and sweet with a honey-like richness **Finish** Good, slightly sweet richness and excellent length **Notes** United Distillers bottling

Age 8 years   **Strength** 40% abv

Sweetness 6   Peatiness 7   Availability 0

Colour Light straw with golden highlights **Nose** Quite light, spirity and aromatic **Flavour** Round, but light, medium-sweet **Finish** Quite good, if a little spirity **Notes** DCL bottling (pre-Guinness)

Distillation 1970   **Strength** 40% abv

Sweetness 5   Peatiness 6   Availability 2

Colour Quite full amber with old gold highlights **Nose** Medium to full-bodied with a freshly hung wallpaper character, medium-dry and quite darkly smoky with a light nuttiness **Flavour** Big-bodied with a dark nuttiness, quite full tannins and medium-dry **Finish** Long, quite spicy and chewy with good richness **Notes** Gordon & MacPhail bottling

Age 27 years   **Distillation** 1966   **Strength** 45.5% abv

Sweetness 5   Peatiness 4   Availability 1

Colour Pale amber with pale gold highlights **Nose** Quite full-bodied, medium-sweet and oaky with an aroma of wet cement, a slight burnt wood character and a touch of mint **Flavour** Quite good body, fairly dominant wood, slightly chewy and medium-dry **Finish** Of reasonable length, with a burnt wood tang and a chewy tail **Notes** Wm Cadenhead bottling, bottled October 1993

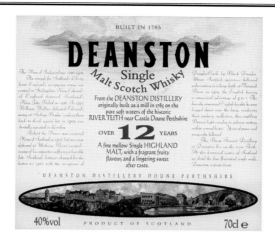

DOUNE, PERTHSHIRE EST. 1965

Founded by the Deanston Distillery Co. Ltd and sold to Invergordon Distillers in 1972. Silent from 1982 until sold to Burn Stewart Distillers in 1990. Four stills.

LOCATION Situated on the south bank of the River Teith within two miles of the centre of Doune village.

NOTES Burn Stewart has decided to use only unpeated barley in the production of Deanston, the company believing there to be sufficient peat for their purposes in the waters of the River Teith. Part of the buildings originally housed a textile mill. This was established in 1748 and was designed by Richard Arkwright of Spinning Jenny fame. Like the distillery, the mill also required good water supplies. The River Teith, as well as supplying all the process water, drives generators which provide all the distillery's electrical power needs - and also export power to the National Grid. The distillery complex includes attractive historic warehouses, many underground, in which are housed 45,000 casks of maturing whisky. The film *Monty Python and the Holy Grail* was shot at nearby Doune Castle.

WATER The River Teith.

Age 12 years **Strength** 40% abv

Sweetness 7 Peatiness 2 Availability 7

Colour Pale straw with lemon highlights **Nose** Medium weight and cerealy with an aroma of chocolate, medium-sweet and fragrant with a mashy character **Flavour** Medium-sweet, good weight, cerealy and smooth **Finish** Quite long and fresh with a touch of honey on the tail **Notes** Burn Stewart bottling

Age 17 years **Strength** 40% abv

Sweetness 4 Peatiness 6 Availability 6

Colour Amber with old gold highlights **Nose** Round, smooth and medium-bodied with good richness, quite lightly peated, nutty and medium-dry **Flavour** Medium-dry, quite full-bodied, round, nutty with a dark smokiness, rich and tangy **Finish** Long, nutty and tangy **Notes** Burn Stewart bottling

Age 25 years **Strength** 40% abv

Sweetness 4 Peatiness 2 Availability 2

Colour Mid-amber with yellow/gold highlights **Nose** Medium-sweet and rich with a soft buttery vanilla character and very lightly peated **Flavour** Medium-dry, round, quite full-bodied and creamy with gentle tannins **Finish** Long, gentle and buttery **Notes** Burn Stewart bottling

Distillation 1977 **Strength** 55.8% abv

Sweetness 4 Peatiness 3 Availability 2

Colour Straw/very pale amber with lemon/yellow highlights **Nose** Fresh and medium-sweet, round with a slight cereal note, lightly peated **Flavour** Medium-dry and round with a gentle smokiness and light oaky tannins **Finish** Fresh, quite zingy, lightly smoky and a hint of coffee **Notes** Wm Cadenhead bottling

Age 8 years **Strength** 40% abv

Sweetness 7 Peatiness 2 Availability 0

Colour Pale straw, pale yellow highlights **Nose** Sweet, with an oily, almost fatty, texture **Flavour** An almost honeyed fruity sweetness - unusual for a distillery so far south **Finish** Quite good, smooth and round **Notes** Invergordon bottling

HIGHLAND
SINGLE MALT *SCOTCH WHISKY*

DUFFTOWN

distillery was established near *Dufftown* at the end of the 19th. The
bright flash of the KINGFISHER can often be seen over the *DULLAN RIVER*, which flows past the *old stone buildings* of the *distillery* on
its way *north* to the *SPEY*. This *single HIGHLAND MALT WHISKY*
is typically *SPEYSIDE* in character with a *delicate, fragrant,*
almost *flowery* aroma and taste which *lingers* on the *palate*.

A G E D **15** Y E A R S

43% vol   Distilled & Bottled in *SCOTLAND* DUFFTOWN DISTILLERY, Dufftown, Keith, Banffshire. *Scotland*   70 cl

DUFFTOWN, BANFFSHIRE EST. 1887

Converted from a former meal mill in 1896 by the Dufftown-Glenlivet Distillery Co. and acquired in 1897 by P. MacKenzie & Co., also owners of Blair Athol distillery, Pitlochry. Purchased by Perth blenders Arthur Bell & Sons in 1933. Originally with two stills extended to four in 1974 and six in 1979. Owned by United Distillers since 1985 and licensed to UMGD from 1992.

LOCATION   Situated in the Dullan Glen on the outskirts of Dufftown near the sixth-century Mortlach parish church.

NOTES   From Dufftown, which has always been a source of good whisky. It is said that Rome was built on seven hills, but Dufftown was built on seven stills. Dufftown was the sixth distillery to be established in Dufftown and the fourth in the 1890's. The original water mill at Dufftown is still in working order. Dufftown, like the malt from its sister distillery, Blair Athol, plays an important role as one of the principal constituents of the Bell's blends.

WATER   Jock's Well in the Conval Hills.

Age 15 years   **Strength** 43% abv

Sweetness 8   Peatiness 3   Availability 6

Colour Pale amber with lemon/gold highlights **Nose** Medium-bodied, medium-sweet, quite rich and fruity with a slight floral note **Flavour** Medium-sweet and fresh, quite rich and delicately peated with a nice sweetness **Finish** Clean and gently smoky with the good sweetness lasting **Notes** United Distillers bottling

Age 10 years   **Strength** 40% abv

Sweetness 8 Peatiness 4 Availability 0

Colour Straw/golden **Nose** Light with hints of burnt rubber and a floweriness in the background **Flavour** Medium-sweet, smooth and slightly fruity **Finish** Lasts well, with good richness, but the rubberiness lingers **Notes** Arthur Bell Distillers bottling

Age 12 years   **Distillation** 1980   **Strength** 43% abv

Sweetness 7 Peatiness 4 Availability 1

Colour Very pale watery straw with pale lemon highlights **Nose** Quite big-bodied, fresh, young and cerealy, green herby and mashy **Flavour** Medium-dry, quite full-bodied, fresh and spicy with a richness at the back **Finish** Long, slightly vegetal and medium-sweet **Notes** Blackadder International bottling

Age 16 years   **Distillation** 1980   **Strength** 55.7% abv

Sweetness 7 Peatiness 3 Availability 2

Colour Amber with old gold highlights **Nose** Quite full-bodied with a dark, nutty, earthy peaty character, medium-sweet, quite rich and with a peppery touch **Flavour** Medium-dry, quite big-bodied, nutty, very rich and quite delicately peated **Finish** Long and medium-sweet with a delicate lightness and a hint of tablet **Notes** Signatory bottling from butt no. 3786 distilled 10 April 1980

Vintage 1980
Single Highland Malt Scotch Whisky
Matured in a sherry butt for 16 years
Distilled at Dufftown Distillery
on 10.4.80   Bottled 5.12.96
Butt. No. 3786   Bottle No. —   of 495
This whisky has been selected, produced and bottled in Scotland for and under the sole responsibility of Signatory Vintage Scotch Whisky Co. Ltd.
Edinburgh EH6 6LJ Scotland
70cl   55.7%vol

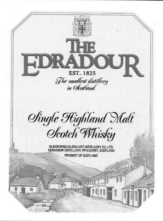

THE EDRADOUR
EST. 1825
*The smallest distillery
in Scotland*

*Single Highland Malt
Scotch Whisky*

GLENFORRES-GLENLIVET DISTILLERY CO. LTD.
EDRADOUR DISTILLERY, PITLOCHRY, SCOTLAND
PRODUCT OF SCOTLAND

PITLOCHRY, PERTHSHIRE EST 1825

Founded on land rented from the Duke of Atholl, Edradour appears little changed by the passing of time. The distillery has gone through several interesting changes of ownership, the most notable of which was becoming a subsidiary of William Whitely & Company, which it remained for most of the 20th century. It is now owned by Campbell Distillers, a subsidiary of the French company Pernod Ricard, who have invested substantially in the development of both the distillery and its single malt.

LOCATION   Situated on the A924, just outside the village of Moulin, at the foot of a steep hill; a collection of old farmstead-like buildings, past which tumbles a fast-flowing burn. An idyllic setting.

NOTES   Scotland's smallest distillery whose actual output is only enough spirit to fill 12 casks per week. The last remaining of the once numerous Perthshire "farm" distilleries and the last actually distilling by hand. It is run by just three people. The output of single malt is just 2,000 cases a year, the balance being kept as "top dressing" principally for the *House of Lords* blend. Also previously known as *Glenforres*, which name is now given to a vatting of several single malts, of which the Edradour is one. An excellent visitor centre.

WATER   A spring on Ben Vrackie

Age 10 years **Strength** 40% abv

Sweetness 9 Peatiness 3 Availability 7

Colour Richly gold, gloriously viscous **Nose** Sweet, almondy aroma with a slight fruitiness **Flavour** A smooth, malty taste with a hint of dryness **Finish** A buttery aftertaste and creamily smooth **Notes** Campbell Distillers bottling

FETTERCAIRN, KINCARDINESHIRE EST. 1824

The Fettercairn distillery originally stood two miles further up the mountain in the heart of a smuggling district, but this was abandoned in 1824 when the present building, converted from a former cornmill, was opened. It was rebuilt in 1887-90 after a fire. Silent 1926-39, when acquired by a subsidiary of National Distillers of America. Extended from two to four stills in 1966. Now owned by JBB (Greater Europe) who market their own bottlings as Old Fettercairn.

LOCATION Situated just off the B974 close to the River Esk on the outskirts of Fettercairn, the distillery rests at the foot of the Cairngorm mountains.

NOTES According to one contemporary account at the turn of the 19th century, the village of Fettercairn was home to 50 weavers, 10 millers, seven shopkeepers, five flaxdressers and one surgeon. There were also numerous distillers who practised their illicit trade on the remote slopes of the nearby Cairngorm Mountains, but these, not surprisingly, did not admit to their trade. In 1829, one John Gladstone bought the nearby Fasque estate. He was the father of William Ewart Gladstone, one of Britain's most illustrious prime ministers and probably the best friend the whisky industry ever had amongst their number. He introduced several reforms crucial to the industry, the most important of which was in 1853 when he abolished the crippling Malt Tax. Another was to permit the selling of bottled whisky to the public. Extensive warehouses contain some 25,000 casks of whisky in differing stages of maturity, some dating back to 1939.

WATER Springs in the nearby Cairngorm Mountains.

Age No age statement **Strength** 40% abv

Sweetness	4	Peatiness	4	Availability	0

Colour Palish straw/golden with yellow edges **Nose** Light and fresh, delicately peated **Flavour** Slightly dry, leafy and smooth with good body **Finish** Clean with a subtle smokiness **Notes** Whyte & Mackay bottling as Old Fettercairn

Age 10 years **Strength** 40% abv

Sweetness	4	Peatiness	4	Availability	6

Colour Straw with good gold highlights **Nose** Quite full, dryish with notes of oaky vanilla and malty **Flavour** Dry, spicy, of medium weight, creamy and smooth **Finish** Dry, long and chewy **Notes** Whyte & Mackay bottling as Old Fettercairn

Distillation 1980 **Strength** 43% abv

Sweetness	3	Peatiness	6	Availability	2

Colour Quite deep amber with ruby-bronze highlights **Nose** Quite big and nutty with a dark, deep burnt character, a hint of rubber and quite gently peated **Flavour** Good body, round and well-peated with a slight burnt character medium-dry with oaky tannins **Finish** Long and smoky with a touch of richness and spicy with an almost salty tail **Notes** Signatory bottling

SINGLE HIGHLAND MALT SCOTCH WHISKY
DISTILLED AT
GLEN ALBYN
DISTILLERY
Proprietors: Mackinlay & Birnie Ltd
DISTILLED **1972** DISTILLED

70cl   SPECIALLY SELECTED, PRODUCED AND BOTTLED BY
GORDON & MACPHAIL   40%vol
ELGIN · SCOTLAND
PRODUCT OF SCOTLAND

CONNOISSEURS CHOICE

INVERNESS EST. 1846

Founded by James Sutherland, the then Provost of Inverness on the ruins of the Muirtown Brewery which had catered for the thirst of the men who built the Caledonian Canal. Rebuilt in 1884 after being used as a flour mill following a period of disuse. Acquired in 1972 by DCL from Mackinlay & Birnie Ltd, a company owned by 14 members of the Mackinlay family of the Leith distillers and 11 members of the local Birnie family, John Birnie having been the manager and distiller in 1892. Managed by SMD until its demolition in 1988, distilling having ceased in 1983. When operational it had two stills.

LOCATION Glen Albyn was situated on the east side of the A9 to the north of Inverness. It faced Glen Mhor distillery across the Great North Road where it crosses the Caledonian Canal.

NOTES The distillery was closed between 1917 and 1919 and used as a US Naval base for the manufacture of mines. For a long time supplies were delivered by sea. Demolished in 1988, along with Glen Mhor, to make way for a supermarket development. Prior to 1745, Inverness had been the chief malting town in Scotland.

WATER Loch Ness.

Distillation 1972   **Strength** 40% abv

Sweetness 7   Peatiness 5   Availability 4

Colour Amber with yellow highlights and a green tinge **Nose** Quite good body, medium-sweet, ripe and fruity, a slight buttery toffee character with a nice dark smokiness **Flavour** Medium-sweet, rich and cerealy with an almost hop-like flavour, good body and delicately peated **Finish** Clean, quite rich and of good length **Notes** Gordon & MacPhail bottling

Age 12 years   **Distillation** 1980   **Strength** 43% abv

Sweetness 7   Peatiness 2   Availability 0

Colour Very pale straw with lemon highlights **Nose** Light, fresh, fruity and medium-dry **Flavour** Medium-sweet, quite full-bodied and round **Finish** Of good length, fresh with a lingering sweetness **Notes** Master of Malt bottling, cask no 294

Distillation 1963   **Strength** 40% abv

Sweetness 7   Peatiness 4   Availability 1

Colour Peaty gold with greenish tinges **Nose** Quite sweet, creamy and fruity with hints of almonds **Flavour** Sweet, nutty and creamy **Finish** Fine, long and delicately sweet **Notes** Gordon & MacPhail bottling

Distillation 1965   **Strength** 40% abv

Sweetness 7   Peatiness 4   Availability 1

Colour Full amber with gold highlights **Nose** Medium-sweet, rich, lanolin and peppery characters with an almost raisiny fruitiness **Flavour** Rich, oaky, of medium weight and quite smooth **Finish** Peppery, oaky and dry **Notes** Gordon & MacPhail bottling

RUTHRIE, ABERLOUR, BANFFSHIRE EST. 1968

Built in 1967-8 by Mackinlay McPherson Ltd, a subsidiary company of Scottish & Newcastle Breweries Ltd. Sold to Invergordon Distillers in 1985 along with its then sister distillery, Isle of Jura. Closed in 1987 and reopened again in 1989 after being purchased by Campbell Distillers, a subsidiary of the French company Pernod Ricard. Four stills.

LOCATION The distillery nestles at the foot of Ben Rinnes, a short way from the A95.

NOTES Campbell Distillers also owns Aberlour and Edradour distilleries. One of three distilleries designed by Delme Evans, the other two being Jura and Tullibardine.

WATER Springs near Ben Rinnes.

Age 12 years **Strength** 40% abv

Sweetness 7	Peatiness 4	Availability 0

Colour Pale, soft golden **Nose** Full and delightfully leafy **Flavour** Full-bodied, lightly peated, slightly sweet **Finish** Elegant and smooth **Notes** Invergordon bottling

Age 11 years **Distillation** 1985 **Strength** 43% abv

Sweetness 7	Peatiness 3	Availability 2

Colour Very pale straw with pale lemon highlights **Nose** Medium-bodied, quite fresh with a slight youthful mashy character, lightly peated with a sweet apple note **Flavour** Medium-sweet, quite smooth and lightly peated with a touch of spice **Finish** Lingeringly sweet with hints of smoke and vanilla tablet on the tail **Notes** Signatory bottling from cask nos. 4072-4

GLENBURGIE

CONNOISSEURS CHOICE

Connoisseurs Choice, a range of single malts from various districts of Scotland.

The distilleries situated in the area of the valley of the River Spey produce some of the finest malt whiskies.

SINGLE SPEYSIDE
MALT SCOTCH WHISKY
DISTILLED AT

GLENBURGIE
DISTILLERY
PROPRIETORS: Jas. & Geo. Stodart Ltd

DISTILLED 1968 DISTILLED

SPECIALLY SELECTED, PRODUCED AND BOTTLED BY

75cl   GORDON & MACPHAIL   40%vol
ELGIN · SCOTLAND
PRODUCT OF SCOTLAND

ALVES, NR FORRES, MORAY EST. 1829

Founded on this site as Kilnflat by William Paul, the grandfather of Dr Listen Paul, a celebrated London surgeon of the latter part of the 19th century. Silent from 1927 to 1935. Controlled by Hiram Walker from 1930, and purchased outright by them in 1936. Now part of Allied Domecq and operated by Allied Distillers Ltd. Two stills.

LOCATION   Sited in a valley to the south of the A95 some five miles to the east of Forres.

NOTES   The distillery did once have two short-necked Lomond stills which produced a heavier malt known as *Glencraig*. Glenburgie is one of the main malts associated with Ballantine's blended whisky. An earlier distillery, possibly founded in 1810, was once on this site.

WATER   Local springs.

Distillation 1948   **Strength** 40% abv
Sweetness 5   Peatiness 6   Availability 1

Colour Deep amber with bronze highlights **Nose** Very big, dark and powerful, with characters of linseed and soft oak with a slightly green touch, medium-dry, with a slight "burnt" character and a pleasant spiritiness **Flavour** Big, rich and smoky with a not too dominant oakiness, the "burnt" character again and quite big tannins **Finish** Long, quite elegant, slightly chewy and gently smoky **Notes** Bottled in 1995 as part of Gordon & MacPhail's *Centenary Reserve* series

Distillation 1960 **Strength** 40% abv

Sweetness 7 Peatiness 5 Availability 2

Colour Pale straw with good yellow highlights **Nose** Woody, slightly sweet and floral **Flavour** Medium-sweet, slightly spicy, oaky, quite heavy **Finish** Oaky of reasonable length **Notes** Gordon & MacPhail bottling

Distillation 1966 **Strength** 57.6% abv

Sweetness 7 Peatiness 5 Availability 3

Colour Quite deep amber with old gold highlights **Nose** Big-bodied, unctuous, creamy oak and medium-sweet with a light peat note **Flavour** Rich and round, with sweet oaky vanilla, medium-sweet and quite delicately peated. **Finish** Long with gently chewy tannins and a slight hint of coffee on the tail **Notes** Gordon & MacPhail bottling from cask no. 3410 distilled 31 March 1996 and 11690 distilled 15 November 1966

GLENCRAIG

Distillation 1970 **Strength** 40% abv

Sweetness 3 Peatiness 1 Availability 2

Colour Mid amber with yellow/gold highlights and a tinge of green **Nose** Light, fresh, fruity, medium-sweet with a greenness **Flavour** Light, clean, medium-dry, very lightly peated with a fresh greenness **Finish** Clean and fresh **Notes** Produced from the Lomond stills and bottled as *Glencraig* by Gordon & MacPhail

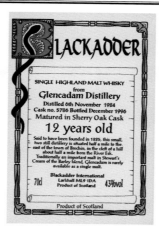

SINGLE HIGHLAND MALT WHISKY
from
Glencadam Distillery
Distilled 6th November 1984
Cask no. 5786 Bottled December 1996
Matured in Sherry Oak Cask
12 years old
Said to have been founded in 1825, this small,
two still distillery is situated half a mile to the
east of the town of Brechin, in the cleft of a hill
about half a mile from the River Esk.
Traditionally an important malt in Stewart's
Cream of the Barley blend, Glencadam is rarely
available as a single malt.

Blackadder International
70cl   Larkhall ML9 1DA   43%vol
Product of Scotland

Product of Scotland

BRECHIN, ANGUS EST 1825

Said to have been founded in 1825, the distillery passed through a number of owners until purchased by Hiram Walker in 1954. Now part of Allied Domecq and operated by Allied Distillers Ltd. Two stills.

LOCATION Situated half a mile to the east of the town of Brechin in the cleft of a hill. It is also about half a mile from the River Esk.

NOTES Presently available only through the independent bottlers. Some of the make goes into *Stewart's Cream of the Barley* blended Scotch whisky.

WATER Springs in the Unthank Hills.

Distillation 1974 **Strength** 40% abv

Sweetness 7   Peatiness 4   Availability 4

Colour Straw/amber with gold/lemon highlights **Nose** Rich, medium-sweet, woody, spirity with a touch of linseed and greenness **Flavour** Medium-bodied, quite rich, soft oak, quite simple and lightly peated **Finish** Light with a touch of spice **Notes** Gordon & MacPhail bottling

Age 12 years **Distillation** 1984 **Strength** 43% abv

Sweetness 6   Peatiness 4   Availability 1

Colour Quite deep amber with old gold highlights **Nose** Full-bodied, dark, burnt and rich brazil-nutty, quite delicately peated with unctuous vanillin **Flavour** Big, dark and full-bodied, rich and round with notes of oaky vanilla **Finish** Long and dark with touches of vanilla and spice **Notes** Blackadder International bottling from Sherry butt no. 5786 distilled 6 November 1984

PRODUCE OF SCOTLAND · THE GLENDRONACH DISTILLERY Cº LIMITED · LICENSED SINCE 1826

FORGUE BY HUNTLY ABERDEENSHIRE, SCOTLAND
BOTTLED IN SCOTLAND BY THE PROPRIETOR

The GLENDRONACH

TRADITIONAL

YEAR **12** OLD

Single Highland Malt Scotch Whisky

MATURED IN SEASONED OAK AND SHERRY CASKS

FORGUE, NR HUNTLY, ABERDEENSHIRE EST. 1826

Glendronach's founder, James Allardes, was a frequent guest of the 5th Duke of Gordon who was largely responsible for the Excise Act of 1823 which was instrumental in creating the modern malt whisky industry. The distillery has had various owners over the years, including Captain Charles Grant, younger son of William Grant of Glenfiddich fame, who purchased it from the Crown in 1920. It remained in that branch of the Grant family until 1960, when George Grey Grant sold it to Wm. Teacher & Sons Ltd. Extended from two to four stills in 1966-7. Now part of Allied Domecq and operated by Allied Distillers Ltd.

LOCATION Situated straddling the Dronach Burn in the valley of Forgue, which supplies the cooling water. The distillery is set amongst tall trees, in which an established colony of rooks is said to bring luck.

NOTES Distilling was undoubtedly carried out in the area in the days before legal distilling came to Glendronach and the noisy rooks would have proved a useful ally to warn of approaching strangers - especially Excise officers. Built in the form of a square and covering four acres, Glendronach is one of the few distilleries where barley is still malted on a malting floor, providing about 15% of the distillery's requirement. It also has coal-fired stills. Glendronach is one of the most important constituents of *Teacher's Highland Cream* Scotch whisky.

WATER "The Source" - a spring four miles east of the distillery.

SHERRY CASK
Age 12 years   **Strength** 40% abv

Sweetness 4   Peatiness 4   Availability 0

Colour Quite dark, richly demerara in colour **Nose** Rich, full and sweet with a smoky edge **Flavour** Rich and full with a slight maltiness **Finish** Long with hints of shortbready-sweetness in the aftertaste **Notes** Discontinued

ORIGINAL
Age 12 years   **Strength** 40% abv

Sweetness 5   Peatiness 5   Availability 0

Colour Straw with gold highlights **Nose** Slightly sweet, biscuity, quite mellow and buttery **Flavour** Medium-sweet, soft, mellow, round **Finish** Slightly spicy, biscuity, good length **Notes** Caledonian Distillers bottling. Discontinued

TRADITIONAL
Age 12 years   **Strength** 40% abv

Sweetness 5   Peatiness 6   Availability 6

Colour Straw with golden highlights **Nose** Quite full, medium-sweet, rich, soft, almost honeyed with a slight oily note **Flavour** Medium-dry, quite rich, full and smooth with a touch of spice, buttery and delicately smoky **Finish** Soft, smooth and long with some smokiness on the tail **Notes** Caledonian Distillers bottling. Traditional is aged in a combination of plain oak and sherry oak casks. It replaced the above two versions

SHERRY CASK
Age 18 years   **Strength** 43% abv

Sweetness 6   Peatiness 3   Availability 1

Colour Deep amber with mahogany highlights **Nose** Full, dark oak, nutty, medium-dry with a slight richness **Flavour** Big-bodied, smooth, rich, oaky, nutty and medium-dry **Finish** Long, dark, oaky with a toasted nutty character **Notes** Caledonian Distillers bottling. Very little remains available

Age 9 years   **Distillation** 1987   **Strength** 58.5% abv

Sweetness 4   Peatiness 7   Availability 2

Colour Amber with old gold highlights **Nose** Full-bodied, rich and medium-dry with a fresh peatiness and a peanut/popcorn character **Flavour** Full, medium-dry and rich with a dark nutty smokiness **Finish** Long, chewy and smoky **Notes** Signatory bottling from butt no. 57 distilled 29 May 1987

SPEYSIDE
SINGLE MALT
SCOTCH WHISKY

GLENDULLAN

distillery, located in a beautiful *wooded valley* was /// built in 1897 and is one of seven *established* in *Dufftown* in the (19th). The *River Fiddich* flows past the *distillery*; originally *providing power* to drive machinery, it is now used /// for cooling. *GLENDULLAN* is a firm, mellow *single MALT SCOTCH WHISKY* with a fruity bouquet and a smooth *lingering* finish.

AGED **12** YEARS

43% vol

Distilled & Bottled in *SCOTLAND*
GLENDULLAN DISTILLERY
Dufftown, Keith, Banffshire, Scotland

70 cl

DUFFTOWN, BANFFSHIRE EST. 1897

The last distillery to be built in Dufftown in the 19th century and the distillery which prompted the "Dufftown is built on seven stills" line. The location was chosen not just for its beauty, but also for its practical convenience. It was sited to take advantage of water power and was also able to share neighbouring Mortlach's private railway siding. Two stills. Acquired by DCL in 1926 and managed by SMD, latterly UMGD, from 1930, the licensees are Macdonald Greenlees & Co. Ltd. Rebuilt 1962. An additional distillery with six stills was built on the field between "Old Glendullan" and the employees' homes in 1971-2. The distance between the two units was defined as "a short one when the weather's good and a long one when it isn't". The old distillery was closed in 1985 and is used as UMGD's maintenance workshops. Now part of United Distillers plc.

LOCATION   Close by the junction of the A941 and A920.

NOTES   Glendullan's process water comes from the River Fiddich. Glendullan was a favourite whisky of King Edward VIII and plays an important role in the *Old Parr* blend.

WATER   Springs in the Conval Hills.

Age 12 years   **Strength** 43% abv

Sweetness 8   Peatiness 4   Availability 6

Colour Pale straw with a touch of green and lemon/yellow highlights **Nose** Quite full, rich appley, slightly spirity with a hint of cereals and lightly peated **Flavour** Medium-dry, rich, sweet oaky vanilla, a touch of greenness, spirity and malty **Finish** Long, smooth, oaky with a delicately smoky tail **Notes** United Distillers bottling

Age 12 years **Strength** 43% abv

Sweetness	5	Peatiness	3	Availability	0

Colour Pale golden with a slightly greenish edge **Nose** Full and fruity with a distinctly sweet oaky hint **Flavour** Full, round, warm, sweet and spicy with a slight flavour of coffee/toffee **Finish** Long and lingering, sweet and memorable **Notes** DCL (pre-Guinness) bottling

Age 10 years **Distillation** 1983 **Strength** 43% abv

Sweetness	8	Peatiness	3	Availability	1

Colour Very pale watery straw with a pale lemon tinge **Nose** Sweet, fruity, quite full-bodied, a touch mashy, quite fresh and delicately peated **Flavour** Quite sweet, fresh with good body and a nice fruity touch **Finish** Quite fresh, of good length with a firm touch of dry tannin **Notes** Blackadder International bottling

The spirit safe

Built between 1898 and 1900 by a partnership of William Simpson, a former manager of Glenfarclas, and James Carle, the local agent for the North of Scotland Bank. Production began on 1 May 1900. Acquired by SMD in 1930. Extended from two to six stills when rebuilt in 1964. The distiller's licence is held by *White Horse* Distillers Ltd. Now part of United Distillers plc.

LOCATION Situated on the A941, the main Elgin to Rothes road.

NOTES A very compact distillery, due to a shortage of capital when it was built. The architect, Charles Doig of Elgin, said at the time that Glen Elgin would be the last to be built on Speyside for more than sixty years. He was right! The next was Glen Keith in 1957. Glen Elgin is an important constituent in the White Horse blend.

WATER Springs near Millbuies Loch.

Age 12 years **Strength** 43% abv

Sweetness 8 Peatiness 4 Availability 1

Colour Pale gold with peaty depths **Nose** Sweet, slightly green with fine, soft oak and hints of honey **Flavour** Soft, pleasantly sweet, smooth and round with honey coming through on the palate **Finish** Smooth, fruity and distinguished **Notes** DCL (pre-Guinness bottling). A more recent version is now available, apparently still 12 years old, but with no age statement on the label

Age 22 years **Distillation** 1971 **Strength** 50.3% abv

Sweetness 7 Peatiness 8 Availability 2

Colour Bright and clear, but grey/green, almost khaki **Nose** Sweet, round, a strange sooty smokiness with a slight green edge and quite good body **Flavour** Big-bodied, medium-sweet, very smoky with a burnt character **Finish** Long, smoky, slightly austere and tannic **Notes** Wm Cadenhead bottling

GLENESK

GLENESK

YEARS 12 OLD
SINGLE MALT
HIGHLAND SCOTCH WHISKY

Wᵐ Sanderson son Ltd.
Distillers, South Queensferry, Scotland
Bottled in Scotland
40% vol 75 cl

HILLSIDE, BY MONTROSE, ANGUS EST. 1897

Glenesk distillery was first known as *Highland Esk* when convert-ed from a former flax-spinning mill in 1897 by Septimus Parsonage & Co. and James Isles of Dundee, its name was changed to *North Esk* in 1899 when acquired by J. F. Caille Heddle. Closed during the First World War. Reopened in 1938, and re-equipped by new owners Associated Scottish Distillers Ltd to produce grain whisky under the name Montrose Distillery. Acquired by DCL in 1954 and operated off and on by SGD until 1964, when it was transferred to SMD and converted back to a malt distillery. A large drum maltings was built in 1968. Renamed Glenesk in 1980.

LOCATION Two miles north of Montrose, half a mile west of the A92 on the south bank of the River Esk.

NOTES Glenesk has also been known as *Hillside,* which is the name United Distillers bottles under in its *Rare Malts* series. The distillery is now closed and unlikely to reopen, however the maltings are in full production for United Distillers. Glenesk was traditionally an important malt to William Sanderson's *VAT 69* blend.

WATER The river North Esk.

Age 25 years **Distillation 1970** years **Strength** 60.1% abv

Sweetness	3	Peatiness	7	Availability	1

Colour Pale straw with pale yellow highlights **Nose** Medium-dry, quite rich with a lemon sherbet touch, firm peatiness at the back and a slight cereal note on the end **Flavour** Quite good body and medium-dry with chewy tannins and a burnt peat character **Finish** Long with a dry cereal note and a chewy burnt smokiness **Notes** United Distillers *Rare Malt* bottling

MARYPARK, BALLINDALLOCH, BANFFSHIRE EST. 1836

Founded by Robert Hay, a tenant farmer at Rechlerich farm, it is said that the plant used was taken from Dandaleith Distillery, near Craigellachie. It came into the family ownership of the Grant family when Hay died in 1865 and John Grant took over the tenancy. It was let to John Smith until 1870, when he left to run his new Cragganmore distillery. The running of the distillery was then taken over by John Grant himself and it has been run by successive generations of the Grant family ever since. The present John Grant is the fifth generation to be in charge, while his father George Grant sits as Chairman of the company. Extended from two to four stills in 1960 and to six in 1976.

LOCATION   South of the A95, almost midway between Grantown-on-Spey and Craigellachie, lying in quite desolate moorland at the foot of Ben Rinnes.

NOTES   Glenfarclas means "valley of the green grass". The whisky ages very well. "Whisky Tom" Dewar waxed most lyrical of a 30 year old he tasted in 1912, although George Grant considers the 15 year old to be perfection - all a matter of personal taste. Glenfarclas has been the pioneer of cask strength whiskies, the company's *Glenfarclas 105*, bottled at 60% abv, long setting the bench mark for such whiskies and having a loyal following worldwide. Glenfarclas used to be casked in a variety of casks, but all new Glenfarclas spirit is now aged in 100% sherrywood at the distillery. Glenfarclas has an excellent reception centre.

WATER   Springs on Ben Rinnes.

Age 10 years   **Strength** 40% abv

Sweetness 9   Peatiness 5   Availability 9

Colour Straw with good gold highlights **Nose** Slightly rubbery, delicately light and sweet, leafy oak with a slight tang of coffee **Flavour** Sweet, malty, full, rich and round **Finish** Slightly spicy, long and characterful **Notes** J&G Grant bottling

GLENFARCLAS 105

Age No age statement   **Strength** 60% abv

Sweetness 7   Peatiness 6   Availability 7

Colour Deep, peaty amber with gold highlights **Nose** Very spirity, slightly astringent, slightly sweet **Flavour** Spirity, malty, a little oily-oak character, quite austere **Finish** Long, flavoursome and, surprisingly, quite dry **Notes** J&G Grant bottling

Age 15 years   **Strength** 46% abv

Sweetness 9   Peatiness 4   Availability 6

Colour Gold/peaty with very bright rich golden highlights **Nose** Full, rich and sweet, with a luscious, unctuous oily-oak character and delicately peated **Flavour** Sweet, rich and creamy, very intense, full bodied and smooth with hints of burnt peat **Finish** Gloriously sweet, gently smoky - long and distinguished **Notes** J&G Grant bottling

Age 21 years   **Strength** 43% abv

Sweetness 9   Peatiness 4   Availability 3

Colour Quite dark amber with rich gold highlights **Nose** Full, rich, sweet vanilla oak with hints of mint **Flavour** Rich, big, full-bodied, delicately smoky **Finish** Lightly smoky, rich and long-lasting **Notes** J&G Grant bottling

Age 25 years   **Strength** 43% abv

Sweetness 9   Peatiness 5   Availability 4

Colour Amber with old gold highlights **Nose** Full, ripe, sweet and round, finely peated with aromas of orange marmalade, honey, coffee and sherry nuttiness **Flavour** Full-flavoured, smooth, sweet with oaky vanilla tannins and coffee and toffee flavours **Finish** Fresh with a smoky nuttiness and long lasting **Notes** J&G Grant bottling

DUFFTOWN, BANFFSHIRE EST. 1887

When Alfred Barnard published his *Whisky Distilleries of the United Kingdom* in 1887, the home of the world's best-selling malt was only just being built. Owned by William Grant & Sons Ltd, it today boasts no less than 28 stills: 10 wash and 18 spirit. No mean achievement for a distillery founded with £120 capital and using second-hand equipment from Cardow distillery; but such has been the success of the family enterprise founded by William Grant of Glenfiddich, the son of a soldier who had served under Wellington.

L O C A T I O N   Situated near the junction of the A941 and the B975 to the north of the centre of Dufftown.

N O T E S   One of only two malt whiskies to be bottled at the distillery (the other being Springbank). The first distillery in Scotland to open a visitor centre, Glenfiddich now attracts 125,000 visitors a year. It welcomed its one millionth visitor, Mr Ronald Pederson from Albany in New York State, on 4 August 1987.

W A T E R   The Robbie Dhu springs

GLENFIDDICH SPECIAL RESERVE
Age No age statement **Strength** 40% abv

Sweetness 8 Peatiness 5 Availability 10

Colour Straw/ gold **Nose** Cooked mash, light, soapy, delicately peated **Flavour** Light, sweet, well-balanced and gentle **Finish** Sweet and of medium length **Notes** William Grant bottling

GLENFIDDICH EXCELLENCE
Age 18 years **Strength** 43% abv

Sweetness 8 Peatiness 4 Availability 2

Colour Straw with pale gold highlights **Nose** Fresh, medium-bodied and round, notes of citrus and a grapey character, a slight bubble-gummy sweetness, lanolin character and lightly peated **Flavour** Soft, smooth, medium-sweet and round with an unctuous lanolin oakiness **Finish** Clean, surprisingly dry, but rich, with a fresh, light peatiness **Notes** William Grant bottling

GLENFIDDICH ANCIENT RESERVE
Age 18 years **Strength** 43% abv

Sweetness 8 Peatiness 3 Availability 4

Colour Straw with greeny/gold highlights **Nose** Rich, medium-sweet, grapey, quite soft and with a slight tang of coffee **Flavour** Medium-sweet, spicy, slightly peppery with a slight green leafiness **Finish** Good, smooth and long with hints of coffee **Notes** William Grant bottling

GLENFIDDICH WEDGWOOD DECANTER
Age 21 years **Strength** 43% abv

Sweetness 9 Peatiness 5 Availability 1

Colour Quite pale straw with good yellow/gold highlights **Nose** Fresh, malty, medium-dry and slightly grapey **Flavour** Soft, warm, grapily fruity, quite big-bodied, spicy and medium-sweet **Finish** Herby, long, sweet and smooth with a soft maltiness at the end **Notes** William Grant bottling

GLENFIDDICH CASK STRENGTH

Age No age statement **Strength** 51% abv

Sweetness 8 Peatiness 6 Availability 4

Colour Straw with pale gold highlights **Nose** Fresh, medium-sweet and quite full-bodied with a quite soft peat character and fruity notes of lemon and apple **Flavour** Medium-sweet, smooth, round, medium-bodied with a gentle peatiness **Finish** Long and fresh with a good smoky backbone

The workforce at Glenfiddich

Vintage 1970
Single Lowland Malt Scotch Whisky
Matured in oak casks for 23 years
Distilled at the Glenflagler Distillery
on 6.10.70   *Bottled 5.94*
Cask nos. 1260 + 7861   Bottle no.   of 350
*This whisky has been selected, produced and bottled in
Scotland for and under the sole responsibility of*
5cl   *Signatory Vintage Scotch Whisky Co. Ltd.* 50.1%vol
Edinburgh EH6 Scotland

MOFFAT, BY AIRDRIE, LANARKSHIRE EST. 1965

Founded within the Moffat grain distillery complex by Inver House Distillers, at the time a subsidiary of Publicker Industries of Philadelphia. The distillery was closed in 1985 and the pot stills dismantled at this time. Inver House was bought from its American parent by its UK directors in 1988. Six stills.

LOCATION At Moffat Mills on the eastern outskirts of Airdrie

NOTES The distillery complex was converted from Moffat Mills paper mill. Originally known as Garnheath.

WATER Lilly Loch.

Age 23 years   **Distillation** 1970   **Strength** 50.1% abv
Sweetness 3   Peatiness 2   Availability 1

Colour Pale to mid-amber with yellow highlights **Nose** Fresh, quite light and delicate, malty, nutty, a dark oaky character and medium-dry **Flavour** Medium-dry, a touch of spice, quite fresh and round with good body and a malic apple touch **Finish** Quite long and round, medium-sweet and fresh **Notes** Signatory bottling - distilled 6 October 1970

OLD MELDRUM, ABERDEENSHIRE EST. 1785

Established by one Thomas Simpson, the first spirit was announced on 1 December 1785 in the *Aberdeen Journal*. Glen Garioch is one of Scotland's oldest distilleries. In two centuries, ownership has passed through various hands, including SMD who acquired it in 1943. It was closed by SMD in 1968 and sold to Stanley P. Morrison, who extended it from two to three stills in 1973. Now operated by Morrison Bowmore Distillers, who are wholly owned by Japanese company Suntory. Glen Garioch closed in October 1995.

LOCATION The distillery is situated in Old Meldrum village on the Banff to Aberdeen road, close by the historic Meldrum House.

NOTES Garioch is pronounced "Geerie". Waste heat was used to grow tomatoes. The Garioch valley, an 18 mile or so stretch of highly fertile land is known as the granary of Aberdeenshire. Glen Garioch was indeed a canny place to build a distillery. Other dates have been given elsewhere for the opening of this distillery, but the *Aberdeen Journal* announcement of December 1785 clearly pre-dates them. This source refers to a "licensed distillery", making it Scotland's longest licensed on the same site. Glen Garioch is housed in a very attractive cluster of old buildings with the pagoda heads of the floor maltings adding to its appeal. The floor maltings supplied about half of the distillery's requirements, the rest being bought in from outside maltsters. Pitsligo Moss peat was used for the malt drying, which was finished by gas-firing. In 1982 Glen Garioch was the first distillery in Scotland to convert its stills to gas-firing.

WATER Springs on Percock Hill.

GLEN GARIOCH

Age 8 years **Strength** 43% abv

Sweetness 4 Peatiness 5 Availability 2

Colour Straw/pale amber with lemon/yellow highlights **Nose** Fresh and clean, slightly perfumed, malty and medium-dry **Flavour** Medium-dry, perfumed, fresh and quite rich **Finish** A spirity youthfulness with a lingering flavour of violets **Notes** Morrison Bowmore bottling

Age 10 years **Strength** 40% abv

Sweetness 4 Peatiness 5 Availability 6

Colour Bright gold **Nose** Delicately peated, flowery and smoky **Flavour** Peaty, dry and slightly pungent **Finish** Good, smooth and delicate **Notes** Morrison Bowmore bottling

Age 12 years **Strength** 40% abv

Sweetness 4 Peatiness 5 Availability 6

Colour Mid-amber with gold/green highlights **Nose** Medium-bodied, delicately peated and floral (almost violets), dry with a slight edge of sweetness **Flavour** Medium-dry, slightly spicy, floral and fresh with good body **Finish** Quite long, spicy and tangy with a green edge **Notes** Morrison Bowmore bottling

Distillation 1984 **Strength** 40% abv

Sweetness 4 Peatiness 5 Availability 3

Colour Straw/amber with yellow/gold highlights **Nose** Medium-bodied with a lemon/citrus note, floral peaty and a heathery perfumed character **Flavour** Quite soft and round , a touch perfumed and a gentle smokiness **Finish** Good with a touch of heather and spice **Notes** Morrison Bowmore bottling

Age 15 years **Strength** 43% abv

Sweetness 3 Peatiness 6 Availability 6

Colour Straw/light amber with yellow/gold highlights **Nose** Medium-bodied, malty, round with a smoky peatiness **Flavour** Quite big-bodied and smooth with a rich edge and smoky character **Finish** Long, almost pungent, a gentle heathery smokiness and slightly chewy **Notes** Morrison Bowmore bottling

Age 21 years **Strength** 43% abv

Sweetness 4 Peatiness 5 Availability 5

Colour Pale with yellow/green highlights **Nose** Medium-sweet and quite smoky **Flavour** Full-bodied, rich, medium-dry, and delicately peated **Finish** Smoky, slightly spicy and quite long with touches of oak **Notes** Morrison Bowmore bottling

CONNOISSEURS
CHOICE

Connoisseurs Choice, a
range of single malts from
various districts of
Scotland

In the Highlands
are situated the greatest
number of malt whisky
distilleries

SINGLE HIGHLAND
MALT SCOTCH WHISKY
DISTILLED AT
GLENGLASSAUGH
Distillery
Proprietors: The Highland Distilleries Ltd.

DISTILLED 1983 DISTILLED

SPECIALLY SELECTED, PRODUCED AND BOTTLED BY
70cl   GORDON & MACPHAIL   40%vol
ELGIN - SCOTLAND
PRODUCT OF SCOTLAND

NR. PORTSOY, BANFFSHIRE EST. 1875

Founded by the Glenglassaugh Distillery Company. Acquired by the Highland Distilleries Co. Ltd in the 1890s. Glenglassaugh was silent from 1907 to 1931 and again from 1936 until it was extensively rebuilt 1959-60. Closed again in 1986, but reopened. Since closed again. Two stills.

LOCATION Sited on the slope of a steep hillside in the Glassaugh Glen close to the sea approximately two miles west of Portsoy.

NOTES During the period 1907 to 1960, Glenglassaugh only produced for a handful of years in all. When rebuilt, the distillery managed to double its output simply by doubling the size of its stills.

WATER The Glassaugh spring

Distillation 1983   **Strength** 40% abv

Sweetness 5   Peatiness 4   Availability 4

Colour Mid-amber with gold highlights **Nose** Quite full, smoky with an oily-oaky character, medium-dry **Flavour** Medium-dry with good richness in the middle, smooth and round with good body **Finish** Long, medium-dry and rich with a nice spiciness **Notes** Gordon & MacPhail bottling

Age 13 years   **Distillation** 1977   **Strength** 59.8% abv

Sweetness 8   Peatiness 4   Availability 2

Colour Straw/pale amber with yellow/gold highlights **Nose** Quite full-bodied, fresh and clean with a touch of cereal and green apple, medium-sweet with a hint of perfume **Flavour** Fresh, green, medium-peated and medium-sweet **Finish** Long and fresh, sweet with a touch of spice and a soft peaty backdrop **Notes** Wm Cadenhead bottling distilled November 1977

OLD KILLEARN, DUMGOYNE, STIRLINGSHIRE EST. 1833

Originally known as *Burnfoot*, Glengoyne has been owned by Lang Brothers since 1876, that company becoming a part of the Robertson & Baxter group in 1965. Rebuilt in 1966/67 and extended from two to three stills.

L O C A T I O N   About twelve or so miles from the centre of Glasgow and about seven from Loch Lomond, Glengoyne nestles in a truly delightful setting at the foot of Dumgoyne Hill, at the north west end of the Campsie Hills.

N O T E S   The distillery is sited on the Highland Line, but, as its water supply comes from north of the Line, it is classified as a Highland malt. The *West Highland Way*, the long-distance footpath which runs from Glasgow to Fort William runs past the distillery. Although first licensed in 1833, the distillery is believed to be somewhat older. The make was triple distilled in Victorian times, but is now double distilled. The make is reduced using natural spring water. Not far from the distillery is the hollow tree in which Rob Roy MacGregor, immortalised by Sir Walter Scott - and Hollywood - is reputed to have hidden while fleeing from the English King's men. The malt used to produce Glengoyne is unpeated. This, coupled with the lack of peat in its source water, makes Glengoyne the least peated of all Scottish malts. The Excise Officer at Glengoyne at the turn of the century was Arthur Tedder, who later became the Chief Inspector of Excise and was knighted. His son, who had grown up at Glengoyne, was eventually to become Air Chief Marshal of the Royal Air Force. When later he was made a baron, he chose as his title Baron Tedder of Glenguin, the old spelling of Glengoyne. The distillery has an excellent visitor centre which sits at the bottom of the 50 foot waterfall which cascades down the side of Dumgoyne Hill.

W A T E R   A burn which falls down Dumgoyne Hill and is known locally as "the Distillery Burn".

Age 10 years **Strength** 40% abv

Sweetness 5 Peatiness 0 Availability 9

Colour Pale straw with lemony gold highlights **Nose** Round, fresh and medium-sweet, quite light and rich with a slight floral note and a touch of greenness at the back **Flavour** Round, smooth, creamy, medium-dry, fresh and clean with good body **Finish** Quite long with a smooth, buttery vanilla character and a touch of greenness on the tail **Notes** Lang Brothers bottling

Age 12 years **Strength** 40% abv

Sweetness 5 Peatiness 0 Availability 4

Colour Pale straw with lemony gold highlights **Nose** Medium-bodied, round and fresh, medium-dry with a sweet-oily oak character and hints of buttery toffee **Flavour** Medium-dry, round, smooth and clean, fresh and medium-bodied with a touch of the toffee character **Finish** Long and fresh, buttery, smooth and clean with a touch of oaky vanilla **Notes** Lang Brothers bottling available in export markets

Age 17 years **Strength** 43% abv

Sweetness 6 Peatiness 0 Availability 5

Colour Pale peaty with yellow/golden highlights **Nose** Rich, sweet oak, light fruit and toffee with an almost liquorice-like character **Flavour** Soft, rich and smooth with sweet oaky vanilla **Finish** Spicy, malty and of nice length, quite chewy **Notes** Lang Brothers bottling.

Age 25 years **Distillation** 1969 **Strength** 47% abv

Sweetness 6 Peatiness 0 Availability 3

Colour Straw/mid-amber with gold/yellow highlights **Nose** Fresh, clean, quite full-bodied and rich with a good unctuous oaky underlay, a hazelnut character, a touch of tarry rope and green apple fruit **Flavour** Quite fresh with a good malty character and a touch of chocolate, firm oaky tannins **Finish** Medium-dry and rich, quite spicy with a note of liquorice on the tail **Notes** Lang Brothers bottling.

Age 25 years **Distillation** 1970 **Strength** 48.5% abv

Sweetness 7 Peatiness 0 Availability 1

Colour Straw/pale amber with gold/yellow highlights **Nose** Quite full, round and soft with a delicate ripeness and a lush fruitiness, a slight note of charred oak and and almost Christmas cake richness **Flavour** Medium-dry, rich, soft and round with a smooth oakiness and a lush, fat texture **Finish** Long and clean with a rich, fruity note **Notes** Bottled as *Glengoyne Vintage 1970*, only 1200 bottles were produced.

Distillation 1985   **Strength** 59.1% abv

Sweetness 6   Peatiness 0   Availability 1

Colour Deep amber with old gold highlights **Nose** Full-bodied, medium-dry, rich and fruity, unctously oily with just a hint of nuttiness, a toffee sweetness and a herby note **Flavour** Medium-sweet, smooth, round, quite full-bodied and nutty **Finish** Long, very gently chewy and quite complex. **Notes** Lang Brothers bottling from cask no. 104 distilled during February 1985 - only available at the distillery

Distillation 1985   **Strength** 57.8% abv

Sweetness 7   Peatiness 0   Availability 1

Colour Deep amber with bronze highlights and a ruby hue **Nose** Full and warm with a dark nuttiness - Brazil nuts -, rich, medium-sweet and with a mahogany character **Flavour** Big-bodied with nice chewy tannins, medium-sweet and nutty **Finish** Powerful, gently chewy and very long **Notes** Lang Brothers bottling from cask no. 103 distilled during February,1985 - only available at the distillery

Age 21 years **Strength** 43% abv

Sweetness 6   Peatiness 0   Availability 4

Colour Deep amber with old gold highlights **Nose** Round, dark and medium-dry, fruity, richly nutty with unctuous oaky vanilla and notes of mint and toffee **Flavour** Full-bodied. medium- sweet, rich round and velvety smooth **Finish** Long, clean, and sweet with a slight hint of mint on the tail **Notes** Lang Brothers bottling

ROTHES, MORAY EST. 1840

Founded by the brothers James and John Grant who had previously been distillers at nearby Aberlour. Amalgamated with George & J.G. Smith of The Glenlivet in 1953. Owned by the Seagram Company of Canada since 1977. Extended from four to six stills in 1973 and to eight in 1977.

LOCATION At the northern end of Rothes.

NOTES The Glen Grant stills are direct-fired gas and all have purifiers fitted, which are said to add extra finesse to the style of spirit produced. It is not generally recognised that Glen Grant is the world's second-best-selling single malt, thanks to its dominant position in Italy, where, as a 5-years-old, it has around 70% of the considerable single malt market. It is also Italy's best-selling whisky. A supply of over-proof Glen Grant is kept in a whisky safe built into the rock at the burnside above the distillery. It is reached through an apple orchard. Taste it cut with water from the burn if you get the chance. Glen Grant was the first distillery to be established in Rothes, and the first industrial building in the north of Scotland to have electric lighting. Although a best-seller through its younger ages, Glen Grant also ages well.

WATER The Glen Grant Burn.

Age 5 years **Strength** 40% abv

Sweetness 4 Peatiness 4 Availability 4

Colour Light gold/copper **Nose** Light, somewhat hard and astringent **Flavour** Drier than most Speyside malts, spirity, slightly peppery **Finish** Reasonable length with a strange heathery perfumed tang **Notes** J & J Grant bottling

Age 12 years **Strength** 43% abv

Sweetness 6 Peatiness 4 Availability 2

Colour Straw/gold with amber highlights **Nose** Light, sweet, slightly fruity with an astringent character **Flavour** Light, medium-sweet, spirity and creamy **Finish** Dry, slightly astringent and lingering **Notes** J.& J. Grant bottling

Age 15 years **Strength** 40% abv

Sweetness 6 Peatiness 4 Availability 5

Colour Peaty/gold with good highlights **Nose** Sweet, lightish, nutty and with a slight fruitiness **Flavour** Medium-sweet, nutty, smooth, slightly smoky **Finish** The smokiness comes through on the finish, which is smooth and mellow **Notes** Gordon & MacPhail bottling

Age 18 years **Strength** 46% abv

Sweetness 5 Peatiness 4 Availability 4

Colour Full amber with gold highlights **Nose** Full, quite rich, slightly green and a little austere, soft oaky vanilla with a little smokiness at the back and hints of apricots and apples **Flavour** Medium-dry, quite full, round and rich with a touch of toffee and maltiness **Finish** Long and rich with a nice edge of greenness **Notes** Wm Cadenhead bottling

Age 21 years **Strength** 40% abv

Sweetness 5 Peatiness 4 Availability 3

Colour Amber with good gold highlights **Nose** Fruity, slightly astringent with a note of green wood **Flavour** Medium-sweet, peppery and oaky **Finish** Smooth, well-balanced, dry, of medium length with good oaky vanilla **Notes** Gordon & MacPhail bottling

Age 31 years **Distillation** 1965 **Strength** 58.4% abv

Sweetness 6 Peatiness 4 Availability 1

Colour Pale amber with pale gold highlights **Nose** Quite full-bodied, sweet and rich with a slightly green, nutty peaty character, smooth with a note of honeyed beeswax **Flavour** Full and medium-sweet with chewy oaky tannins **Finish** Long with characters of vanilla and oak **Notes** Signatory bottling for the USA from cask no. 5849 distilled 1 November 1965

KEITH, BANFFSHIRE EST. 1957

Originally part of an oat mill of uncertain age, it was converted into a distillery by Chivas Brothers Ltd, a subsidiary of The Seagram Company of Canada, between 1957 and 1960. It was originally designed for triple distillation, but converted to the more normal double distillation in 1970.

LOCATION By the Linn Pool near the centre of Keith.

NOTES The first distillery to be founded in Scotland since the boom years of the late 19th century. It was also the first distillery in Scotland to have a gas-fired still and the first to use a micro-processor to control the whole operation.

WATER The Balloch Hill springs.

Distilled before 1983 **Strength** 43% abv

Sweetness 6 Peatiness 3 Availability 6

Colour Pale amber with lemon highlights **Nose** Medium-bodied and medium-sweet with firm peat and soft rich lanolin, a touch mashy and an unctuous oakiness **Flavour** Medium-sweet, soft oak, rich, creamy and smooth **Finish** Rich and smooth with a slight toffee touch **Notes** Seagram bottling

Age 22 years **Distilled** 1967 **Strength** 45.6% abv

Sweetness 7 Peatiness 3 Availability 1

Colour Bright straw with gold/green highlights **Nose** Quite full, rich, oily, nutty and oaky with a slight citrus note **Flavour** Rich, medium-sweet, gently peated and with an oily creaminess **Finish** Long and sweet with a touch of vanilla **Notes** Wm Cadenhead bottling

PENCAITLAND, EAST LOTHIAN EST. 1837

East Lothian is one of the heartlands of Scottish farming and Glenkinchie and its staff have been involved in agricultural activities since its inception. The distillery managers also looked after the adjoining farm and one manager, who fed his beasts on the distillery by-products, won the Supreme Championship for his Aberdeen Angus cattle at Smithfield, Edinburgh and Birmingham in the 1940s and 50s. Established by John and George Rate, Glenkinchie was disused between 1853 and 1880, when it was revived by the Glen Kinchie Distillery Co. Owned by SMD since 1914, Glenkinchie was one of the founding distilleries in SMD, and licensed to John Haig & Company. Now a part of United Distillers plc. Two stills.

LOCATION Due south of Pencaitland, the distillery is in a hollow in the hills and, although the chimney can be seen from some distance, the road end could easily be missed as the sign was traditionally overgrown.

NOTES The distillery has a unique museum of distilling which was originated around 1968 by Alistair Munro, a former manager, the work being continued by his successors. This includes an enormous model of a Highland malt distillery which was built to a scale of one-sixth of actual size for the Empire Exhibition in 1924-5. Glenkinchie has also been known as *Kinchie* and is probably also the same distillery as *Milton* of which records exist of being operated by John and George Rate from 1825 to 1834. Glenkinchie has long been an important malt to the Haig blend.

WATER Reservoirs in the Lammermuir Hills.

Age 10 years   **Strength** 43% abv
Sweetness 2   Peatiness 5   Availability 7

Colour Pale straw/golden with yellow highlights **Nose** Fresh, dry, pleasantly peated and slightly spirity **Flavour** Dry, malty, quite spicy, full and smooth **Finish** Long, lingering, delicately smoky and quite rich **Notes** United Distillers bottling

MINMORE, BALLINDALLOCH, BANFFSHIRE   EST. 1824

George Smith established his distillery in 1824 at Upper Drummin farm, being the first distiller in the Highlands to take out a licence after the passing of the Excise Act of 1823. In 1858, after the original distillery had been destroyed by fire, a new one was built at Minmore on land obtained from the Duke of Gordon. The Glenlivet was amalgamated with J & J Grant of Glen Grant in 1953 and later with Longmorn-Glenlivet Distilleries Ltd in 1970. The enlarged Glenlivet group of companies was purchased by the Seagram Company of Canada in 1977. Eight stills.

LOCATION   Situated on the slopes of the Braes of Glenlivet, the local hills.

NOTES   The very district of Glenlivet is rich in history. It was here that, in 1594, the King's army under the Earl of Huntly defeated the Covenanters commanded by the Duke of Argyll. The real name of the very English-sounding Smiths was Gow. They had been support-ers of the Jacobites and Bonnie Prince Charlie, but after his defeat at Culloden in 1746, the family apparently changed their name to avoid the oppression which followed. Although many others have laid claim to the "Glenlivet" appellation, following legal action taken by the Glenlivet distillery's then owners in the 1880s, there is only one whisky which can rightly be called *The Glenlivet*. So famous had the name Glenlivet already become by then that the wags of the day christened it "the longest glen in Scotland". Such was the reputation for quality that The Glenlivet had gained, that whiskies that had not even been distilled anywhere near the Livet glen were claiming its provenance on their labels. The words "The Glenlivet" together today only appear on the company's own bottlings.

WATER   Josie's Well.

Age 12 years **Strength** 40% abv

Sweetness 8 Peatiness 4 Availability 10

Colour Straw with a definite greenness to its edge **Nose** Leafy, floral, slightly malty, very fragrant **Flavour** Sherry cask on palate with typical honeyed shortbread-sweet flavour **Finish** Good length **Notes** George & J.G. Smith bottling

Age 12 years **Strength** 40% abv

Sweetness 3 Peatiness 6 Availability 4

Colour Amber with gold highlights and a dark tinge **Nose** Slightly dumb, floral, violet character and medium-dry **Flavour** Quite dry with quite big oaky tannins, a slight touch of richness and quite full-bodied **Finish** Long with quite chewy dry tannins and an earthy peatiness **Notes** Gordon & MacPhail bottling

Age 18 years **Strength** 43% abv

Sweetness 6 Peatiness 5 Availability 3

Colour Quite deep amber with bronze highlights **Nose** Quite full-bdied, medium-sweet with a dark, soft nuttiness, a good, peaty character with a lightly honeyed, almost Christmas cake richness and a gentle peaty fruitiness **Flavour** Big-bodied, smooth, round, soft, rich and medium-sweet, slightly toffeeyed and gently peated **Finish** Rich with a touch of spice, a light, elegant smoky touch to the tail and surprisingly dry **Notes** Glenlivet Distillers bottling

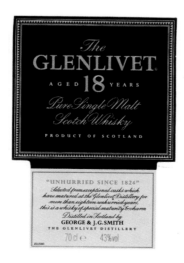

Age 15 years **Strength** 57% abv

Sweetness 8 Peatiness 6 Availability 4

Colour Amber with old gold highlights **Nose** Quite full, sweet, rich and malty **Flavour** Rich, Full-bodied and round with a touch of tannin, malty and quite sweet **Finish** Big-bodied, spicy, gently tannic, warm **Notes** Gordon & MacPhail bottling

Age 21 years **Strength** 40% abv

Sweetness 6 Peatiness 7 Availability 4

Colour Full amber with good gold highlights **Nose** Sweet and fruity (peaches) with touches of oaky vanilla **Flavour** Smooth, medium-sweet, round and full-bodied, gently malty **Finish** Long and toffee-like **Notes** Gordon & MacPhail bottling

Age 21 years **Distillation** 1973 **Strength** 56% abv

Sweetness 7 Peatiness 4 Availability 2

Colour Quite full amber with pale bronze highlights **Nose** Rich, oaky and nutty, of light to medium weight (quite closed) **Flavour** Rich, quite full-bodied with big, nutty tannins and medium-sweet **Finish** Long and chewy with a light smoky touch **Notes** Signatory bottling; Butt 3946 distilled 19 April 1973

Age 15 years **Distillation** 1977 **Strength** 59.5% abv

Sweetness 6 Peatiness 7 Availability 3

Colour Mid-amber with bronze highlights and a tinge of ruby **Nose** Quite full and rich, medium-dry with a burnt oak character **Flavour** Full-bodied, rich and medium-sweet with quite big tannins and a quite full smokiness **Finish** Long, chewy and quite tannic with a smoky tail **Notes** Gordon & MacPhail bottling; cask nos. 11302/3 distilled 6 June 1977

GLENLIVET DISTILLERY.

Vintage 1963
Single Highland Malt Scotch Whisky
Matured in sherry casks for 30 years
Distilled at the Glenlochy Distillery
on 14.3.63   Bottled 12.93
Cask no. 762   Bottle no.158 of 250
This whisky has been selected, produced and bottled in
Scotland for and under the sole responsibility of
Signatory Vintage Scotch Whisky Co. Ltd.
Edinburgh EH6 Scotland
70cl   52.2%vol

FORT WILLIAM, INVERNESS-SHIRE EST. 1898

Glenlochy was always very up-to-date. All the fittings in 1898 were "arranged throughout with a view to saving labour". A visitor reported, in 1907, that Glenlochy possessed "every modern facility for enabling it to be worked with a minimum of labour". Joseph Hobbs of Associated Scottish Distillers sold it in 1940. Eight years later, he established the Great Glen cattle ranch, an area of 54 square kilometres where beef cattle fend for themselves, as they do on the US prairies. The ranch is still in operation. Glenlochy was silent from 1917 to 1924 and again from 1926 to 1937. It was bought by DCL in 1953 when the unit was transferred to SMD. It had two stills.

LOCATION   Situated within Fort William on the north bank of the River Nevis, to the west of the A82.

NOTES   The distillery closed for good in 1983.

WATER   The River Nevis.

Age 30 years   **Distillation** 1963   **Strength** 52.2% abv

Sweetness 3	Peatiness 6	Availability 1

Colour Mid amber with gold highlights **Nose** Light, quite fresh with a cooked apple character and quite dry **Flavour** Quite dry with a smoky oak and coffee character **Finish** Good length and delicately smoky **Notes** Signatory bottling

Distillation 1974   **Strength** 40% abv

Sweetness 7	Peatiness 4	Availability 2

Colour Palish amber with copper highlights **Nose** Spirity, sweet, woody, fruity **Flavour** Sweet, woody and creamy with a note of spice **Finish** Short with a strange woody aftertaste **Notes** Gordon & MacPhail bottling

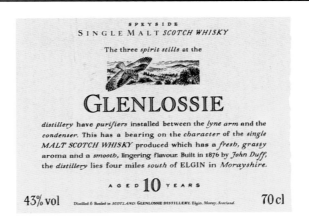

SPEYSIDE
SINGLE MALT *SCOTCH WHISKY*

The three *spirit stills* at the

GLENLOSSIE

distillery have *purifiers* installed between the *lyne arm* and the *condenser*. This has a bearing on the *character* of the *single MALT SCOTCH WHISKY* produced which has a *fresh, grassy* aroma and a *smooth*, lingering flavour. Built in 1876 by *John Duff*, the *distillery* lies four miles *south* of ELGIN in *Morayshire*.

AGED **10** YEARS

43% vol   Distilled & Bottled in *SCOTLAND* GLENLOSSIE DISTILLERY, Elgin, Moray, Scotland.   70 cl

THOMSHILL, BY ELGIN, MORAY   EST. 1876

Built in 1876 by John Duff, tenant of the Fife Arms, Lhanbryde, and previously manager of the Glendronach distillery. A controlling interest was obtained by SMD in 1919 and the distillery was taken over completely by DCL in 1930. Extended from four to six stills in 1962. The make is important to John Haig's blends, the distillery being licensed to that company. Now part of United Distillers plc.

LOCATION Sited at Thomshill on an unclassified road to the west of the A941, two miles south of Elgin.

NOTES A purifier has been installed between the lyne arm and the condenser on each of the three spirit stills. Electricity only replaced steam as late as 1960 as the means of power generation at the distillery. A fire at the distillery in 1929 caused some damage. One of the appliances that fought the blaze was the distillery's own engine. Dating from the 1860s and originally horse drawn, it can still be seen at the distillery. The site now houses two distilleries, the other being the much newer Mannochmore, built in 1971.

WATER The Bardon Burn.

Age 10 years   **Strength** 43% abv

Sweetness 6   Peatiness 3   Availability 6

Colour Quite pale straw with lemon yellow highlights **Nose** Fresh, cerealy and green, fragrant with a touch of perfume **Flavour** Fresh with a touch of oaky tannin, quite green and gently smoky, medium-dry with richness in the middle of the palate **Finish** Lasts quite well - clean, fresh and spicy **Notes** United Distillers bottling

Distillation 1968 **Strength** 40% abv

Sweetness 7 Peatiness 4 Availability 2

Colour Palish gold with good bright highlights **Nose** Sweet, fruity, slightly musty, nutty **Flavour** Sweet, fruity, musty and spicy **Finish** Nice fruitiness, good length and with a nuttiness on the tail **Notes** Gordon & MacPhail bottling

Distillation 1969 **Strength** 40% abv

Sweetness 7 Peatiness 4 Availability 2

Colour Straw/amber with gold highlights **Nose** Medium-bodied, quite rich with a tang of gunpowder and a warm nuttiness **Flavour** Quite rich, medium-bodied, lightly peated with a nice sweet edge and a slightly oily texture **Finish** Of reasonable length, rich with a touch of greenness **Notes** Gordon & MacPhail bottling

Age 16 years **Distillation** 1980 **Strength** 43% abv

Sweetness 7 Peatiness 5 Availability 1

Colour Pale straw with pale lemon highlights **Nose** Surprisingly fresh and youthful, quite full-bodied and clean with a note of mintiness, an edge of richness and a good, burnt peat character **Flavour** Medium-sweet, clean and fresh with good body and a creamy peatiness **Finish** Long and creamy with a slightly perfumed peatiness **Notes** Blackadder International bottling from cask no. 1365 distilled 7 March 1980

GLEN MHOR

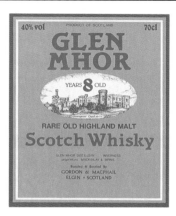

INVERNESS EST. 1892

Founded by ex-Provost John Birnie and James Mackinlay of Charles Mackinlay & Co., Glen Mhor began production on 8 December 1894. It became a part of DCL in 1972, John Walker & Co. having long had a large shareholding in the company, from which date it was operated by SMD. Closed in 1983 and subsequently demolished to make way for a shopping complex.

LOCATION The distillery was situated at the north end of the Caledonian Canal where it intersects with the Great North Road (the A9) at the north west of Inverness, across the road from Glen Albyn.

NOTES The name Glen Mhor means "Great Glen". It was the first distillery in Scotland to introduce mechanical maltings. Glen Mhor, like its sister Glen Albyn, is alas no more.

WATER Loch Ness.

Age 8 years   **Strength** 57% abv

Sweetness 4   Peatiness 4   Availability 2

Colour Straw/amber with good gold highlights **Nose** Lightly peated with an edge of sweetness **Flavour** Medium-sweet, slightly woody and quite full-bodied **Finish** Spicy, creamy, long and almost leafy **Notes** Gordon & MacPhail bottling

Age 14 years   **Distillation** 1978   **Strength** 43% abv

Sweetness 4   Peatiness 6   Availability 0

Colour Straw with lemon highlights **Nose** Medium-bodied and quite rich with an appley sweetness and a slight floral touch **Flavour** Quite dry and smooth with big, full, dark, nutty tannins **Finish** Long with a salty smokiness **Notes** Master of Malt bottling; cask nos. 4041/2 distilled 21 September 1978

GLENMORANGIE
SINGLE HIGHLAND
MALT SCOTCH WHISKY

ESTABLISHED 1843   PRODUCE OF SCOTLAND

TEN YEARS OLD

The GLENMORANGIE
DISTILLERY COY. TAIN, ROSS-SHIRE
BOTTLED IN SCOTLAND

TAIN, ROSS-SHIRE EST. 1843

Converted from the Morangie Brewery of McKenzie & Gallie by William Mathieson. Rebuilt in 1887 and again in 1979, when it was extended from two to four stills. Glenmorangie has been owned by Macdonald & Muir (who were renamed Glenmorangie plc in 1996), the Leith blenders, since 1918.

LOCATION   Sited on the Dornoch Firth on the A9 between Tain and Edderton, looking across the Firth towards the hills of Sutherland.

NOTES   One of the smallest of all Highland distilleries. All of the make is used by the owners, none being made available as fillings. A noted feature of the distillery is that the stills have very tall necks, at 16 ft 10 ins (5.14m), the tallest in Scotland.

WATER   Springs in the Tarlogie Hills above the distillery.

Age 10 years   **Strength** 40% abv

Sweetness 4   Peatiness 4   Availability 10

Colour Good light gold/pale straw **Nose** Fresh, medium-bodied, steely with floral notes and a touch of peat **Flavour** Light, fresh, slightly smoky with an oily creaminess **Finish** Sweet with good length **Notes** Macdonald & Muir bottling

Age 18 years   **Strength** 43% abv

Sweetness 4   Peatiness 4   Availability 6

Colour Honey-amber with good gold highlights **Nose** Fresh, salty, nutty (almonds), with an edge of sweetness, quite full and round **Flavour** Smooth, medium-dry, fresh, good nut-oily glycerine, quite full-bodied **Finish** Medium-dry, spicy, long and almost creamy **Notes** Macdonald & Muir bottling

THE NATIVE ROSS-SHIRE GLENMORANGIE
Age 10 years **Distillation** 1980 **Strength** 57.6% abv

Sweetness 4 Peatiness 4 Availability 1

Colour Bright pale amber, yellow-gold highlights **Nose** A touch of sweetness, fresh, quite full, dried hay, lanolin and vanilla **Flavour** Quite rich, round, medium-dry oaky-vanilla, quite full, fat and soft **Finish** Fresh, clean, aromatic and quite long **Notes** Macdonald & Muir bottling. Cask no. 4336; distilled 15.5.80; bottled 5.9.90. Branded as *The Native Ross-shire Glenmorangie*

Distillation 1963 (Bottled 1988) **Strength** 43% abv

Sweetness 4 Peatiness 4 Availability 1

Colour Quite pale peaty/straw with gold and green highlights **Nose** Rich, full malty, oaky with sweet appley fruit **Flavour** Sweet, full spicy, quite green with a toffee-like richness **Finish** Long, spicy, caramelly and fine **Notes** Macdonald & Muir bottling. Matured in a Bourbon cask, as all Glenmorangie is, for 22 years and "finished off" for the last year in an oloroso sherry cask

PORT FINISH GLENMORANGIE
Age No stated age **Strength** 56.5% abv

Sweetness 4 Peatiness 3 Availability 1

Colour Quite full amber with bronze highlights **Nose** Medium-bodied, quite fresh with a slightly green mint character and richness with notes of vanilla, butterscotch and toffee **Flavour** Medium-dry, rich, spicy, fresh, soft round and with good body **Finish** Rich, smooth, spicy and with a long chocolate-sweet tail with a fresh, green edge **Notes** Macdonald & Muir bottling

GLENMORANGIE
PORT WOOD FINISH

This unusual whisky is the direct result of pioneering work into the role of wood in malt whisky maturation. Initially matured in American oak casks for at least 12 years, Glenmorangie Port Wood Finish has been racked into selected port "pipes" for the last few years of its maturation. The results of this "finishing" are truly exceptional.

MADEIRA WOOD FINISH GLENMORANGIE
Age no age statement   **Strength** 43% abv
Sweetness   3   Peatiness   3   Availability   5

Colour Pale amber with yellow/pale gold highlights **Nose** Quite full-bodied, but quite delicate, a dark winey character, fresh, rich and medium-sweet with a slight green citrus edge **Flavour** Sweet, rich and quite full with notes of vanilla and a gentle peatiness **Finish** Quite long and elegantly ethereal, rich with a dry note **Notes** Glenmorangie bottling

PORT WOOD FINISH GLENMORANGIE
Age no age statement   **Strength** 43% abv
Sweetness   4   Peatiness   3   Availability   5

Colour Quite deep amber with ruby/bronze highlights and a purple hue **Nose** Medium-bodied and rich, with notes of mint, butterscotch and oaky vanilla **Flavour** Medium-dry with an edge of richness, of good weight and gently peated **Finish** Long, nutty and rich with a slight green edge **Notes** Glenmorangie bottling

SHERRY WOOD FINISH GLENMORANGIE
Age no age statement   **Strength** 43% abv
Sweetness   4   Peatiness   3   Availability   5

Colour Amber with old gold highlights **Nose** Quite big-bodied, fresh and nutty, medium-sweet, round and quite rich with vanilla and a honeyed beeswax note **Flavour** Smooth, fresh and medium-dry, full-bodied and round with slightly chewy oaky tannins and a gentle, slightly green peatiness **Finish** Long, gently chewy and clean **Notes** Glenmorangie bottling

Age 10 years   **Strength** 57.2% abv
Sweetness   5   Peatiness   4   Availability   4

Colour Amber with yellow highlights **Nose** Fresh, clean and medium-dry with floral and citrus notes, round and delicately peated with a light, sweet, vanilla tablet/toffee character **Flavour** Medium-sweet, smooth, round and delicately nutty (almonds) with good body **Finish** Long and fresh with a sweet oakiness **Notes** Bottled as *Glenmorangie 100° Proof*

ELGIN, MORAY EST. 1897

Like its sister distillery, Glenmorangie, a former brewery, having been built in 1815. It was closed in 1910 and passed into the ownership of Macdonald & Muir, which is now known as Glenmorangie plc, in 1923. It was rebuilt in 1958, when it was converted from two to four stills.

LOCATION Situated in a hollow on the bank of the River Lossie, on the western outskirts of Elgin.

NOTES Close by the distillery is Gallowcrook Hill, which was, as its name implies, the scene of public hangings in days gone by. Some of the make goes into Macdonald & Muir's *Highland Queen* blend. The old steam engine that formerly powered the distillery is still in place.

WATER River Lossie.

Age 12 years   **Strength** 40% abv

Sweetness 7 Peatiness 3 Availability 7

Colour Pale gold **Nose** Clean, fresh, aromatic and slightly peppery **Flavour** Light, creamy, heathery and medium-sweet **Finish** Delicate, of reasonable length and soft **Notes** Macdonald & Muir bottling

Age 16 years   **Strength** 43% abv

Sweetness 7 Peatiness 2 Availability 5

Colour Amber with gold highlights **Nose** Fresh, medium-bodied with an appley character, sweet soft bubble-gummy vanilla, good richness and a hint of perfume **Flavour** Round with oaky tannins, quite a rich fruity character and good body **Finish** Smooth, spicy and medium-sweet with a rich chewy tail **Notes** Macdonald & Muir bottling

GLEN MORAY

Age 13 years **Distillation** 1980 **Strength** 43% abv
Sweetness 4 Peatiness 6 Availability 1

Colour Pale straw with pale lemon highlights **Nose** Light to medium-bodied, fresh and medium-sweet, a green, almost floral character and quite lightly peated **Flavour** Good body, fresh and medium-sweet, slightly green with a good background of peatiness **Finish** Fresh, clean and smoky with a richness in the middle **Notes** Blackadder International bottling

Age 27 years **Distillation** 1962 **Strength** 55.1% abv
Sweetness 7 Peatiness 3 Availability 1

Colour Rich, mid-dark amber with good gold highlights **Nose** Quite full-bodied, toffee & chocolate, medium-sweet, lightly peated with warm, oaky vanilla **Flavour** Medium-sweet, quite full-bodied, spicy, nutty, almost austere with oaky tannins **Finish** Smooth, medium-dry and quite firm with a smoky touch; it lingers well **Notes** Wm Cadenhead bottling

Age 13 years **Distillation** 1982 **Strength** 56.0% abv
Sweetness 6 Peatiness 3 Availability 1

Colour Pale straw with pale yellow highlights **Nose** Medium-bodied, quite softly peated with an appley fruitiness, touches of perfume and oaky vanilla and a sherbetty freshness **Flavour** Medium-bodied and medium-sweet with a hint of perfumed peatiness **Finish** Quite fresh and clean with good length **Notes** Adelphi bottling

ROTHES, MORAY EST. 1878

Built by William Grant & Co. Amalgamated in 1887 with the Islay Distillery Company (owners of Bunnahabhain distillery) to form The Highland Distilleries Ltd. Enlarged in 1963 from four to six stills, and from six to ten in 1980.

LOCATION A short way up the glen formed by the Burn of Rothes which flows from the Mannoch Hills.

NOTES The first spirit ran from the stills in 1897 on the night of the Tay rail bridge disaster. The distillery experienced "one of the most disastrous distillery fires" on 15 May 1922 when No. 1 Bonded Warehouse was destroyed, along with 2,500 casks (800,000 litres of maturing spirit): a stream of burning whisky flowed out of the stricken building and into the burn. Glenrothes, as the make is usually known, is one of the malts at the heart of the *Famous Grouse* and *Cutty Sark* blends.

WATER Springs in the hills above the distillery.

Age 15 years **Distillation** 1979 **Strength** 43% abv
Sweetness 7 Peatiness 3 Availability 5

Colour Mid-amber with gold highlights **Nose** Rich, soft and round with an unctuous sweetness, a slight nutty character and a touch of fresh citrus **Flavour** Full-bodied, soft, round and medium-sweet with gentle tannins **Finish** Long, quite fresh, delicately peated, rich and smooth **Notes** Berry Bros & Rudd bottling. The bottle, label and individual carton for this presentation was lauded and received many prizes in the 1994 industry awards.

GLEN ROTHES

Age 8 years **Strength** 40% abv

Sweetness 8 Peatiness 3 Availability 4

Colour Full mid-amber with gold highlights **Nose** Full-bodied, quite spirity, rich, dark, lightly peated and medium-sweet **Flavour** Medium-sweet, very rich and toffee-like, light to medium-peated **Finish** Warm, sweet and of good length **Notes** Gordon & MacPhail bottling

Age 16 years **Strength** 46% abv

Sweetness 8 Peatiness 3 Availability 2

Colour Deep gold, quite peaty in depth **Nose** Fruity, sweet, slightly oaky **Flavour** Full-bodied, richly sweet, possibly a little woody **Finish** Long and complex with a dry tail **Notes** Wm Cadenhead bottling

Age 19 years **Distillation** 1974 **Strength** 43% abv

Sweetness 8 Peatiness 3 Availability 0

Colour Pale straw with yellow/gold highlights **Nose** Soft, medium-sweet, caramel/toffee and malty with quite good body and a shortbread character **Flavour** Sweet, malty, soft with gentle tannins, sweet oaky vanilla and quite big-bodied **Finish** Sweet and rich vanilla with good length **Notes** Master of Malt bottling - cask no. 11810 distilled 9 July 1974

Age 27 years **Distillation** 1966 **Strength** 51.3% abv

Sweetness 7 Peatiness 3 Availability 1

Colour Very dark amber with an almost black heart and bronze/ruby highlights **Nose** Big-bodied, dark nutty oak with spirit at the back, almost a beeswax note, rich and medium-dry **Flavour** Big and dark with quite gentle tannins, full-bodied and smooth **Finish** Long, quite spirity and rich **Notes** Signatory bottling - butt no. 13512 distilled 3 November 1966

Distillation 1978 **Strength** 40% abv

Sweetness 7 Peatiness 4 Availability 2

Colour Straw/pale amber with yellow highlights **Nose** Light to medium-bodied, sweet, with a honeyed nuttiness, delicately peated and a little spirity **Flavour** Quite full-bodied, medium-sweet and quite smooth with a good smoky character **Finish** Good length, quite fresh, clean and rich **Notes** 1995 Gordon & MacPhail *Centenary Reserve* bottling

CAMPBELTOWN, ARGYLL EST. 1832

Since it was founded as *Scotia* in 1832 by Stewart, Galbraith & Co., Glen Scotia has gone through many changes of ownership, the most recent being when Gibson International, who had owned it since the 1980s, went into receivership towards the end of 1994. It has two stills of classic swan-necked design.

LOCATION   In the centre of the town, at the junction of High Street with Saddell Street.

NOTES   One of only two distilleries remaining in Campbeltown (the other being Springbank); somewhat fewer than the 19 which existed at the start of the economic recession of the 1920s and early 30s, during which time all were closed. Glen Scotia and Springbank were the only two to reopen. After £1,000,000 had been spent upgrading the distillery between 1979 and 1982, it was closed again until 1989 when it reopened, only to cease production late in 1994 following Gibson International's receivership. The distillery and all maturing stocks have since been purchased by Glen Catrine Bonded Warehouse Ltd, but it remains closed and is said to be for sale by its new owners.

WATER   The Crosshill Loch and two wells bored 80 feet down into the rocks below the distillery.

Age 8 years   **Strength** 40% abv

Sweetness 8   Peatiness 6   Availability 2

Colour Golden with hints of peaty water **Nose** Slightly peaty, complex, but delicate **Flavour** Lightish, smoky, richly sweet and slightly spirity **Finish** Soft and long **Notes** Gibson International bottling

Age 14 years **Strength** 40% abv

Sweetness 4 Peatiness 3 Availability 3

Colour Straw with yellow/gold highlights **Nose** Clean, medium-bodied with a slight bubble-gummy sweetness, a touch of perfume and a hint of greenness **Flavour** Round, smooth and gentle, quite good body and medium-dry with the bubble-gummy note and a soft peatiness **Finish** Long, clean and slightly tangy with a hint of smokiness **Notes** Glen Catrine bottling

Age 27 years **Distillation** 1966 **Strength** 51.5% abv

Sweetness 4 Peatiness 2 Availability 2

Colour Pale straw with yellow/lemon highlights **Nose** Fresh and medium-dry with a leafy greenness, a delicate nuttiness and a slight oaky unctuousness **Flavour** Medium-dry, fresh and clean with a good richness and an almost chocolatey maltiness **Finish** Clean, quite crisp and lightly tangy with good length and concentration **Notes** Signatory bottling - cask nos. 1271-2 distilled April 1966

Age 16 years **Distillation** 1977 **Strength** 57.6% abv

Sweetness 5 Peatiness 6 Availability 2

Colour Pale amber with yellow/gold highlights **Nose** Medium-bodied, fresh and off-dry with hints of Orange Pekoe tea and a light, earthy peatiness **Flavour** Quite rich, medium-dry with a touch of spice, gentle tannins, a firm peatiness and a flavour of tea **Finish** Quite tangy, softly smoky and of good length **Notes** Wm Cadenhead bottling

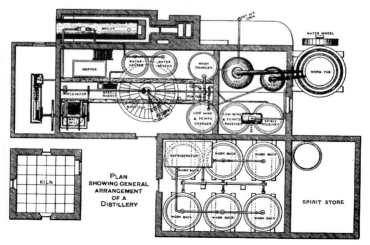

PLAN SHOWING GENERAL ARRANGEMENT OF A DISTILLERY

ROTHES, MORAY EST. 1878

Established by James Stuart & Company. Owned by W & A Gilbey since 22 September 1887 and now part of the Grand Metropolitan Group. Rebuilt in 1970 when it was extended from two to four stills.

LOCATION   The distillery stands just below the ruins of Castle Rothes, the ancient seat of the Leslie family, the Earls of Rothes.

NOTES   James Stuart & Company also once owned Macallan distillery, a short distance away at Craigellachie. Like Knockando, Glen Spey is an important constituent of the J & B blends. The original unit covered an area of 2 acres the distillery beginning life as an extension to a mill which was the company's original business as a grain merchant. The maturation warehouse was very innovative for its day, 10,000 square feet covered by two arched corrugated iron spans and supported by decorative iron pillars. Regrettably, on 10 January 1892, there was an exceptionally heavy snowfall and the roof collapsed under the weight of a covering of two feet of snow.

WATER   The Doonie Burn.

Age 8 years   **Strength** 40% abv

Sweetness 7   Peatiness 3   Availability 0

Colour Pale amber with lemon highlights and a definite green tinge **Nose** Quite light and mashy, gently smoky with a greenness at the back **Flavour** Medium-sweet, fragrant, cerealy, spirity, quite fresh and smooth **Finish** Nice sweetness, spirity and spicy **Notes** W & A Gilbey bottling

MULBEN, BANFFSHIRE EST. 1898

The foundation stone was laid on 29 May 1897, on one of the fields belonging to Tauchers Farm, and the first brew was brewed on 16 June 1898. One of the original owners was James Buchanan, later Lord Woolavington of Black & White fame. Merged with DCL in 1925, the distillery came under SMD's wing in 1930. Rebuilt in 1965-6 when it was increased from two to six stills. Closed in May 1983. Sold to Allied Distillers in 1989 and reopened. Now part of Allied Domecq and operated by Allied Distillers Ltd.

LOCATION On the A95, four miles west of Keith

NOTES Experiments in the continuous distillation of malt whisky were carried out here around 1910.

WATER Springs in the local hills.

Distillation 1979 **Strength** 40% abv

Sweetness 7 Peatiness 3 Availability 4

Colour Light amber with gold highlights **Nose** Medium weight with good richness, nutty, medium-sweet with an aroma of dried apricots and delicately peated **Flavour** Nutty, oaky, medium-sweet with a touch of spice **Finish** Fresh, smooth, good length with a nice light nuttiness **Notes** Gordon & MacPhail bottling

Age 16 years **Distillation** 1977 **Strength** 63.8% abv

Sweetness 5 Peatiness 6 Availability 4

Colour Straw/pale amber with yellow highlights **Nose** Fresh, round and slightly green, medium-sweet with slight floral and aromatic notes **Flavour** Medium-sweet, round and quite full-bodied with a floral note and quite big tannins, gently smoky **Finish** Long, smooth and delicately smoky **Notes** Wm Cadenhead bottling

THE HOSH, CRIEFF, PERTHSHIRE EST. 1775

Glenturret, previously called *Hosh,* is the second to take that name. It was renamed Glenturret in 1875, some 20 or so years after the nearby original distillery of that name closed. The distillery which, with two stills, is one of Scotland's smallest, was silent from 1923 to 1959. It was revived by James Fairlie who, with the later assistance of his son, Peter, has established Glenturret as one of the world's most sought-after single malts and the Glenturret distillery as a superb tourist attraction.

LOCATION On the banks of the River Turret north west of Crieff on a secondary road which leads from the A85 round Crieff to Monzie and Gilmerton.

NOTES Now part of Highland Distillers Co. plc. Although the present buildings were erected in 1775, illicit distilling took place at least as early as 1717. The Drummond Arms Hotel in Crieff was the building in which Prince Charles Edward Stuart (Bonnie Prince Charlie) held his stormy council of war on 3 February 1746. Apart from being possibly the oldest distillery in Scotland (see *Littlemill*) and certainly the oldest in the Highlands, Glenturret has another impressive claim to fame in the *Guinness Book of Records.* A legend even in her own lifetime, Towser, the distillery's rodent operative, was credited with catching a world-record 28,899 mice. Born at the distillery on 21 April 1963, Towser died on 20 March 1987, not far short of her 24th birthday - a very good age for a cat! As well as the mice, Towser was also more than a match for rats, baby rabbits and even pheasants.

WATER Loch Turret.

Age 8 years **Strength** 40% abv

Sweetness 6 Peatiness 4 Availability 1

Colour Very pale straw with yellowy green highlights **Nose** Full, fruity, quite spirity, malty and dryish **Flavour** Lightweight, medium-dry, round, smooth and slightly nutty **Finish** Lightly spicy, grapey, of medium length **Notes** Glenturret bottling

Age 10 years **Strength** 57.1% abv

Sweetness 6 Peatiness 4 Availability 1

Colour Very pale straw with pale yellow/green highlights **Nose** Full-bodied, slightly sweet, floral and slightly meaty **Flavour** Quite full-bodied, round, smooth, creamy, slightly meaty and medium-dry **Finish** Smooth, dry and quite long with soft edges **Notes** Glenturret bottling

Age 12 years **Strength** 40% abv

Sweetness 7 Peatiness 3 Availability 6

Colour Straw/amber with good greeny gold highlights **Nose** Rich and sherried with oaky vanilla, medium-sweet **Flavour** Rich, medium-sweet, sweet oaky vanilla, full-bodied and smooth **Finish** Long and sherried **Notes** Glenturret bottling

Age 15 years **Strength** 40% abv

Sweetness 7 Peatiness 3 Availability 4

Colour Golden/copper coloured with good yellow highlights **Nose** Big-bodied, full, spicy and medium-sweet with oaky vanilla and characters of liquorice, citrus and mint **Flavour** Full, rich, sweet and slightly peppery with hints of mint and liquorice - very complex **Finish** Smooth, spicy, long and memorable **Notes** Glenturret bottling

Age 18 years   **Strength** 40% abv

Sweetness 7 Peatiness 3 Availability 4

Colour Straw/amber with yellow/gold highlights **Nose** Rich, medium-bodied and slightly perfumed with characters of honey, toffee and green coffee **Flavour** Round, smooth, medium-sweet with a slight apple and coffee tang **Finish** Smooth, sweet and rich with a slight tang of fennel **Notes** Glenturret bottling

Age 21 years   **Strength** 40% abv

Sweetness 7 Peatiness 3 Availability 1

Colour Light mid-amber with old gold highlights **Nose** Rich and quite full-bodied, a greenness and liquorice/aniseed, medium-sweet **Flavour** Medium-sweet, lightly peated, rich aniseed and creamily smooth with a touch of oaky vanilla **Finish** Fresh, clean and long with a touch of sweetness **Notes** Glenturret bottling

Age 25 years   **Strength** 43% abv

Sweetness 6 Peatiness 3 Availability 1

Colour Straw with yellow/gold highlights **Nose** Quite fresh, medium-bodied and medium-sweet, a slight oaky oiliness and a nice citrus character **Flavour** Quite full-bodied and sweet with touches of vanilla and tannin **Finish** Long and sweet, tannic and quite fresh **Notes** Glenturret bottling

Distillation 1966   **Strength** 40% abv

Sweetness 6 Peatiness 3 Availability 1

Colour Pale to mid-amber with gold highlights **Nose** Rich and quite full-bodied, medium-sweet oaky vanilla with a tang of orange and delicately peated **Flavour** Medium-dry, quite full-bodied, oaky, spicy with characters of liquorice and vanilla, quite round **Finish** Quite long and complex, with rich liquorice/aniseed and a tail of oaky tannin **Notes** Glenturret bottling

Distillation 1968 **Strength** 40% abv

Sweetness	6	Peatiness	3	Availability	1

Colour Straw with yellow/lemon highlights **Nose** Medium-sweet, grapey and rich with slight chocolate and nutty characters, caramel toffee and bubble-gummy notes **Flavour** Medium-sweet, quite good body, rich and smooth with a coffee/toffee tang **Finish** Long, tangy with a coffee/toffee note, quite rich and clean **Notes** Glenturret bottling

Distillation 1972 **Strength** 40% abv

Sweetness	7	Peatiness	3	Availability	2

Colour Pale straw with good greeny-gold highlights **Nose** Rich oaky vanilla, malty, medium-sweet and delicate **Flavour** Rich, soft, round with hints of smokiness and medium-sweet **Finish** Smooth, pleasantly soft and with reasonable length **Notes** Glenturret bottling

Age 17 years **Distillation** 1980 **Strength** 53.7% abv

Sweetness	8	Peatiness	4	Availability	2

Colour Pale amber with yellow/lemon highlights **Nose** Sweet and fresh with an almost lemon citrus note, medium-bodied and quite lightly peated **Flavour** Sweet and rich with a quite soft peatiness, smooth and gentle **Finish** Long and lingering with smoky peat coming through on the finish **Notes** Blackadder International bottling from cask no 4906 distilled 7 April 1980

5,000 DAYS
Age 5,000 days old **Strength** 40% abv

Sweetness	6	Peatiness	3	Availability	2

Colour Pale amber with yellow highlights **Nose** Good body, fresh with a slight floral note, lightly peated and a hint of tablet **Flavour** Soft, smooth, quite sweet, coffee flavour and lightly smoky **Finish** Medium-sweet, quite soft and of good length **Notes** Glenturret bottling in miniatures

10,000 DAYS
Age 10,000 days old **Strength** 40% abv

Sweetness	6	Peatiness	4	Availability	1

Colour Mid-amber with yellow/gold highlights **Nose** Quite full, sweet, rich and fruity with a touch of greenness, an oaky lanolin character and a hint of green coffee **Flavour** Good body, quite zesty, fresh and medium-dry with a slight greenness **Finish** Clean, of good length with a touch of coffee **Notes** Glenturret bottling in miniatures

CONNOISSEURS CHOICE

Connoisseurs Choice, a range of single malts from various districts of Scotland.

In the Highlands are situated the greatest number of malt whisky distilleries.

SINGLE HIGHLAND MALT SCOTCH WHISKY
DISTILLED AT
GLENUGIE
DISTILLERY
Trade Mark of Proprietors: Long John Distillers Ltd

DISTILLED **1966** DISTILLED

Specially selected, produced and bottled by and under the responsibility of

70cl **GORDON & MACPHAIL** 40%vol
REGD. BOTTLER · ELGIN · SCOTLAND
PRODUCT OF SCOTLAND

PETERHEAD, ABERDEENSHIRE EST. 1831

Built by Donald McLeod & Company, Glenugie passed through the hands of a number of different owners. More recently, in 1970, it was owned by a company called Long John International, which was purchased by Whitbread & Co. Ltd in 1975, who were also at the time owners of Laphroaig distillery. Unlike many distilleries which were originally breweries, Glenugie was converted into a brewery for a while before being turned back to distilling. Two stills.

LOCATION   About three miles south of Peterhead, Glenugie sits close to the sea, below the A92.

NOTES   The distillery buildings, with their cast-iron frames, are of an unusual and interesting design. Closed in 1983, the buildings have since been sold for use other than distilling.

WATER   Springs in the local hills.

Distillation 1966   **Strength** 40% abv

Sweetness 7   Peatiness 4   Availability 2

Colour Quite full amber with old gold highlights **Nose** Full and rich, quite sweet and delicately peated with a ripe fruitiness **Flavour** Medium-sweet, rich and oaky with a green tang **Finish** Clean and lightly smoky with oaky characters **Notes** Gordon & MacPhail bottling

Vintage 1978
Single Highland Malt Scotch Whisky
Matured in oak casks for 15 years
Distilled at the Glenury Royal Distillery
on 22.11.78 *Bottled 23.11.93*
Cask no. 9770 *Bottle no. of 290*
This whisky has been selected, produced and bottled in Scotland for and under the sole responsibility of Signatory Vintage Scotch Whisky Co. Ltd. Edinburgh EH6 Scotland
70cl 62.3%vol

STONEHAVEN, KINCARDINESHIRE EST. 1825

Built to provide a market for barley in a period of agricultural depression by Barclay, McDonald & Co. It was closed from 1925 to 1937, having been sold for £7,500 to Joseph Hobbs the preceding year. He, in turn, sold it to Associated Scottish Distilleries Ltd in 1938 for £18,500. Glenury acted as the "control office" for all of ASD's distilleries and the site was landscaped and roads were built into the unit. ASD was bought by DCL in 1953 and Glenury was worked from that date by SMD. The licensees were John Gillon & Co. Ltd. Glenury was extensively rebuilt from 1965-6, at which time it was doubled from two to four stills. Glenury was closed in 1985. Its licence was cancelled in 1992 and the site sold for development.

LOCATION On the north bank of the Cowie Water, on the northern outskirts of Stonehaven.

NOTES The water supply was also that of the town of Stonehaven. Glenury's founder, Captain Robert Barclay, was the local member of Parliament. Through influence he was given permission by King William IV to call his whisky "Royal".

WATER The Cowie Water.

Age 15 years **Distillation** 1978 **Strength** 62.3% abv
Sweetness 4 **Peatiness** 2 **Availability** 2

Colour Very pale with hints of watery-green and lemon-green highlights **Nose** Quite full-bodied, malty and almost dry with an apple hint and fresh lanolin characters **Flavour** Medium-dry, round and smooth with a touch of spice and greenness; gentle tannins and lightly peated **Finish** Long, smooth and quite sweet **Notes** Signatory bottling from cask no. 9770

Age 12 years **Strength** 40% abv

Sweetness 2 Peatiness 7 Availability 2

Colour Mid-amber with gold highlights **Nose** Medium-bodied, quite dry, dark and smoky with a dry burnt character **Flavour** Dry, peaty, quite smooth and fragrant with a slight floral character at the back **Finish** Long, smoky and quite fresh **Notes** Gordon & MacPhail bottling

Age 12 years **Strength** 40% abv

Sweetness 3 Peatiness 6 Availability 0

Colour Gold/copper **Nose** Light, spirity, malty and quite dry **Flavour** Light, medium-dry and slightly smoky **Finish** Smoky, but quite short **Notes** DCL (pre-Guinness) bottling

Age 14 years **Distillation** 1978 **Strength** 43% abv

Sweetness 6 Peatiness 3 Availability 1

Colour Very pale straw with pale lemon highlights **Nose** Light and fresh, medium-dry with a touch of richness and an appley character **Flavour** Medium-sweet, good body, a slightly green character with good richness **Finish** Lasts well: good, rich and delicate with a dry tail **Notes** Blackadder International bottling

Age 15 years **Distillation** 1978 **Strength** 62.3% abv

Sweetness 7 Peatiness 7 Availability 1

Colour Very pale watery straw with pale yellow highlights **Nose** Medium-dry and fresh with a mashy/cerealy character, a slight citrus tang and a light dark smokiness **Flavour** Rich and medium-sweet with a good under-pinning of peat and dry, oaky tannins **Finish** Long, quite chewy, rich and lingering **Notes** Master of Malt bottling

KIRKWALL, ORKNEY EST. 1798

Said to have been founded by David Robertson, Highland Park is Scotland's most northerly distillery. It had several different owners, before coming into the hands of James Grant and family in the late 1800s. Enlarged from two to four stills in 1898 and operated by James Grant & Co. until 1935, when the company was purchased by the Highland Distilleries Co. Ltd.

LOCATION   Sited on a hillside overlooking Scapa Flow to the south and Kirkwall to the north.

NOTES   The distillery is built on the spot where the legendary 18th century smuggler Magnus Eunson's bothy stood. A local minister as well as a distiller, he apparently kept a stock of whisky under his pulpit. Hearing that his church was about to be searched by the Excisemen, he had the kegs removed to the manse where they were shrouded in white cloth. A coffin lid was placed next to the cloth and Eunson and his "mourners" knelt in prayer. The whispered word "smallpox" quickly ended any idea of a search by the Excisemen.

WATER   From springs below the level of the distillery. The water has to be pumped uphill!

Age 12 years   **Strength** 40% abv

Sweetness 2   Peatiness 7   Availability 9

Colour Pale straw with pale yellow depths **Nose** Pleasantly peaty, dryish and with a hint of smokiness **Flavour** Well balanced and almost dry **Finish** Long, distinguished and lightly smoky **Notes** Highland Distillers' bottling

Age 10 years **Distillation** 1983 **Strength** 58.6% abv

Sweetness 2 Peatiness 7 Availability 3

Colour Pale amber with yellow/gold highlights **Nose** Fresh, creamy and delicately smoky with a slightly green apple touch **Flavour** Smooth, gently smoky, fruity and floral, medium-dry with a creamy richness **Finish** Quite big, long and fragrant, almost chewy and gently smoky **Notes** Gordon & MacPhail bottling. Distilled 14 April 1983

Age 18 years **Distillation** 1975 **Strength** 52.1% abv

Sweetness 2 Peatiness 6 Availability 2

Colour Pale amber with beige highlights **Nose** Quite good body, round with a touch of perfume and a cereal character, medium-dry, delicate creamy peatiness **Flavour** Quite dry, round, creamily smooth, delicately peated with oaky tannins and a hint of treacle **Finish** Quite big, delicately smoky, elegant and long **Notes** Signatory bottling

Age 21 years **Distillation** 1972 **Strength** 56.5% abv

Sweetness 4 Peatiness 6 Availability 2

Colour Very deep amber with dark bronze highlights **Nose** Big-bodied, full, dark and nutty (Brazil nuts) with a burnt oak character and almost dry **Flavour** Big, dark and medium-sweet with a creamy peatiness, a salty tang and big tannins **Finish** Long, chewy, nutty and medium-sweet **Notes** Wm Cadenhead bottling

Vintage 1975
Single Orkney Island Malt Scotch Whisky
Matured in oak casks for 18 years
Distilled at the Highland Park Distillery
on *31.3.75*   *Bottled 10.93*
Cask no. 4277   *Bottle no.   of 260*
This whisky has been selected, produced and bottled in Scotland for and under the sole responsibility of Signatory Vintage Scotch Whisky Co. Ltd. Edinburgh EH6 Scotland
70cl   52.1%vol

Distillation 1989   **Strength** 58% abv

Sweetness 5   Peatiness 6   Availability 2

Colour Very pale straw with pale lemon/yellow highlights.
Nose Fresh, clean and medium-dry with a slightly meaty character, a smooth peatiness and an almost fruity note **Flavour**
Medium-sweet with good body, a gentle edge of tannin and rich with a smooth peaty character **Finish** Long and gently smoky with a rich sweetness **Notes** Clydesdale Original bottling

Distillation 1970   **Strength** 40% abv

Sweetness 3   Peatiness 7   Availability 4

Colour Quite deep amber with bronze highlights **Nose** Full-bodied, fresh, rich and round with a peaty saltiness, medium-dry with a dark oaky, almost burnt Christmas cake character
Flavour Big-bodied, smooth with quite gentle tannins, medium-dry and smokily peaty **Finish** Full, rich, salty, long and tangy **Notes** Gordon & MacPhail *Centenary Reserve* bottled 1995

Age 19 years **Distillation** 1977 **Strength** 43% abv

Sweetness 3   Peatiness 5   Availability 2

Colour Very pale, watery straw with pale lemon highlights
Nose Fresh, clean and medium-sweet with a note of rich mint, round with a delicate peatiness **Flavour** Fresh, quite dry and smooth with good body **Finish** Long, elegant and ethereal
Notes Signatory bottling from cask nos. 5778/9 distilled 29 December 1977

40% vol. *Product of Scotland* 70 cl.

IMPERIAL
TRADEMARK OF PROPRIETORS: ALLIED DISTILLERS LTD

Single Highland Malt

Scotch DISTILLED 1979 *Whisky*

IMPERIAL
Built in 1897, the year of
Queen Victoria's Diamond
Jubilee, the Imperial
Distillery stands
majestically among the
dark woods of Carron,
in a fold of the hills
which encompass the
glittering Spey.

Specially selected,
produced and bottled by
and under the
responsibility of
Gordon & Macphail,
Elgin, Scotland.
Regd. Bottler.

CARRON, MORAY EST. 1897

Built by Thomas Mackenzie in 1897, ownership was transferred to Dailuaine-Talisker Distilleries the following year. It closed in 1899 and was silent until 1919. Became a part of DCL in 1925 and closed again. Re-opened under the control of SMD when rebuilt in 1955. Doubled to four stills in 1965. Closed again in 1985 and sold to Allied Lyons in May, 1989, when it was reopened. Now part of Allied Domecq and operated by Allied Distillers Ltd.

LOCATION On an unclassified road between the A95 and B9102, some two miles south west of Aberlour in a hollow on the banks of the Spey and next to the former Carron station.

NOTES The distillery was designed by architect Charles Doig of Elgin of red Aberdeen bricks within a framework of iron beams and frames. One of the malt kilns was surmounted by an enormous imperial crown which flashed and glittered in the sun. The crown, which by then had rusted, was taken down in 1955. It was one of the distilleries where experimentation on the technique of drying distillery effluent for use as cattle feed was pioneered.

WATER The Ballintomb Burn.

Distillation 1979 **Strength** 40% abv

Sweetness 6 Peatiness 7 Availability 4

Colour Amber with yellow/gold highlights **Nose** Quite full-bodied, medium-dry with a clean green freshness and a good peatiness **Flavour** Medium-sweet with a green edge, quite rich dark chocolatey and a firm peatiness **Finish** Clean, long, medium-sweet and delicately smokey **Notes** Gordon & MacPhail bottling

Distillation 1970   **Strength** 40% abv

Sweetness 6	Peatiness 7	Availability 2

Colour Bright amber with good gold highlights **Nose** Medium-peaty, medium-sweet, oaky, lightly mashy with green fruit at the back **Flavour** Almost medium-dry, quite full-bodied, peaty, smooth and oily-creamy **Finish** Smooth, quite long, a touch smoky and with a peanut character **Notes** Gordon & MacPhail bottling

HOGMANAY DRAM

Age 16 years   **Distillation** 1976   **Strength** 43% abv

Sweetness 5	Peatiness 7	Availability 0

Colour Very pale straw with a green tinge **Nose** Quite full, smoky, aromatic and medium-dry with a green fruitiness **Flavour** Slightly off-dry, smoky and full-bodied **Finish** Long, smoky and smooth **Notes** Master of Malt *Hogmanay Dram 1992* - cask no 7559

Age 12 years   **Strength** 65% abv

Sweetness 7	Peatiness 6	Availability 3

Colour Slightly hazy, pale straw/yellow **Nose** Full, sweetish, malty and spirity **Flavour** Quite sweet, smooth, almost creamy, lightly smoky **Finish** Long, quite spicy, strong and quite scented, strangely chocolatey **Notes** James MacArthur bottling

Age 14 years **Distillation** 1979 **Strength** 64.9% abv

Sweetness 6	Peatiness 5	Availability 4

Colour Very pale straw with yellow/lemon highlights **Nose** Warm, with an unusual spiritiness, very fruity and medium-sweet **Flavour** Warm, soft, smooth, woody and tangy, medium-sweet and gently smoky **Finish** Quite long, fresh and gently smoky **Notes** Wm Cadenhead bottling

SPEYSIDE
SINGLE MALT
SCOTCH WHISKY

The *Oyster Catcher* is a common *sight*
around the

INCHGOWER

distillery, which stands *close* to the *sea*
on the mouth of the *RIVER SPEY*
near *BUCKIE*. *Inchgower*,
established in 1824, produces *one* of the
most *distinctive single* malt whiskies
in *SPEYSIDE*. It is a malt for the
discerning drinker ~ a complex aroma
precedes a *fruity, spicy*
taste 🦪 with a hint of *salt*.

AGED **14** YEARS

43% vol   Distilled & Bottled in *SCOTLAND*
INCHGOWER DISTILLERY,
Buckie, Banffshire, Scotland   70cl

BUCKIE, BANFFSHIRE EST. 1871

Built by Alexander Wilson and Company as "The great distillery of Inchgower" to replace *Tochineal,* which had become outdated and cramped. The company celebrated its centenary on 12 July 1922. It was purchased by Buckie Town Council for £1,000 in 1936 and sold on to Arthur Bell & Sons in 1938, reputedly for £4,000. Doubled to four stills in 1966. Now part of United Distillers plc.

LOCATION   On the north side of the A98 between Fochabers and Buckie.

NOTES   A farm on the hill above the distillery was once the home of a noted local smuggler by the name of Macpherson. His still, well hidden at the back of the hill, was only discovered when some stray Highland cattle dislodged a large piece of turf, thus exposing the still to the farmer driving his cattle home. Sad to say for Macpherson, the farmer was quick to tip off the Excisemen and claim his reward.

WATER   Springs in the Menduff Hills.

Age 14 years   **Strength** 43% abv

Sweetness 7	Peatiness 3	Availability 6

Colour Straw with lemon yellow highlights **Nose** Medium-sweet, good richness with vanilla and a greenness at the back **Flavour** Smooth, creamy vanilla, medium-sweet with a fresh greenness **Finish** Long, clean and fresh with a hint of coffee on the tail **Notes** United Distillers bottling

Age 12 years **Strength** 40% abv

Sweetness 8 Peatiness 6 Availability 0

Colour Pale golden/straw **Nose** Slightly sweet and peaty **Flavour** Rich, sweet and full-bodied with a delicate peatiness **Finish** Distinguished, long and delicately sweet **Notes** Arthur Bell (pre-Guinness) bottling

Age 13 years **Strength** 43% abv

Sweetness 7 Peatiness 3 Availability 1

Colour Pale amber/straw with lemon highlights **Nose** Quite good body, fresh, quite sweet, gently peated and gently nutty **Flavour** Clean, quite zingy, medium-sweet, fruity and rich with good body **Finish** Quite long, fresh and clean **Notes** Master of Malt bottling

Distillation 1966 **Strength** 61.6% abv

Sweetness 7 Peatiness 4 Availability 1

Colour Mid amber with old gold highlights **Nose** Sweet with an aroma of unctuous oily oak, almost buttery and quite a fresh, ripe green fruitiness **Flavour** Medium-sweet with good body, chewy oaky tannins and a smooth, slight toffee note **Finish** Rich toffee, good length with a touch of menthol **Notes** Scotch Malt Whisky Society bottling; cask no. 16.5; bottled May 1994

THE SCOTCH
MALT WHISKY SOCIETY
THE VAULTS · LEITH · SCOTLAND

SOCIETY CASK NO
18.5

DATE DISTILLED   NOV 66
DATE BOTTLED   MAY 94
PROOF STRENGTH 107.8° 61.6% vol e
CONTENTS BY VOL. 70cl.
PRODUCE OF SCOTLAND · BOTTLED IN LEITH · SCOTLAND

INCHMURRIN

SINGLE HIGHLAND MALT

SCOTCH WHISKY

Distilled by
THE LOCH LOMOND DISTILLERY
DUNBARTONSHIRE SCOTLAND

70cl℮   40%vol
PRODUCT OF SCOTLAND

ALEXANDRIA, DUNBARTONSHIRE EST. 1965

One of two styles of malt produced by the Loch Lomond distillery, built in 1965/66 by the Littlemill Distillery Company Ltd. Closed 1984 and reopened in 1987 after being purchased by Glen Catrine Bonded Warehouse Ltd. Two stills.

LOCATION Alexandria is at the southern end of Loch Lomond on the A82 Glasgow to Fort William road.

NOTES An earlier distillery of the same name existed at Arrochar, at the other end of Loch Lomond from 1814 to 1817. The stills are of an unusual design, allowing them to produce two very different styles of malt whisky, the other style being *Rhosdhu* (see p. 190).

WATER Loch Lomond.

Age 10 years   **Strength** 40% abv
Sweetness 4   Peatiness 6   Availability 4

Colour Amber with old gold highlights **Nose** Youthful, fresh, mashy, rich and medium-dry with a good weight of peat **Flavour** Quite sweet and fresh with good weight and a nice green note to the peat character **Finish** Long, clean and rich **Notes** Glen Catrine bottling

Age 9 years   **Distillation** 1985   **Strength** 64% abv
Sweetness 4   Peatiness 3   Availability 2

Colour Pale watery straw with lemon highlights **Nose** Young, mashy, vegetal and dry with just a hint of sweetness at the back **Flavour** Medium-sweet, vegetal and mashy with a citrus note, slightly harsh and austere **Finish** Earthy, quite short and spirity **Notes** Wm Cadenhead bottling, distilled March 1985

GLASGOW ROAD, DUMBARTON EST. 1938

Inverleven was built in 1938 by Hiram Walker & Sons, Scotland, within the site of the Dumbarton grain distillery complex. Licensed to George Ballantine & Son Ltd. Now part of Allied Domecq, but closed in 1991.

LOCATION Next to the River Clyde in the centre of Dumbarton.

NOTES Two stills for malt whisky production at Dumbarton. There was also a third Lomond-type still which produced a heavier style of spirit known as *Lomond*.

WATER Loch Lomond.

INVERLEVEN
Distillation 1979   **Strength** 40% abv

Sweetness 6	Peatiness 1	Availability 4

Colour Mid-amber with gold highlights **Nose** Quite light and cereal with a touch of apple fruit, medium-dry with an edge of richness **Flavour** Medium-sweet with good richness and a smooth, creamy character **Finish** Long, spicy, quite sweet and tangy **Notes** Gordon & MacPhail bottling - followed by 1984

LOMOND
Age 30 years   **Strength** 60% approx. abv

Sweetness 2	Peatiness 3	Availability 0

Colour Pale straw/amber with yellowy green highlights **Nose** Quite full-bodied, good richness and still with a touch of greenness **Flavour** Full, spirity, dry, but with a richness at the back, the greenness of the aroma is still present **Finish** Long, quite light and spicy **Notes** A *Lomond* cask sample supplied by Whyte & Mackay for a tasting tutored by Richard Paterson held at Christie's, Glasgow

CASK STRENGTH 61.5% VOL. 5 CL

LOCHRANZA, ISLE OF ARRAN EST. 1995

Harold Currie had a dream, when he retired as managing director of Chivas Bothers, to create his own distillery. He found a site at Lochranza in the north of the island of Arran and built a modern distillery with the architectural appearance and feel of much older buildings. Very small, it dovetails perfectly with the rest of the island which has been described as "Scotland in Miniature".

LOCATION Immediately to the east of the village of Lochranza in the north of the island.

NOTES The only distillery on the Isle of Arran, the last (legal) distillery, at Lagg in the south, closed in 1837. The manager, Gordon Mitchell, has a number of ducks which swim in the water-cooling pond. There are also a pair of Golden Eagles which nest on the crags above the distillery and caused the initial building works to stop while they tended to their young. Whilst waiting for their own spirit to be ready for sale, the company are marketing a range of whiskies, including vatted and single malts under their own labels.

WATER Loch na Davie.

Age 1 year **Distillation** 1995 **Strength** 61.5% abv

Sweetness 9 Peatiness 2 Availability 1

Colour Pale straw with pale yellow/pale lemon highlights **Nose** A herby character with a definite oregano note, soft, quite sweet, quite full-bodied with a fresh greenness and a soft peaty character. Complexity is developing quite fast **Flavour** Medium-sweet with good body, soft and smooth and with a slight vegetal greenness **Finish** A salty tang, sweet and long, developing well with a slight hint of oaky vanilla showing on the tail **Notes** Bottled as "1 Year Old Spirit 1996" (aged in barrel)

CRAIGHOUSE, ISLE OF JURA, ARGYLL EST. 1810

After passing through several different owners in its early years, Jura blossomed in the late 1800s when it came into the hands of Messrs James Ferguson & Sons in 1875, being rebuilt at a cost of £25,000. However, it closed in the early 1900s because, it is said, of an argument over the rent, after which the distiller upped and went, taking his still and equipment with him. Jura was abandoned until the late 1950s when a rebuilding programme was begun. The first spirit for more than 50 years flowed in 1963. Enlarged from two to four stills in 1978. Now owned by Invergordon Distillers plc, which in turn was taken over by JBB (Greater Europe) plc in 1994.

LOCATION Across from Islay on the leeward east coast of Jura, on a bay where a string of islands forms a natural breakwater.

NOTES Records are said to trace distilling on Jura as far back as 1502. After the distillery had been rebuilt in the 1870s it gained a reputation for being one of the most efficient in Scotland. However it was once discovered that the spent wash from the stills was finding its way into a local cattle trough. The effect on the animals, it is said, was most interesting.

WATER Loch a' Bhaile Mhargaidh (Market Loch).

Age 10 years **Strength** 40% abv

Sweetness 3 Peatiness 7 Availability 8

Colour Pale straw with very slight green tinges **Nose** Full, pleasantly dry **Flavour** Very delicate, lightly smoky with a pleasant oily nuttiness **Finish** Very smooth and lingers well **Notes** Invergordon Distillers bottling

TOWERS ROAD, AIRDRIE, LANARKSHIRE EST. 1965

Killyloch was a second still at Moffat distillery which produced a malt for blending purposes only (see *Glen Flagler*). The whisky was supposed to be named *Lillyloch,* from the water source on the outskirts of Airdrie, but at the time of filling, it was discovered that the cask stencil had been mis-spelt. As the whisky was intended for blending purposes only, it was decided to leave the name as Killyloch.

L O C A T I O N Within the Glen Flagler complex at Moffat distillery.

N O T E S Prior to June 1994, its make had never been bottled as a single malt.

W A T E R Lillyloch.

Age 22 years **Distillation** 1972 **Strength** 52.6% abv

Sweetness 4 Peatiness 2 Availability 0

Colour Pale mid-amber with lemon/gold highlights **Nose** Medium-bodied, cereally, a fairly harsh spirit character and a slightly green, almost leafy, dry and with a creamy oiliness **Flavour** Medium-dry, soft with good richness, a touch of spice and medium-bodied with gentle tannins **Finish** Medium-length with good sweetness, a light smokiness and a fresh green note **Notes** Signatory bottling, distilled 21 March 1972 and bottled June 1994

CONNOISSEURS CHOICE

Connoisseurs Choice, a range of single malts from various districts of Scotland.

The lowlands traditionally produce smooth soft and mellow whiskies.

SINGLE LOWLAND
MALT SCOTCH WHISKY
DISTILLED AT
KINCLAITH
DISTILLERY
Trade Mark of Proprietors: Long John Distillers Ltd
DISTILLED **1967** DISTILLED
Specially selected, produced and bottled by and under the responsibility of
70cl **GORDON & MACPHAIL** 40%vol
REG'D BOTTLER · ELGIN · SCOTLAND
PRODUCT OF SCOTLAND

MOFFAT STREET, GLASGOW EST. 1957

Built 1957/58 by Strathclyde & Long John Distilleries Ltd, at that time a subsidiary of the American company Seager Evans & Co. Ltd. Sold to Whitbread & Co. Ltd in 1975 and dismantled in 1976 to make way for an enlarged Strathclyde grain distillery. Two stills.

LOCATION   In the centre of Glasgow within the Strathclyde Grain Distilling complex.

NOTES   The last of Glasgow's once numerous malt whisky distilleries.

WATER   The local Glasgow water supply, which comes from Loch Katrine.

Age 20 years   **Strength** 46% abv

Sweetness 6   Peatiness 3   Availability 1

Colour Very pale straw with yellow/green highlights **Nose** Quite sweet oak, rich and full-bodied **Flavour** Creamy, smooth and medium-sweet **Finish** Peppery and spicy with a dry, clean tail **Notes** Wm Cadenhead bottling

Distillation 1966   **Strength** 40% abv

Sweetness 6   Peatiness 3   Availability 2

Colour Amber with old gold highlights **Nose** Medium-bodied, lightly peated and medium-sweet with a leather and shoe wax aroma **Flavour** Medium-sweet and quite full-bodied with gentle oaky tannins and a leathery smokiness **Finish** Long, rich and creamy with dry tannins and almost chewy **Notes** Gordon & MacPhail bottling - followed by 1967

KNOCKANDO, MORAY EST. 1898

Built by the Knockando-Glenlivet Distillery Co. Owned by J Thomson & Co. from 1900-3. Acquired by W & A Gilbey in 1904. Now managed by Justerini & Brooks, a subsidiary of IDV.

LOCATION South of the B9102 between Knockando and Archiestown, sited on the banks of the River Spey.

NOTES Much of the make is used in the J & B blend. An individual feature of the malt is that its bottle states both its year of distillation and date of bottling. If you believe that whisky, like wine, has vintage years, then Knockando is worthy of close study. Knockando is "cnoc an dhu" in Gaelic which means "little black hillock".

WATER The Cardnach Spring.

Distillation 1982 **Strength** 43% abv

Sweetness	7	Peatiness	3	Availability	7

Colour Straw with yellow/lemon highlights **Nose** Medium-bodied, medium-sweet and leafy with with rich unctuous oaky vanilla notes, an almost grapey fruitiness and delicately peated **Flavour** Good body, quite sweet and fresh with gentle tannins and peatiness **Finish** Long, smooth and sweet with a , slightly chewy tail and hints of green coffee **Notes** J&B bottling 1996

KNOCKANDO EXTRA RESERVE

Age 21 years **Strength** 43% abv

Sweetness	7	Peatiness	3	Availability	1

Colour Straw, lightly peaty with pale greeny-gold highlights **Nose** Lightly peated, medium-dry, rich and leafy with pleasantly oaky vanilla **Flavour** Medium weight, slightly green, medium-sweet and round **Finish** Smooth, not quite medium-sweet, delicately spicy and quite long **Notes** J&B bottling in 1995

KNOCK, BANFFSHIRE EST. 1893

Knockdhu, as the distillery is known, was the first to be built by the DCL, being licensed to John Haig & Co. Closed in 1983. Sold late 1988 to the Knockdhu Distillery Company Ltd, a subsidiary of Inver House Distillers plc and reopened in 1989. Two stills.

LOCATION   West of the B9022, seven miles north of Huntly.

NOTES   Built of local grey granite by Gordon & Macbey, architects of Elgin. The water supply, owned by the company, is piped from Knock Hill and is also supplied to the villagers of Knock. The distillery was occupied by a unit of the Indian Army from 1940 to 1945. As Inver House want to avoid confusion with, or suggestion of another malt, the single malt from Knockdhu is now marketed under the Gaelic name *An Cnoc*.

WATER   A spring on the southern slopes of Knock Hill.

Age 12 years   **Strength** 43% abv
Sweetness 6 Peatiness 7 Availability 4

Colour Straw/amber with gold highlights **Nose** Fresh, medium-bodied, malty and medium-sweet with a touch of greenness **Flavour** Sweet, round, quite full-bodied and lightly peated **Finish** Long, smooth and sweet with a green smokiness **Notes** Inver House bottling as *An Cnoc*

Distillation 1974   **Strength** 40% abv
Sweetness 9 Peatiness 3 Availability 4

Colour Pale straw/gold with yellow highlights **Nose** Fatty, slightly sweet, quite full-bodied **Flavour** Sweet, malty and slightly peppery **Finish** Quite long and slightly oily **Notes** Gordon & MacPhail bottling as *Knockdhu*

PURE MALT SCOTCH WHISKY
from
LADYBURN
Distillery

Proprietors: William Grant & Sons Ltd.

75 cl   Bottled by Wm. Cadenhead,
18 Golden Square, Aberdeen
Scotland   **46% vol**

GIRVAN, AYRSHIRE EST. 1966

Opened in 1966 by William Grant & Sons Ltd, Ladyburn has not produced any spirit since 1976. Four stills.

LOCATION   Ladyburn is part of the complex which includes the Girvan grain distillery.

NOTES   William Grant & Sons are also the proud owners of the Speyside malts Glenfiddich and The Balvenie, but Ladyburn is much harder to come by, as it is only occasionally released through the independent bottlers none being available from the owners although there is a rumour that William Grant & Sons have 30 casks laid down for future bottling.

WATER   Penwapple reservoir.

Age 20 years   **Strength** 46% abv

Sweetness 4   Peatiness 4   Availability 1

Colour Pale straw with lemon/gold highlights **Nose** Malty, lightly peated, leafy and slightly rich with an oily character **Flavour** Almost dry, smooth, round, soft and peaty; quite simple, but with good body **Finish** Slightly smoky, a touch of spice and of reasonable length **Notes** Wm Cadenhead bottling

LAGAVULIN

* visits by appointment only

NEAR PORT ELLEN, ISLAY, ARGYLL   EST. 1816

Originally two legal distilleries were set up on the site, the first in 1816 was Lagavulin, founded by John Johnson. The second, the following year, was established by Archibald Campbell and is believed to have been known as Kildalton. In Alfred Barnard's report on his visit of 1887, he stated that the make was "principally sold in Glasgow, England and the Colonies". Lagavulin has long been important to *White Horse* blended whisky, becoming part of DCL in 1927 and managed by SMD from 1930. Rebuilt in 1962 when the stills from Malt Mill (see below) were incorporated. Four stills. Now part of United Distillers plc.

LOCATION   Occupying a site of six acres, Lagavulin stands at the head of a small bay. The ruins of Dunyvaig Castle are next door.

NOTES   Lagganmhouillin, or Lagavulin, means "mill in the valley". Distilling on the site is thought to date from as early as 1742 when there were ten small bothies there. One of United Distillers' *Classic Malts* portfolio. Mackie & Co., owners at the turn of the century, were also the agents for *Laphroaig* next door. When they lost the agency in 1907, they built a new distillery within the Lagavulin complex to produce a similar style of whisky. Called Malt Mill, it had its own maltings which had a haircloth-floored kiln fired only with open peat fires. The Lagavulin mash tun was utilised, but there were two independent wash backs and two pear-shaped stills. Malt Mill closed in 1960 and the stills incorporated in Lagavulin.

WATER   The Solan Lochs.

Age 16 years   Strength 43% abv

Sweetness 3	Peatiness 10	Availability 10

Colour Deep amber with rich gold highlights **Nose** Distinctive, pungent, burnt heather, very peaty and full-bodied **Flavour** Big, peaty, dry, very smooth and powerfully complex **Finish** Long and smoky with an almost burnt character, very persistent **Notes** United Distillers bottling

LAGAVULIN

Age 12 years **Strength** 40% abv

Sweetness 3 Peatiness 10 Availability 0

Colour Golden brown, like a peat-stained burn **Nose** Big, powerful, burnt mahogany, lots of peat **Flavour** Full, heavy and smokily powerful with a strangely sweet edge **Finish** Explosive, spicy and smokily pungent **Notes** DCL (pre-Guinness) bottling

Age 15 years **Distillation** 1978 **Strength** 64.4% abv

Sweetness 5 Peatiness 9 Availability 2

Colour Pale amber with a greenish tinge and yellow highlights **Nose** Full and pungent with ozone, burnt heather and a rich, slightly creamily unctuous character **Flavour** Seaweed with great richness and quite big tannins, quite sweet, powerful and pungent **Finish** Long, lingering, smoky and rich **Notes** Wm Cadenhead bottling

Age 15 years **Distillation** 1980 **Strength** 63.3% abv

Sweetness 3 Peatiness 8 Availability 1

Colour Deep amber with bronze highlights and a ruby hue **Nose** Full-bodied, dark, powerful and pungent (but its inherent character is partly masked by the influence of the Oloroso cask), rubber/liquorice and burnt heather roots **Flavour** Big-bodied, pungently smoky, with good richness and quite gentle, tarry tannins **Finish** Long, dark, smoky and tangy **Notes** Scotch Malt Whisky Society bottling as cask no. 111.1

LAPHROAIG®

**SINGLE ISLAY MALT
SCOTCH WHISKY**

10
Years Old

**The most richly flavoured of
all Scotch whiskies**

ESTABLISHED
1815

DISTILLED AND BOTTLED IN SCOTLAND BY

D. JOHNSTON & CO., (LAPHROAIG), LAPHROAIG DISTILLERY, ISLE OF ISLAY.

40%vol IMPORTADOR WENCESLAO PAZ MARTINEZ
DOMICILIO C HADDU S/N R.S. NUM 40.1.125 ML **70cl**

L00205

NEAR PORT ELLEN, ISLAY, ARGYLL   EST. 1815

Said to have been founded by Donald and Alex Johnston. Originally a farm distillery, records show distilling took place on the site in 1812. By 1815, when the forerunner of today's distillery opened, distilling had overtaken farming in importance to the Johnston family. Laphroaig remained in the Johnston family until 1954, when the then proprietor, Ian Hunter, bequeathed it to Bessie Williamson. At this time she was company secretary, having worked in the business for many years, and went on to become a most important and respected figure in the Scotch whisky industry before she retired as managing director in 1972. Miss Williamson sold Laphroaig to Long John Distillers Ltd, part of the Seager Evans group, between 1962 and 1967 and the business is now part of Allied Domecq and operated by Allied Distillers Ltd. Enlarged from two to four stills in 1923, to six in 1968-9 and to seven in 1974.

LOCATION   Situated on a small bay, frequented by otters, swans and a heron, it has been greatly influenced by the sea throughout its history.

NOTES   Generally accepted as being the most individually flavoured of all single malts. Although Laphroaig, like all the distilleries on the island, is built on the coast, it has always been maintained that it is not only the sea air, but also the peat which accounts for the distinctiveness of the make. The peat used by the distillery has a high proportion of moss in its content and this is said to give Laphroaig its particular flavour. Laphroaig has its own floor maltings. Part of the site occupied by the modern Laphroaig distillery includes that of the old Ardenistle distillery (1837- c. 1848).

WATER   The Kilbride Dam.

Age 10 years   **Strength** 40% abv

Sweetness 2   Peatiness 10   Availability 10

Colour Palish amber with slightly greenish tones **Nose** Dry, heavy and peaty with a heathery smokiness **Flavour** Full of character, very peaty and smoky with iodine/medicinal notes **Finish** Lingering, smoky, smooth and unique **Notes** Caledonian Distillers bottling

Age 15 years   **Strength** 43% abv

Sweetness 2   Peatiness 10   Availability 6

Colour Amber/peaty with good gold highlights **Nose** Peaty, full and medicinal with a slightly fruity edge **Flavour** Soft, smoky, round and smooth with a slightly sweet middle to the palate **Finish** Long, smoky and refined **Notes** Caledonian Distillers bottling

Age 10 years   **Strength** 57.3% abv

Sweetness 2   Peatiness 10   Availability 6

Colour Amber with gold highlights **Nose** Big, full-bodied and powerful with a dark, burnt heather peaty character, an ozone/wrack medicinal note and a slight hint of richness **Flavour** Smooth and big-bodied with a chewy tarriness, smoky and dry, but with an edge of richness **Finish** Long, tangy, smoky and slightly chewy, powerful and complex **Notes** Bottled by Allied Domecq as *Original Cask Strength Laphroaig - Straight from the Wood*

Distillation 1979 **Strength** 54% abv

Sweetness 1 Peatiness 10 Availability 2

Colour Pale amber with pale gold highlights. **Nose** Big and with a dark peatiness with a sea character to the smokiness and notes of iodine and creosote. **Flavour** Big, powerful and darkly peaty with a dry, chewy peatiness, a touch of richness and antiseptic notes. **Finish** Long, quite rich and very smoky **Notes** Limited Editions cask sample from cask no 5962

Distillation 1979 **Strength** 43% abv

Sweetness 2 Peatiness 10 Availability 2

Colour Straw with yellow highlights **Nose** Big, powerful, pungently peaty with a soft edge to it, notes of bandages and antispetic and a slightly floral note **Flavour** Big and very smoky with chewy tannins and a slightly astringent note to the peat **Finish** Long, explosively smoky and salty, a contemplative tipple. **Notes** Celtic Connections bottling

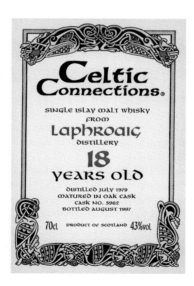

SPEYSIDE
SINGLE MALT
SCOTCH WHISKY

LINKWOOD

distillery stands on the *River Lossie*,
close to *ELGIN* in *Speyside*. The *distillery*
has retained its *traditional atmosphere*
since its *establishment* in 1821.
Great care has always
been taken to *safeguard* the
character of the *whisky* which has
remained the same through the
years. Linkwood is one of the
FINEST Single Malt Scotch Whiskies
available - *full bodied* with a *hint* of
sweetness and a *slightly smoky aroma*.

YEARS **12** OLD

43% vol   Distilled & Bottled in *SCOTLAND*. LINKWOOD DISTILLERY Elgin, Moray, *Scotland*.   70 cl

ELGIN, MORAY EST. 1821

Built by Peter Brown in 1821 and named after the estate on which it was built. The *Elgin Courant* of 10 April 1874 reported that the old buildings of Linkwood distillery were being pulled down and that new, more extensive buildings were being erected. By 1887 Linkwood had a 2,000 gallon wash still and a 1,850 gallon spirit still and was producing 50,000 gallons a year. It was bought by SMD in 1933 and rebuilt twice more: in 1962 and again in 1971, when a second distillery unit was built alongside the original extending it from two to six stills. Now part of United Distillers plc.

LOCATION   On the A941 south of Elgin and on the River Lossie.

NOTES   A very picturesque distillery with a reservoir of water for cooling purposes, which is inhabited by swans, alongside the buildings. It is surrounded by woodlands, hence the name. Roderick Mackenzie, who was manager from 1945 to 1963, believed that the character of the spirit depended not just on the vessels in which it was made, but also on everything in their immediate environment. He is even reputed not to have permitted the removal even of spiders' webs in case the character of the whisky were to alter as a result.

WATER   Springs near Millbuies Loch.

Age 12 years   **Strength** 43% abv

Sweetness 7   Peatiness 5   Availability 6

Colour Straw/amber with lemon highlights **Nose** Medium to full-bodied, medium-sweet with an appley character and a soft smokiness at the back **Flavour** Good weight, medium-sweet, fruity and lightly smoky **Finish** Long and spicy with a nice edge of sweetness **Notes** United Distillers bottling

Age 12 years   **Strength** 40% abv

Sweetness 8   Peatiness 4   Availability 0

Colour Clear golden, like sunlit peat-stained loch water over a sandy bottom **Nose** Fruity, with a sweetness reminiscent of apples **Flavour** Pleasantly light, round, sweet and slightly spicy **Finish** Long and elegant **Notes** DCL (pre-Guinness) bottling

Age 15 years   **Strength** 40% abv

Sweetness 7   Peatiness 5   Availability 4

Colour Quite full mid-amber with a tinge of green and gold highlights **Nose** Quite full-bodied, musty apples and oak with a fresh smokiness **Flavour** Medium-sweet and full-bodied with a touch of spice and oaky vanilla **Finish** Smooth and appley with a dry smoky finish **Notes** Gordon & MacPhail bottling

Age 21 years   **Strength** 40% abv

Sweetness 8   Peatiness 6   Availability 3

Colour Quite deep amber with bronze highlights **Nose** Smooth, dark and nutty with a touch of demerara sugar, medium-sweet and rich with a musty apple aroma **Flavour** Sweet, quite full-bodied and smooth with a delicate, but firm, peatiness **Finish** Long and sweet with just a hint of smokiness on the tail **Notes** Gordon & MacPhail bottling

Distillation 1979   **Age** 14 years   **Strength** 58.5% abv

Sweetness 3   Peatiness 6   Availability 2

Colour Deep, treacly amber with deep bronze/ruby highlights **Nose** Big-bodied, burnt wood peatiness, a dark nuttiness, medium-dry with the soft aroma of one of Leith's old tea warehouses **Flavour** Big, burnt and almost dry with chewy tannins **Finish** Soft, rich, long, chewy and off-dry **Notes** Wm Cadenhead bottling

LITTLEMILL

PRODUCT OF SCOTLAND

LITTLEMILL

Established 1772

SINGLE LOWLAND MALT
SCOTCH WHISKY

DISTILLED AND BOTTLED IN SCOTLAND BY
LITTLEMILL DISTILLERY CO. LTD.
BOWLING, DUNBARTONSHIRE, SCOTLAND

70cl ℮   40%vol

BOWLING, DUMBARTONSHIRE EST. 1772

The distillery has had numerous owners over its two centuries of operation, although its origins are somewhat obscure. Littlemill could be Scotland's oldest distillery. It is possible that whisky was distilled on the site as long ago as the 14th century, when the Colquhouns built Dunglas Castle to guard crossing the Clyde. About 1750, George Buchanan, a wealthy maltster from Glasgow bought Littlemill when he purchased the Auchterlonie estate and in 1772 he had to build houses for the Excise officers. Annual production in 1821 is recorded as 20,000 gallons. Rebuilt in 1875, Littlemill used triple distillation until the 1930s. The distillery closed in 1984 and was reopened by Gibson International in 1989. Following that company's failure late in 1994, Littlemill is now owned by Glen Catrine Bonded Warehouse Ltd but is again closed. It has two stills.

LOCATION Between the main road, the A82 and the River Clyde at the foot of the Kilpatrick Hills, 12 miles from Glasgow city centre towards Dumbarton.

NOTES Although strictly speaking a Lowland distillery, this is another which takes its water supply from north of the Highland Line. The present stills are of a most unusual design.

WATER A spring in the Kilpatrick Hills.

Age 8 years · **Strength** 40% abv

Sweetness 6 Peatiness 1 Availability 5

Colour Straw with yellow/gold highlights **Nose** Quite young, slightly mashy with an unpeated green, new-mown grassiness, medium-dry and with quite good body **Flavour** Fresh, quite mashy, medium-sweet and clean with good body **Finish** Quite rich and clean, of good length with just a suggestion of darkness at the end **Notes** Glen Catrine bottling

MONTROSE, ANGUS EST. 1957

Established on the site of Deuchar's brewery in 1957 by Joseph Hobbs, formerly of Associated Scottish Distillers, as a grain and malt distillery and blending and bottling plant. It was to be run by Hobbs under the operational company, MacNab Distilleries Ltd. It was sold to Destilerias y Crianza de Whisky SA of Madrid in November 1973. Originally four pot stills and one Coffey (grain) still, the latter was closed in 1970.

LOCATION At the north end of Montrose, at the junction of the coastal Aberdeen to Dundee road (the A92) and the A935 from Montrose to Brechin.

NOTES All of the make used to be bottled at the distillery by MacNab Distilleries. A small loch once existed opposite the distillery, hence the name. Most of the malt went to export, in bulk as well as bottle, with Spain being the main market because of the company's Spanish owners. Some of the whisky was available in bottle locally. The stills ceased production in the mid-1980s and the plant is now closed. The buildings are in the process of being redeveloped.

WATER A bore well beneath the distillery.

Age 10 years **Strength** 40% abv

Sweetness 3 Peatiness 5 Availability 1

Colour Light straw with gold highlights **Nose** Quite light, floral, leafy and slightly sweet **Flavour** Medium-dry, round and spicy, of medium weight **Finish** Leafy with hints of coffee, quite smooth **Notes** MacNab Distilleries bottling

NEAR ELGIN, MORAY   EST. 1894

Built by the Longmorn Distillery Company, which was amalga-mated with The Glenlivet and Glen Grant Distilleries and Hill, Thomson & Co. Ltd to form The Glenlivet Distilleries Limited. Owned by the Seagram Company of Canada since 1977. Extended from four to six stills in 1972 and eight in 1974.

LOCATION On the A941 Elgin to Rothes and Craigellachie road.

NOTES Professor R J S McDowall considered Longmorn to be one of the four finest malts. The name Longmorn comes from the Gaelic "Llanmorgund" meaning "place of the holy man", the distillery reputedly being on the site of an ancient abbey. The distillery houses an old steam engine which is occasionally used and it also has a dis-used water wheel. This malt is much favoured by blenders as a "top dressing" for their blends.

WATER Local springs.

Age 15 years   **Strength** 45% abv

Sweetness 6   Peatiness 4   Availability 6

Colour Mid-amber with gold highlights **Nose** Rich, full-bodied with soft oak and a cooked apples/grapey fruitiness, slightly peppery **Flavour** Quite full-bodied, round, soft and smooth, medium-sweet with a delicate edge of smokiness and gentle tannins **Finish** Rich, smooth and elegant with just a touch of smokiness **Notes** Seagram bottling

Age 12 years **Strength** 40% abv

Sweetness 6 Peatiness 5 Availability 4

Colour Amber with old gold highlights **Nose** Medium-bodied, a light sweet smokiness, a touch of creamy toffee and an almost menthol character **Flavour** Medium-dry, round, slightly creamy and smooth with a dark nuttiness **Finish** Long and nutty with a slight fragrant smokiness and a floral tail **Notes** Gordon & MacPhail bottling

Age 12 years **Strength** 58.6% abv

Sweetness 8 Peatiness 3 Availability 1

Colour Pale/mid-amber with pale yellow/gold highlights **Nose** Sweet, unctuous banana fruitiness with quite good body and delicately peated **Flavour** Sweet, round, soft and full-flavoured, gently tannic with a good, clean chocolatey peatiness **Finish** Long, sweet, rich and lingering with a smooth oaky vanilla background **Notes** Blackadder International Limited Editions bottling

CAMPBELTOWN, ARGYLL EST. 1973

Longrow is a particular type of malt produced occasionally from one of the stills within Springbank distillery.

LOCATION In the centre of Campbeltown.

NOTES Although the current brand was introduced only in 1973, the name was originally given to a distillery that once stood next door to Springbank, said to have been founded in 1824. It had closed by 1896. The old Longrow distillery site is now Springbank's car park. Very little Longrow has ever been released, and we understand from the brand's owners that it will be at least a couple of years before any more malt of this style is ready for release.

WATER Crosshill Loch and a spring on the premises.

Distillation 1973 **Strength** 43% abv

Sweetness 4 Peatiness 7 Availability 0

Colour Pale gold with green edges **Nose** Peaty and quite full with an edge of sweetness **Flavour** Smoky and dry with a touch of sweetness, slightly woody **Finish** Long and round with the smokiness to the end **Notes** J & A Mitchell & Co. Ltd bottling

Distillation 1974 **Strength** 46% abv

Sweetness 3 Peatiness 6 Availability 0

Colour Pale straw with a green tinge and lemon yellow high-lights **Nose** Dry and of medium weight with a smoky peatiness and a salty/seaweed character **Flavour** Smooth, round, of medium weight with an edge of sweetness, an earthy peatiness and a salty tang **Finish** Long and lightly smoky with a nice sweetness on the tail **Notes** J & A Mitchell & Co. Ltd bottling

PRODUCE OF — SCOTLAND

ESTABLISHED 1824

The

MACALLAN

Single Highland Malt Scotch Whisky

YEARS **10** OLD

DISTILLED AND BOTTLED BY
THE MACALLAN DISTILLERS LTD.
CRAIGELLACHIE · SCOTLAND

BOTTLED
IN
SCOTLAND

40% vol — 35cl e

CRAIGELLACHIE, MORAY EST. 1824

Until the bridge at Craigellachie was built by Thomas Telford in 1814, the ford across the Spey at Easter Elchies was one of the few on the river. It was much used by cattle drovers, and whisky distilled at the old farm distillery which preceded the licensed distillery was a popular feature of the river crossing for them. The licensed distillery was founded by Alexander Reid in 1824. Macallan, although now a public limited company, was until recently, controlled by the successors of Roderick Kemp who purchased it in 1892. The distillery was extended in the early 1950s and again in 1959, but the demand for Macallan fillings was such that it was doubled from six to twelve stills in 1965, increased to eighteen in 1974 and to twenty-one in 1975. The stills are small. Operatioanl control passed to Highland Distilleries plc in 1996. Highland Distilleries and Japanese company Suntory, both of which have had shareholdings in Macallan for some years, are now the majority shareholders, the former family interests no longer controlling the company.

LOCATION On a hillside overlooking the Spey with the old Easter Elchies house now magnificently refurbished as corporate offices.

NOTES The company's own bottlings are sold as *The Macallan*. The makers of The Macallan have championed the use of Sherry casks for maturing whisky and have helped to reverse the trend away from their use. All The Macallan's make is now aged in various types of Sherry wood. Old vintages of The Macallan are much sought after and very valuable. One bottle was bought for £12,000 in 1997.

WATER From bore holes.

Age 7 years **Strength** 40% abv

Sweetness 8 Peatiness 2 Availability 1

Colour Pale amber with yellow/lemon highlights **Nose** Young, cerealy, rich and medium-sweet, a slight unctuous-oily character and medium-bodied with a slightly green touch **Flavour** Quite light and sweet with a caramelly-tablet flavour **Finish** Quite short and sweet **Notes** Macallan bottling for Giovanetti in the Italian market

Age 10 years **Strength** 40% abv

Sweetness 7 Peatiness 4 Availability 10

Colour Fairly full amber with old gold highlights **Nose** Quite full-bodied with a slight green touch, good peatiness, a slightly rich sweet, sherried nutty vanilla character **Flavour** A chewy nuttiness with a vanilla overlay, quite full-bodied, smooth, quite rich and medium-sweet **Finish** Quite clean and long with a slight burnt nutty character **Notes** Macallan bottling

Age 18 years **Distillation** 1967 **Strength** 43% abv

Sweetness 6 Peatiness 3 Availability 1

Colour Rich and deeply golden **Nose** Rich, sherry-sweet with oaky-vanilla **Flavour** Sweet and round, rich, velvety smooth and less spirity than the 10 years old **Finish** Long, sweet and very distinguished **Notes** Macallan bottling

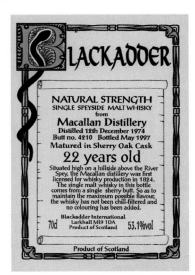

Age 18 years **Distillation** 1971 **Strength** 43% abv

Sweetness 8 **Peatiness** 3 **Availability** 2

Colour Rich amber with good gold highlights **Nose** Medium-sweet , quite full-bodied and with a slight oily nuttiness **Flavour** Medium-dry, nutty, round and medium-bodied **Finish** Clean and fresh with a nice touch of richness and slightly smoky **Notes** Macallan bottling

Age 18 years **Distillation** 1976 **Strength** 43% abv

Sweetness 7 **Peatiness** 3 **Availability** 6

Colour Full amber with old gold highlights **Nose** Quite full-bodied, rich and medium-sweet, nutty and honeyed with a beeswax character **Flavour** Full-bodied, round with gently chewy tannins, rich and medium-sweet with the beeswax unctuous texture **Finish** Long and rich with a touch of spice and pleasantly chewy **Notes** 1995 Macallan bottling

Age 20 years **Distillation** 1974 **Strength** 53.9% abv

Sweetness 5 **Peatiness** 6 **Availability** 2

Colour Deep amber with old gold highlights **Nose** Full-bodied, dark and nutty, medium-sweet with an edge of richness and a sooty, burnt peat character **Flavour** Medium-sweet, rich, soft and very smooth with gentle tannins **Finish** Nutty and peaty with a touch of spiciness **Notes** Wm Cadenhead bottling

Age 25 years **Distillation** 1963 **Strength** 43% abv

Sweetness 7 **Peatiness** 3 **Availability** 2

Colour Deep oaky amber with lovely gold highlights **Nose** Full, rich and nutty with a sherry-sweetness **Flavour** Big, rich, medium-sweet, creamy ,oaky and velvety smooth **Finish** Long, lightly spicy and nutty, finishes dry **Notes** Macallan bottling

Age 19 years **Distillation** 1976 **Strength** 54.1% abv

Sweetness 7 **Peatiness** 4 **Availability** 2

Colour Amber with bright gold highlights **Nose** A Christmas cake richness, yeasty and biscuity with an almost winey freshness and ripeness, medium-bodied and quite lightly peated **Flavour** Medium-dry with good body and creamily smooth with a firm peaty character **Finish** Long, quite smoky and slightly chewy **Notes** Blackadder International bottling from Bourbon cask no. 2873 distilled 18 October 1976

AGED **12** YEARS

DISTILLED, MATURED AND BOTTLED IN SCOTLAND
HIGHLAND
GLEN DEVERON
SINGLE MALT
SCOTCH WHISKY

MACDUFF DISTILLERY

BANFF, BANFFSHIRE EST. 1962

Built 1962-3 by a consortium which included George Crawford, Morty Dykes and Brodie Hepburn. Acquired by William Lawson in 1972, which in turn became part of the General Beverage Corporation, the Luxembourg company which controls Martini & Rossi's world interests. Extended from two to three stills in 1966 and to four in 1968. Now subsidiary of Bacardi Limited, Hamilton, Bermuda.

LOCATION Situated to the east of Banff on the east bank of the River Deveron, about half a mile from the Moray Firth.

NOTES William Lawson bottlings take the name *Glen Deveron* from the River Deveron valley rather than that or the distillery itself, which is known as Macduff. A five-year-old version is sold in Italy. It can be obtained bottled by independents as *Macduff*.

WATER The Gelly Burn

Age 12 years **Strength** 40% abv

Sweetness 7 Peatiness 3 Availability 6

Colour Pale straw with bright golden highlights **Nose** Fresh, leafy, quite full **Flavour** Medium-sweet, very smooth **Finish** Distinguished and lasts very well **Notes** Wm Lawson bottling as Glen Deveron

Age 20 years **Distillation** 1976 **Strength** 43% abv

Sweetness 6 Peatiness 4 Availability 2

Colour Very pale, watery straw with pale lemon highlights **Nose** Quite light and peppery with a spicy, delicate, herby oakiness, medium-dry with a round fruitiness **Flavour** Medium-dry with smooth and gently chewy oaky tannins **Finish** Quite delicately peated and medium-dry **Notes** Blackadder International bottling as *Macduff* from cask no. 1683

MANNOCHMORE

ELGIN, MORAY EST. 1971

Established by SMD in 1971 and licensed to John Haig & Co., Mannochmore was built on the same 25 acre (10 hectare) site as the older Glenlossie (1876). Mannochmore does not utilise a purifier between the lyne arm and condenser as does Glenlossie. Part of United Distillers plc. Mothballed in 1985, but reopened in 1989.

LOCATION   Sited next to Glenlossie at Thomshill on an unclassified road to the west of the A941, two miles south of Elgin.

NOTES   Previously not often available as a single, Mannochmore is important to a number of blends, including Haig. Owners United Distillers are now finishing certain whiskies in very heavily charred casks, which helps give a very dark style of whisky. See below.

WATER   The Bardon Burn.

Age 12 years   **Strength** 43% abv

Sweetness 5	Peatiness 3	Availability 6

Colour Very pale, almost watery with lemon highlights **Nose** Quite full, cerealy and yeasty with green fruit, medium-dry and quite lightly peated **Flavour** Medium-dry, mashy, quite fresh, clean and aromatic **Finish** Light and clean with a hint of coffee, lasts well **Notes** United Distillers bottling as Mannochmore

Age 10 years   **Strength** 40% vov

Sweetness 4	Peatiness 6	Availability 5

Colour A very deep black heart with an amber/garnet edge and a ruby hue **Nose** Full, rich, dark & nutty with a slight winey sweetness **Flavour** Quite full-bodied, medium-dry and smooth with slightly chewy tannins **Finish** Long and gently chewy. **Notes** Bottled by United Distillers as *Loch Dhu "The Black Whisky"*, it has been finished in a heavily charred oak cask

MILLBURN

RARE MALTS
SELECTION

Each individual vintage has been specially selected from Scotland's finest single malt stocks of rare or now silent distilleries. The limited bottlings of these scarce and unique whiskies are at natural cask strength for the enjoyment of the true connoisseur.

NATURAL
CASK STRENGTH
SINGLE MALT
SCOTCH WHISKY
AGED **18** YEARS
DISTILLED IN 1975 AT THE
MILLBURN
DISTILLERY
ESTABLISHED 1825
INVERNESS
58.9%vol 70cle
PRODUCE OF SCOTLAND
LIMITED BOTTLING

MILLBURN ROAD, INVERNESS EST. 1807

Said to have been founded by a Mr Welsh. The earliest recorded reference held by United Distillers dates from 1825, when James Rose and Alexander Macdonald were named as the licence holders. Used as a flour mill in 1853, it was rebuilt and reopened on 28 September 1876. It was then remodelled internally in late 1898. Owned from 1921 to 1937 by gin distillers, Booth's, who were themselves taken over by DCL in that year. Management was transferred to SMD in 1943. There were two stills.

LOCATION Millburn was located about one mile east of the centre of Inverness, on the banks of the Mill Burn from which the distillery and the district take their name.

NOTES Fire broke out on 26 April 1922, but the local fire brigade, "greatly assisted" by the Cameron Highlanders, saved the still house and storage warehouses. The commander of the 3rd Battalion, Lt-Col. David Price Haig, had owned the distillery until 1921. The site was sold for property development in 1988 and the buildings remain as the Beefeater Distillery Restaurant.

WATER Loch Duntelchaig.

Age 18 years   **Strength** 58.9% abv

Sweetness 5 Peatiness 7 Availability 1

Colour Very pale amber with pale lemon highlights **Nose** Medium to full-bodied with a dark, deep smoky character, quite pungent and medium-dry **Flavour** Quite round with good peaty smokiness and a touch of bitter chocolate **Finish** Long and clean with an edge of richness, quite smoky with quite gentle oaky tannins **Notes** United Distillers bottling

Distillation 1966 **Strength** 40% abv

Sweetness 6 Peatiness 6 Availability 1

Colour Deep, syrupy golden **Nose** Woody, spirity and dryish **Flavour** Round and medium-sweet, slightly woody with a touch of fruit **Finish** A little flat spot, then finishes well and dry **Notes** Gordon & MacPhail bottling

Distillation 1971 **Strength** 40% abv

Sweetness 6 Peatiness 5 Availability 3

Colour Mid-amber/straw with gold/yellow highlights **Nose** Rich, medium-sweet, delicately peated with touches of oily nuttiness **Flavour** Medium-dry, gently smoky, medium to full-bodied, smooth and round **Finish** Soft with a touch of spiciness, quite long and gently smoky **Notes** Gordon & MacPhail bottling followed by 1972

Age 11 years **Distillation** 1983 **Strength** 59.7% abv

Sweetness 7 Peatiness 4 Availability 3

Colour Mid-amber with yellow/gold highlights **Nose** Medium-bodied with a slight richness, medium-sweet with a green smokiness **Flavour** Medium-sweet, rich and round with gentle peatiness and a slight nuttiness **Finish** Sweet and rich, quite full and smooth **Notes** Wm Cadenhead bottling

NEAR ELGIN, MORAY EST. 1824

Said to have been founded by Pearey & Bain, Miltonduff came into the ownership of Hiram Walker in 1936 and is now a part of the Allied Domecq group. The distillery was extended in the mid-1890s and was largely rebuilt 1974-5. Licensed to George Ballantine & Son Ltd and operated by Allied Distillers Ltd. Six Miltonduff stills and two Lomond stills, which were installed in 1964 and dismantled in 1981. The Lomond stills produced a different style of malt known as *Mosstowie.*

LOCATION West of the B9010 to the south of Elgin. A short distance away across the River Lossie are the ruins of Pluscarden Priory.

NOTES In the 18th and 19th centuries, the waters of the Black Burn supplied scores of illicit stills in the Glen of Pluscarden, the fertile barley-rich plain being ideal for their situation. Miltonduff is the principal malt associated with Ballantine's Scotch whisky.

WATER Reputedly the Black Burn.

Age 12 years **Strength** 40% abv

Sweetness 9 Peatiness 3 Availability 5

Colour Straw/golden with greenish edges **Nose** Medium to full-bodied, fragrant, slightly floral and sweet **Flavour** Sweet, fruity, full and round **Finish** Almost delicate, refined and long **Notes** Allied Distillers bottling

MOSSTOWIE
Distillation 1975 **Strength** 40% abv

Sweetness 6 Peatiness 4 Availability 3

Colour Amber with old gold highlights **Nose** Medium-bodied and medium-sweet with touch of toffee and quite delicately peated **Flavour** Round, smooth and medium-sweet with a slight fruitiness, a touch of spice, good weight and softly smoky Fisnish Long, clean and delicately smoky **Notes** Gordon & MacPhail bottling

SPEYSIDE
SINGLE MALT
SCOTCH WHISKY

MORTLACH

was the first of seven
distilleries in *Dufftown*. In the
(19th *farm animals* kept in
adjoining byres were fed on
barley left over from processing
Today *water* from springs in
the *CONVAL HILLS* is used to
produce this delightful
smooth, fruity single
MALT SCOTCH WHISKY.

AGED **16** YEARS

Distilled & Bottled in SCOTLAND
MORTLACH DISTILLERY
Dufftown, Keith, Banffshire, Scotland

43% vol   70 cl

DUFFTOWN, BANFFSHIRE   EST. 1823

The first of Dufftown's "seven stills". Founded by James Findlater. For a time it was owned by J & J Grant of Glen Grant who removed the distilling utensils. It lay unoccupied for some years, the barley granary serving as a Free Church during the Disruption until a Free Church building could be erected. Extended from three to six stills in 1897. Acquired by John Walker & Son in 1923, by which time it was the largest distillery in the area. Walker's joined DCL in 1925 and management of Mortlach passed to SMD in 1936. The old Mortlach was demolished and rebuilt in the early 1960s, reopening in 1964. Now part of United Distillers plc.

LOCATION   Sited at the junction of the A941 and B9014 on the eastern outskirts of Dufftown.

NOTES   In the hollow in which the distillery lies (Mortlach means bowl-shaped valley) was fought the battle, in 1010, at which the Scots King Malcolm II defeated the Danes. Tradition has it that the distillery is on the site of an illicit still which drew its water from a spring called Highland John's Well. Except in 1944, Mortlach had permission to stay open during the Second World War.

WATER   Springs in the Conval Hills.

Age 16 years   **Strength** 43% abv

Sweetness 7   Peatiness 5   Availability 6

Colour Deep amber with old gold highlights **Nose** Full-bodied, deep, dark and nutty, gently peated **Flavour** Full, rich, dark and nutty, big-bodied, smooth and round with soft oaky vanilla notes **Finish** Long, full-flavoured, smooth and darkly sherry cask-nutty **Notes** United Distillers bottling

Distillation 1984 **Strength** 40% abv

Sweetness 6 Peatiness 6 Availability 3

Colour Straw with yellow/pale lemon highlights **Nose** Medium-bodied and medium-sweet with a good dollop of dark peatiness and a slight green apple character **Flavour** Quite big-bodied and medium-sweet with a dark peatiness and gentle tannins **Finish** Long and elegant with a touch of spice and a good balance between sweetness and peatiness **Notes** 1995 Gordon & MacPhail *Centenary Reserve* bottling

Age 21 years **Strength** 40% abv

Sweetness 8 Peatiness 5 Availability 4

Colour Deep, syrupy amber with dark gold highlights **Nose** Quite dry, woody, slightly astringent and fairly pungent **Flavour** Medium-sweet, slightly woody, but very smooth and round, full and thick in consistency **Finish** Long and velvety with touches of "sticky" sweetness **Notes** Gordon & MacPhail bottling

Age 15 years **Strength** 40% abv

Sweetness 6 Peatiness 6 Availability 4

Colour Light to mid-amber with gold highlights **Nose** Medium-sweet, rich, toffee with a fresh peat character **Flavour** Medium-dry, rich, quite smoky and nutty **Finish** Quite fresh, tangy, nutty and long **Notes** Gordon & MacPhail bottling

Age 12 years **Distillation** 1984 **Strength** 43% abv

Sweetness 6 Peatiness 6 Availability 2

Colour Straw with yellow highlights **Nose** Quite big-bodied, rich and medium-sweet with unctuous vanilla and a slight floral note, medium peat **Flavour** Medium-sweet with a fresh, firm and fragrant peatiness and of good body **Finish** Long and clean with a floral note to the sweetness **Notes** Signatory bottling from cask no. 2941 distilled 11 October,1984

Age 50 years **Distillation** 1942 **Strength** 40% abv

Sweetness 5 Peatiness 5 Availability 1

Colour Full amber with old gold highlights **Nose** Full, rich and dark, medium-sweet, oaky vanilla with a lightly charred smoky character **Flavour** Full-bodied, round and rich with an edge of dryness, medium-dry with oaky tannins **Finish** Long, spicy and delicately smoky with firm tannins **Notes** Gordon & MacPhail bottling

CONNOISSEURS
CHOICE

Connoisseurs Choice, a
range of single malts from
various districts of
Scotland.

In the Highlands
are situated the greatest
number of malt whisky
distilleries.

SINGLE HIGHLAND
MALT SCOTCH WHISKY
DISTILLED AT
NORTH PORT-BRECHIN
DISTILLERY
Proprietors: Mitchel Bros. Ltd

DISTILLED 1974 DISTILLED

SPECIALLY SELECTED, PRODUCED AND BOTTLED BY
70cl GORDON & MACPHAIL 40%vol
ELGIN · SCOTLAND
PRODUCT OF SCOTLAND

BRECHIN, ANGUS EST. 1820

Founded by David Guthrie, a local farmer, Alfred Barnard referred to it as Brechin Distillery. It originally traded as Townhead Distillery Co., the company name changing to Brechin Distillery Co. in 1823. Barnard wrote "The district around Brechin being highly cultivated, barley of the highest quality is grown and carted" to the distillery, "where nothing but the best barley is malted". Run by SMD since 1922 and licensed to John Hopkins & Co. Ltd, the distillery had two stills. It was closed in 1983 and since demolished

LOCATION Sited north west of the town centre of Brechin.

NOTES North Port took its name from the north gate in the ancient city walls, now long since vanished. It was very much a "family" employer, with sons following fathers into the business.

WATER Loch Lee, which is also the town's supply.

Distillation 1970 **Strength** 40% abv

Sweetness	7	Peatiness	6	Availability	1

Colour Gold with yellow highlights **Nose** Sweet with heather honey aromas and rich **Flavour** Medium-sweet, full and round **Finish** Strangely slightly astringent, but lasts well **Notes** Gordon & MacPhail bottling

Age 17 years **Distillation** 1976 **Strength** 64.1% abv

Sweetness	4	Peatiness	6	Availability	3

Colour Pale amber with yellow highlights **Nose** Quite light with a burnt oak tang and a touch of perfume, a slight earthy peatiness and medium-dry **Flavour** Quite big and medium-dry with slightly bitter oaky tannins **Finish** Long with a tail of richness and toffee **Notes** Wm Cadenhead bottling

STAFFORD STREET, OBAN, ARGYLL   EST. 1794

Oban distillery was built, fortress-like, jammed between the cliff, on which sits McCaig's Folly, and the main street, by the Stevenson family, founders also of the town of Oban. It was rebuilt between 1883 and 1887 by Walter Higgin. It became part of DCL in 1925 and has been operated by SMD since 1930. The still house was rebuilt 1969-72 and has two stills. Now part of United Distillers plc.

L O C A T I O N   In the centre of Oban overlooking the harbour.

N O T E S   During enlargement in August 1890, a cave was discovered which contained bones from the Mesolithic era (4500-3000 BC). These remains are now to be found at the National Museum of Antiquities in Edinburgh. Oban's nose and flavour are reminiscent of Bowmore. One of United Distillers' *Classic Malts* portfolio.

W A T E R   Two lochs in Ardconnel, one mile inland from the town.

Age 14 years	**Strength** 43% abv	
Sweetness 5	**Peatiness** 7	**Availability** 7

Colour Very pale straw with gold highlights **Nose** Medium-sweet and lightly peated, quite rich with a slight burnt heather character **Flavour** Smooth, lightly sweet and creamy with a very delicate peatiness **Finish** Smoky, dry and delicate **Notes** United Distillers bottling

Age 12 years	**Strength** 40% abv	
Sweetness 4	**Peatiness** 7	**Availability** 0

Colour Dark amber with a syrupy texture **Nose** Clean, slightly spirity with a delicate peaty/heather aroma **Flavour** Very smooth, slightly peppery and hints of heather **Finish** Good length and a smoky aftertaste **Notes** DCL (pre-Guinness) bottling

MUIR OF ORD, ROSS-SHIRE EST. 1838

Ord distillery was founded as the Ord Distillery Company, which was taken over by James Watson & Co. of Dundee in 1896. Watson's in turn was acquired by John Dewar & Sons of Perth in 1923. Dewar's joined DCL in 1925, and the management of the distillery was taken over by SMD from 1930. The floor maltings were converted to Saladin maltings in 1961. Extensively rebuilt and extended from two to six stills in 1966. A large drum maltings was built on an adjacent site in 1968 and supplies malted barley to many other distilleries in the north of Scotland. Ord is now a part of United Distillers plc and licensed to John Dewar & Sons Ltd.

LOCATION About 15 miles to the north of Inverness on the western side of the A832, immediately to the west of Muir of Ord.

NOTES *The New Statistical Account of Scotland* recorded in 1840 that "distilling of aquavitae" was the sole manufacture of the district. Ord, which was built on the site of a smugglers' bothy, is the only distillery remaining in the area. There were nine other licensed distilleries operating during the last century. The distillery was lit by paraffin lamps until it gained access to the national electricity grid after the Second World War, but water power was still used for some operations as late as the 1960s. A visitor centre was opened in 1992. In the late 1950s and early 1960s, Ord was used for a programme of experiments which studied the differences between batches of spirit produced respectively by heating with coal, oil and steam. A colourful local smugglers' tale tells of Excisemen taking a confiscated cask of whisky upstairs to their room for safe-keeping while staying overnight in a local inn, the Bogroy Hotel, in nearby Beauly. A hole was drilled through the ceiling under the cask from the bar below and the whisky was "liberated" while the Excisemen slept.

WATER Loch nan Eun and Loch nam Bonnach.

Age 12 years   **Strength** 40% abv

Sweetness 6 Peatiness 5 Availability 6

Colour Mid-amber with yellow/green highlights and just a tinge of green **Nose** Quite fresh and lightly peated with a green fruitiness, medium-dry with a hint of creamy richness **Flavour** Medium-dry, quite rich and fresh, full and round with a touch of pepperiness **Finish** Long, fresh and quite rich with a dry tail **Notes** United Distillers bottling as *Glen Ord*

Age 12 years   **Strength** 40% abv

Sweetness 7 Peatiness 5 Availability 0

Colour Gold/straw with amber tints **Nose** Full-bodied, slightly dry, but with an overlying richness **Flavour** Quite full, big-bodied, round and medium-sweet **Finish** Very smooth, long and smoky **Notes** DCL (pre-Guinness) bottling as *Ord*

Age 27 years   **Distillation** 1962   **Strength** 55.4% abv

Sweetness 7 Peatiness 5 Availability 1

Colour Amber with good gold highlights **Nose** Full, round, medium-sweet and quite mellow with a touch of oily-nuttiness **Flavour** Fresh, clean, soft, a touch oaky, quite round and full **Finish** Dry, smooth, slightly austere and nutty **Notes** Wm Cadenhead bottling

SPEYSIDE
SINGLE MALT
SCOTCH WHISKY

PITTYVAICH

distillery is situated in the
DULLAN GLEN on the *outskirts*
of Dufftown, near to the *historic*
Mortlach Church which dates back
to the C6th The distillery draws
water from two nearby

springs - *CONVALLEYS* and
BALLIEMORE. Pittyvaich single
MALT SCOTCH WHISKY
has a *perfumed, fruity*
nose and a *robust* flavour with
a *hint* of *spiciness*.

AGED **12** YEARS

Distilled & Bottled in SCOTLAND.
PITTYVAICH DISTILLERY
Dufftown, Keith, Banffshire, Scotland

43% vol   70 cl

DUFFTOWN, BANFFSHIRE   EST. 1975

Built by Arthur Bell & Sons Ltd as a sister to Dufftown and operated in conjunction with it. Four stills. Now part of United Distillers plc. Closed in 1993.

LOCATION   Situated in the Dullan Glen on the outskirts of Dufftown near the sixth-century Mortlach Parish Church.

NOTES   The make uses the same water source as Dufftown and gives a similar whisky.

WATER   The distillery draws its process water from two springs, Convalleys and Balliemore.

Age 12 years   **Strength** 43% abv

Sweetness 4 Peatiness 6 Availability 6

Colour Amber with old gold highlights **Nose** Round, quite full and malty, spicy, peppery and almost meaty with a coffee tang at the back **Flavour** Medium-dry, quite full-bodied and dark flavoured with a touch of tannin **Finish** Long, chewy and quite big **Notes** United Distillers bottling

Age 12 years   **Strength** 56.6% abv

Sweetness 4 Peatiness 7 Availability 2

Colour Straw/amber with pale gold highlights **Nose** Quite peaty and soft with a damp oak character and a touch of green, unripe coffee **Flavour** Medium-dry, a coffee/chocolate character and smoky peatiness with a touch of spice **Finish** Long, lingering, spicy, smooth and nutty **Notes** Wm Cadenhead bottling

Age 12 years **Strength** 54% abv

Sweetness 5 Peatiness 7 Availability 3

Colour Medium to pale amber with lemon highlights **Nose** Medium-bodied, spirity and a hint of toffee/coffee with a greenness at the back, medium peated **Flavour** Medium-dry with a coffee flavour, quite full-flavoured, round and smooth **Finish** Creamy, quite sweet tangy and long with a soft touch of smokiness on the tail **Notes** James MacArthur bottling from cask number 15096

Age 13 years **Strength** 58% abv

Sweetness 4 Peatiness 7 Availability 4

Colour Deep, cough linctus-amber with bronze highlights **Nose** Big-bodied, dark, rich, malty, cerealy and a touch of rubber with a smoky burnt character **Flavour** Big, dark, rich, cerealy and smoky with a little spice **Finish** Quite spirity, long and smoky with a rich centre **Notes** Wm Cadenhead bottling

Age 18 years **Distillation** 1976 **Strength** 53.3% abv

Sweetness 8 Peatiness 2 Availability 2

Colour Pale straw/amber with pale gold highlights **Nose** Fresh and sweet with an almost grapey richness, a slightly unctuous lanolin aroma, a ripe apple character and lightly smoky **Flavour** Quite sweet, full and smooth with a green ripeness **Finish** Long, sweet and clean with a light smokiness on the tail **Notes** Blackadder International bottling

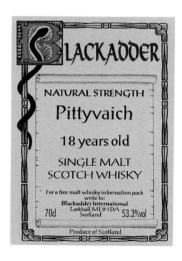

DISTILLED

≈ *1978* ≈

CASK

≈ 63.3% ≈
VOL·

NATURAL HIGH STRENGTH

NATURAL
CASK
STRENGTH

1978

63.3%
VOL

70cl

SINGLE MALT

SCOTCH WHISKY

FROM

PORT ELLEN

DISTILLERY

LOW ROBERTSON & CO LIMITED

SPECIALLY SELECTED, PRODUCED AND BOTTLED BY
GORDON & MACPHAIL
ELGIN·SCOTLAND

PRODUCT OF SCOTLAND

CASK No.
2698

DISTILLED
21/4/78

BOTTLED
September 1994

PORT ELLEN, ISLAY, ARGYLL EST. 1825

Founded by Alexander Ker Mackay, with the support of landown-er Walter Campbell, shortly after the Excise Act of 1824. Acquired by John Ramsay and run by him, and his heirs, until 1920, when sold to John Dewar & Sons Ltd and James Buchanan & Co., both of which companies merged with DCL in 1925. Port Ellen's management was transferred to SMD in 1930. Although silent from 1929 to 1966, the maltings continued in use. The distillery was extensively rebuilt in 1967, when it was increased from two to four stills. A large new maltings was erected in 1973. The distiller's licence was held by Low, Robertson & Co. Ltd. Although the distillery ceased production permanently in May 1983, the maltings now serves all the Islay distilleries, and also nearby Jura, following an his-toric concordat between the producing companies in 1987.

LOCATION   Situated about half a mile from the centre of Port Ellen, the maltings building now dominates the shoreline.

NOTES   The Excise Act of 1824 enforced the introduction of the spirit safe in distilleries. Tests had to be made to ensure that it had no harmful effects on the make. The official experiments were car-ried out in Port Ellen. The maltings were visited by Her Majesty Queen Elizabeth on 11 August 1980 and a commemorative bottling was produced.

WATER   The Leorin Lochs.

Distillation 1980 **Age** 16 years **Strength** 59% abv

Sweetness 2 Peatiness 9 Availability 2

Colour Pale straw with pale yellow/lemon highlights **Nose** Big-bodied and sea-influenced (ozone & salt spray) with dry notes of cereal and a dark, smoky peatiness **Flavour** Big, powerful and dry, but with a richness, very smoky and with quite chewy tannins **Finish** Long and smoky with just a hint of sweetness **Notes** Signatory bottling

Distillation 1970 **Strength** 40% abv

Sweetness 2 Peatiness 9 Availability 2

Colour Peaty/gold with bright highlights **Nose** Big-bodied, pungent and peaty with a slight rubbery character and dry **Flavour** Big, powerful, burnt peat with an edge of sweetness, very distinctive **Finish** Long, pungent and smoky **Notes** Gordon & MacPhail bottling

Distillation 1971 **Strength** 40% abv

Sweetness 1 Peatiness 9 Availability 3

Colour Bright gold/amber with golden/yellow highlights **Nose** Smoky peat, ozone, burnt heather roots with a very slight hint of sweetness **Flavour** Quite full, round, smoky, quite smooth and almost medicinal **Finish** Dry and smoky with the burnt heather roots lingering **Notes** Gordon & MacPhail bottling

Age 14 years **Distillation** 1977 **Strength** 59.7% abv

Sweetness 0 Peatiness 9 Availability 3

Colour Mid-amber with old gold highlights **Nose** Big, pungently smoky and dry with an earthy burnt peat character **Flavour** Big, powerful dark peatiness, a real "peat reek", and dry with a slight richness **Finish** Long and very peaty **Notes** Gordon & MacPhail bottling; cask no. 2017, distilled 14 April 1977

WICK, CAITHNESS EST. 1826

Established by James Henderson. Became part of DCL in 1925, having been purchased by John Dewar & Sons a couple of years earlier. Closed between 1930 and 1951, then revived. In 1955 it was bought by Hiram Walker, now part of Allied Domecq, who rebuilt the distillery in 1959. Pulteney distillery was sold to Inver House Distillers in June 1995. It has two stills.

LOCATION The most northerly distillery on the UK mainland, it is sited on the southern side of Wick, close to the North Sea coast.

NOTES Available only from the independent bottlers. One of the malts associated with *Ballantine's* blended Scotch whisky.

WATER The Loch of Hempriggs.

Age 12 years **Strength** 40% abv

Sweetness 6 Peatiness 5 Availability 5

Colour Very pale straw with pale, watery-green highlights **Nose** Soft, medium-bodied and medium-dry with a fresh, gentle, east coast touch of the sea and an almost grapey richness **Flavour** Medium-dry, fresh, clean and smooth, with good richness and an edge of sweetness **Finish** Very clean and fresh; lingering with a slightly salty touch on the lips **Notes** Inver House bottling as *Old Pulteney*

Age 8 years **Strength** 40% abv

Sweetness 3 Peatiness 8 Availability 4

Colour Palish gold with tinges of green **Nose** Delicately pungent with faint tangs of ozone **Flavour** Quite pungent, smoky and clean **Finish** Smoky, dry and refreshing **Notes** Gordon & MacPhail bottling as *Old Pulteney*

OLD RHOSDHU

Single Highland Malt

40% vol   SCOTCH WHISKY   70 cl e

PRODUCE OF SCOTLAND

DISTILLED AND MATURED AT
LOCH LOMOND DISTILLERY·ALEXANDRIA·SCOTLAND

ALEXANDRIA, DUNBARTONSHIRE EST. 1965

One of two styles of malt produced by the Loch Lomond distillery, built in 1965/66 by the Littlemill Distillery Company Ltd. Closed 1984 and reopened in 1987 after being purchased by Glen Catrine Bonded Warehouse Ltd. Two stills.

LOCATION Alexandria is at the southern end of Loch Lomond on the A82 Glasgow to Fort William road.

NOTES An earlier distillery of the same name existed at Arrochar, at the other end of Loch Lomond from 1814 to 1817. The stills are of an unusual design, allowing them to produce two very different styles of malt whisky, the other being called *Inchmurrin* (see p. 150).

WATER Loch Lomond.

Age 10 years   **Strength** 40% abv

Sweetness 6   Peatiness 4   Availability 4

Colour Amber with old gold highlights **Nose** Fresh, medium-dry and youthful with a cereal note and quite gentle dark peat **Finish** Medium-sweet with a touch of richness, of good body, with delicate peat and a cereal note **Finish** Long with a slight burnt note **Notes** Glen Catrine bottling as *Old Rhosdhu*

Age 9 years   **Distillation** 1985   **Strength** 60.5% abv

Sweetness 6   Peatiness 4   Availability 2

Colour Straw with lemon yellow highlights **Nose** Quite full, young, spirity and mashy, a dry earthy smokiness with just an edge of sweetness **Flavour** Medium-sweet, mashy and vegetal, medium-bodied **Finish** Sweet, cerealy, of medium length and with a burnt toffee tail **Notes** Wm Cadenhead bottling

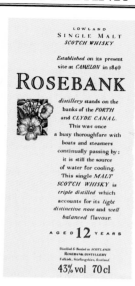

LOWLAND
SINGLE MALT
SCOTCH WHISKY

Established on its present
site at *CAMELON* in 1840

ROSEBANK

distillery stands on the
banks of the *FORTH*
and *CLYDE CANAL.*
This was once
a busy thoroughfare with
boats and steamers
continually passing by;
it is still the source
of water for cooling.
This single *MALT
SCOTCH WHISKY* is
triple distilled which
accounts for its *light
distinctive nose* and *well
balanced* flavour.

A G E D **12** Y E A R S

Distilled & Bottled in *SCOTLAND*
ROSEBANK DISTILLERY
Falkirk, Stirlingshire, Scotland

43% vol   70 cl

FALKIRK, STIRLINGSHIRE EST. 1840

The distillery, established by James Rankine, was converted from the maltings of the earlier Camelon distillery. It was rebuilt by his son in 1864. It was Rankine's objective to distil a whisky which would stand comparison with his competitors' finest makes. By the 1890s, there was an extraordinary demand for Rosebank and customers were put on allocation. In 1914 the Rosebank Distillery Ltd, as it was then called, was one of the original founders of Scottish Malt Distillers Ltd. Now part of United Distillers plc, Rosebank was closed in May 1993.

LOCATION   Sited on the banks of the Forth and Clyde Canal where the A803 intersects with the canal to the west of Falkirk.

NOTES   The make was triple distilled with one wash still and two spirit stills. The licensees were The Distillers Agency Ltd.

WATER   Carron Valley Reservoir.

Age 12 years   **Strength** 43% abv

Sweetness 2   Peatiness 4   Availability 6

Colour Straw/light amber with gold and lemon highlights **Nose** Medium-bodied and spirity with a touch of greenness, lightly oily, medium-dry with a good edge of richness **Flavour** Light and smooth, dryish with a mashy character **Finish** Smooth, dry and oaky with a pleasant lightness **Notes** United Distillers bottling

ROSEBANK

Age 12 years   **Strength** 43% abv

Sweetness 2 Peatiness 5 Availability 0

Colour Palish gold/amber with green tinges **Nose** Light and spirity, a little astringent **Flavour** Dry, a little spirity with a touch of spice **Finish** Quite good length, if somewhat fiery **Notes** DCL (pre-Guinness) bottling

Age 17 years   **Strength** 43% abv

Sweetness 2 Peatiness 4 Availability 0

Colour Mid-amber with a touch of green **Nose** Medium-bodied and dryish, but with a richness at the back, a green nuttiness and malty with an almost honeyed touch **Flavour** Dry, spicy, quite full-bodied, round, soft and smooth **Finish** Long and quite rich with a toffee-like tail **Notes** Master of Malt bottling - cask no. 5064

Age 19 years **Distillation** 1974   **Strength** 43% abv

Sweetness 1 Peatiness 4 Availability 0

Colour Mid-amber with pale gold highlights **Nose** Medium-bodied, quite fresh and slightly perfumed, medium-dry with a sweet oak note and a malty fruitiness **Flavour** Dry, fresh and quite lightly peated with an underpinning of vanilla **Finish** Fresh, quite clean and smoky **Notes** Master of Malt bottling from cask no. 5049, distilled 30 November 1974

Distillation 1969 **Strength** 51.7% abv

Sweetness 5 Peatiness 3 Availability 2

Colour Pale straw/amber with pale gold highlights **Nose** Malty, cerealy and soft with a slight oily oakiness and quite full with an edge of richness **Flavour** Quite full-bodied, sweet and rich, lightly peated with a green, fresh edge **Finish** Long, sweet and rich with a touch of chocolate **Notes** Signatory bottling

HIGHLAND

SINGLE MALT *SCOTCH WHISKY*

ROYAL BRACKLA

distillery, established in 1812, lies on the
southern shore of the MORAY FIRTH at *Cawdor* near *Nairn*.
Woods around the *distillery* are home to the *SISKIN*:
although a *shy bird*, it can often be seen *feeding* on *conifer* seeds.

In 1835 a *Royal Warrant* was granted to the *distillery* by King William IV,
who enjoyed the *fresh, grassy, fruity* aroma of this *single malt whisky*.

AGED **10** YEARS

43% vol   Distilled & Bottled in *SCOTLAND*. ROYAL BRACKLA DISTILLERY, Cawdor, Nairn, *Scotland*.   70 cl

CAWDOR, NEAR NAIRN EST. 1812

Founded by Captain William Fraser of Brackla House. A map of the Cawdor Estate dated 1773 shows a "malt brewhouse" on the site. The distillery was sold to John Bisset & Co. Ltd, which became part of DCL in 1943, when management was transferred to SMD. It was rebuilt between 1964 and 1965 and the number of stills was increased from two to four in 1970. Closed in 1985, Royal Brackla reopened in 1991.

LOCATION Sited to the north west of the B9090, one mile south of Nairn.

NOTES Despite being regularly fined by HM Customs & Excise for irregularities, Brackla was the first distillery to be granted a Royal Warrant in 1835. It was referred to at that time as *Brackla* or "The King's Own Whisky". Some of the older buildings were converted to a visitor centre in 1982/83, the distillery being three-quarters of a mile from Cawdor Castle. During demolition in November 1994 of Number 4 Warehouse, which had not been used for some years, a hive of wild bees was discovered in one of the warehouse walls. The hive was between 10 and 15 feet across and it was estimated that the bees had inhabited this site for approximately 70 years. Demolition of that wall was postponed until the Spring of 1995, when the queens were removed to another site temporarily. The bees have been returned to beehives in the shape of pagoda roofs which are sited close to the original site of Number 4 Warehouse.

WATER The Cawdor Burn.

Age No age statement **Strength** 40% abv

Sweetness 6 Peatiness 7 Availability 7

Colour Pale straw with pale yellow highlights **Nose** Medium-bodied, quite peaty and round with a slight liquorice character **Flavour** Medium-sweet, rich and slightly spicy with a good smoky peatiness and good body **Finish** Quite clean and fresh with almost a hint of bitter chocolate on the end **Notes** United Distillers bottling

Age 10 years **Strength** 43% abv

Sweetness 7 Peatiness 5 Availability 6

Colour Quite pale straw with yellow highlights **Nose** Fresh, clean and medium-sweet with a fruitiness and a floral note, with gentle peat in the background **Flavour** Round, medium-sweet and quite full-bodied with a green fruity character **Finish** Long, fresh and clean **Notes** United Distillers bottling

Age 18 years **Strength** 46% abv

Sweetness 8 Peatiness 5 Availability 2

Colour Pale straw with good yellow highlights and a definite green tinge **Nose** Round, sweet and fruity **Flavour** Sweet, smooth, round and rich **Finish** Velvety smooth, long and distinguished **Notes** Wm Cadenhead bottling

Age 18 years **Distillation** 19798 **Strength** 43% abv

Sweetness 6 Peatiness 6 Availability 2

Colour Amber with yellow highlights **Nose** Full-bodied, rich and dark with a walnutty character, medium-dry with a slightly perfumed note to the peatiness **Flavour** Big, round, rich, medium-sweet and full-bodied with a slightly tarry note to the tannins **Finish** Long and elegant with a slightly chewy smokiness **Notes** Blackadder International bottling from cask no 5279 distilled 9 January 1979

Distillation 1970 **Strength** 40% abv

Sweetness 6 Peatiness 6 Availability 3

Colour Pale mid-amber with yellow gold highlights **Nose** Good body with oak, cold apples and a peaty smokiness **Flavour** Medium-dry, oaky, quite mellow and smooth with a slight oiliness and a medium peatiness **Finish** Reasonable oaky finish with a touch of richness **Notes** Gordon & MacPhail bottling

CRATHIE, BALLATER, ABERDEENSHIRE EST. 1845

Originally known as *New Lochnagar*, as another Lochnagar distillery had been built nearby in 1826. This had closed by 1860. Lochnagar obtained the Royal Warrant after its owner, John Begg, had invited Queen Victoria and Prince Albert to view the distillery in 1848. The distillery was rebuilt in 1906 and acquired by John Dewar & Sons Ltd in 1916, passing to the DCL in 1925 and operated by SMD, now UMGD, from 1930. Part of United Distillers plc.

LOCATION On Royal Deeside overlooking Balmoral Castle and about one mile from the Queen's Bedroom, from which the young Queen Victoria is said to have looked out at the distillery.

NOTES The story the locals tell is of John Begg looking out of the window one evening and seeing a few figures making their way towards the distillery through the gathering dusk. The figures turned out to be Queen Victoria, her husband, children and lady-in-waiting. The Royal party had just arrived for their first stay at Balmoral, and Begg had delivered the Queen a note inviting her on a not-to-be-missed tour round his new distillery. Prince Albert was particularly interested, being enthusiastic about all new technology. Royal Lochnagar is now the only remaining distillery of the several that used to operate on Deeside. There is a very popular visitor centre, converted from the old distillery farm steading. Scottish children try to trick one another by asking how deep Lochnagar is. The catch is that Lochnagar is not a loch, but a mountain. At 3789 ft (1155m) its bulk dominates the countryside around Balmoral.

WATER Springs in the foothills of Lochnagar.

Age 12 years   **Strength** 40% abv

Sweetness 7   Peatiness 4   Availability 5

Colour Mid-amber with old gold highlights **Nose** Medium-bodied, soft and round with creamy sweet vanilla oak notes **Flavour** Soft, gently peated and round with creamy sweet vanilla oak notes **Finish** Fresh, lingering and medium-sweet with a slightly smoky tang **Notes** United distillers bottling

Age 12 years   **Strength** 40% abv

Sweetness 8   Peatiness 4   Availability 0

Colour Pale straw with bright gold highlights **Nose** Pleasantly sweet, slightly peppery and fruity **Flavour** Sweet, clean, creamy and slightly peppery **Finish** Smooth and with good length **Notes** DCL (pre-Guinness) bottling

ROYAL LOCHNAGAR SELECTED RESERVE
Age No statement   **Strength** 43% abv

Sweetness 8   Peatiness 3   Availability 3

Colour Deep peaty amber with good gold highlights **Nose** Rich, wet oak, vanilla, sweet and lightly sherried **Flavour** Full, round and rich, mellow, nutty and creamy **Finish** Long, slightly spicy and very smooth **Notes** As Royal Lochnagar Selected Reserve, it has no age statement because it is produced from selected casks and the age could vary from bottling to bottling

RARE MALTS
SELECTION

Each individual vintage has been specially selected from Scotland's finest single malt stocks of rare or now silent distilleries. The limited bottlings of these scarce and unique whiskies are at natural cask strength for the enjoyment of the true connoisseur.

NATURAL CASK STRENGTH
SINGLE MALT SCOTCH WHISKY

AGED **23** YEARS

DISTILLED IN 1970 AT THE
ST MAGDALENE DISTILLERY
ESTABLISHED 1765
LINLITHGOW

58.43%vol 70cle
PRODUCE OF SCOTLAND
LIMITED BOTTLING

LINLITHGOW, WEST LOTHIAN EST. PRE-1797

Said to have been founded in the 18th century on the lands of St Magdalene's Cross, the former site of an annual fair and of St Magdalene's Hospital. The earliest record is of Adam Dawson as distiller in 1797. It was taken over by DCL on 16 November 1912, prior to which the owning company was A & J Dawson Ltd. St Magdalene was one of the five founding distilleries of SMD in July 1914.

LOCATION Sited at the eastern end of Linlithgow, where the railway line, running alongside the Union Canal, intersects with the A706 to Edinburgh.

NOTES Linlithgow was a centre of milling and malting in the 17th century and brewing and distilling in the 18th century. The distillery closed in 1983 and its buildings have been converted into housing.

WATER The town's domestic supply, which comes from Loch Lomond.

Age 23 years **Strength** 58.1% abv

Sweetness 2 **Peatiness** 3 **Availability** 1

Colour Amber with gold highlights and a tinge of green **Nose** Gentle, soft and medium-dry with a bread yeasty aroma and a slightly oaky acetone character **Flavour** Big-bodied, quite dry, but with an edge of richness, tannic and yeasty **Finish** Long, quite powerful and quite tannic **Notes** United Distillers bottling

ST MAGDALENE

Distillation 1965   **Strength** 40% abv

Sweetness 1   Peatiness 4   Availability 2

Colour Light to mid-amber with gold highlights and just a tinge of green **Nose** Quite fresh with a light oak character, quite lightweight and dry, a little spirity **Flavour** Dry with oaky tannins, of medium weight and lightly smoky **Finish** Dry, oaky and chewy with dry tannins **Notes** Gordon & MacPhail bottling

Age 10 years   **Distillation** 1982   **Strength** 62.3% abv

Sweetness 2   Peatiness 2   Availability 2

Colour Pale straw with lemon/yellow highlights **Nose** Fresh, clean, fruity and spirity, medium-dry with a slight touch of oak and a light mashy character **Flavour** Medium-dry with good richness and round with quite good body **Finish** Good length, rich and smooth **Notes** Wm Cadenhead bottling

Distillation 1980   **Strength** 40% abv

Sweetness 3   Peatiness 3   Availability 1

Colour Straw with pale lemon/pale gold highlights **Nose** Quite good body with a fresh, almost fruity richness, off-dry, lightly peated and green with a slight edge of sweetness **Flavour** Smooth, mashy, malty, clean, medium-dry and quite rich **Finish** Quite long and rich with a slightly green freshness **Notes** 1995 Gordon & Macphail *Centenary Reserve* bottling

KIRKWALL, ORKNEY EST. 1885

Built by Macfarlane & Townsend. Owned by Hiram Walker (now part of Allied Domecq) since 1954. Two stills. The wash still was replaced by a *Lomond* still in 1959, this producing a heavier spirit than the more traditional long-necked stills. Operated by Allied Distillers Ltd.

LOCATION   Sited on the Lingro Burn two miles south west of Kirkwall on the A964 at the head of Scapa Bay.

NOTES   Scapa Flow was where the German Fleet was scuttled at the end of the First World War. When whisky chronicler Alfred Barnard visited the distillery in 1886, it had been open for just a year. He wrote about it as being "one of the most complete little Distilleries in the Kingdom". The stills were described as being of "the newest type and heated by steam instead of fire, and are both fitted with "collapse" valves, which allow air to enter in the event of a vacuum being formed". For a malt with such a pronounced astringent nose in its youth, the palate is, unusually, surprisingly sweet. Scapa is one of the main malts associated with *Ballantine's* blended Scotch whisky.

WATER   The Lingro Burn and nearby springs.

Distillation 1983   **Strength** 40% abv
Sweetness 2 Peatiness 4 Availability 4

Colour Mid-amber with old gold highlights **Nose** Fresh, clean, malty and slightly green with a slight nuttiness and medium-dry **Flavour** Almost dry, quite full-bodied, slightly spicy and tangy, gently smoky **Finish** Long and clean with a touch of richness **Notes** Gordon & MacPhail bottling, followed by 1984 and 1985

Age 14 years **Distillation** 1979 **Strength** 43% abv

Sweetness 6 Peatiness 5 Availability 0

Colour Pale straw with yellow/lemon highlights **Nose** Round, smooth and medium-sweet, slightly unctuous with a fresh floral character and rich with a maltiness at the back **Flavour** Medium-dry, quite full and round, quite smooth with tannic oak **Finish** Long and full, quite rich with a toffee tail **Notes** Master of Malt bottling from cask no. 3851/2 distilled 9 May 1979

Age 24 years **Distillation** 1965 **Strength** 50.1% abv

Sweetness 8 Peatiness 6 Availability 1

Colour Straw with lemony gold highlights **Nose** Sweet, quite fresh and rich with a creamy peatiness and an underpinning of oak **Flavour** Quite sweet, softly peated, light and quite delicate **Finish** Smooth and smoky with a lanolin character **Notes** Wm Cadenhead bottling, September 1990

Age 8 years **Strength** 57% abv

Sweetness 8 Peatiness 7 Availability 2

Colour Peaty/amber with good gold highlights and a greenish tinge **Nose** Spirity, somewhat astringent, young and peaty **Flavour** Sweet, rich, full-bodied, lightly oaky and malty **Finish** Good, spicy and long lasting **Notes** Gordon & MacPhail bottling

Distillation 1979 **Strength** 56.3% abv

Sweetness 8 Peatiness 6 Availability 1

Colour Straw with yellow/lemon highlights **Nose** Full-bodied, fruity (strawberries), bubble-gummy, medium sweet and finely peated **Flavour** Sweet, round, quite spicy, smooth, almost grapey **Finish** Long, sweet and clean **Notes** Scotch Malt Whisky Society bottling; cask no. 17.13; bottled May 1994

ROTHES, MORAY EST. 1897

Built by John Hopkins & Co. for the Speyburn-Glenlivet Distillery Company Ltd. Local tradition has it that the walls were built of stones "extracted by man and beast" from the bed of the River Spey. DCL bought John Hopkins & Co. in 1916, but the Speyburn-Glenlivet Distillery Co. Ltd was not wound up until 1962, when Speyburn's management was transferred to SMD. It was the first distillery to install a drum maltings, this unit being closed in 1968. The distillery has two stills and is now owned by Inver House Distillers, who purchased it in 1991.

LOCATION   Situated a quarter of a mile north west of the B9105 on the northern outskirts of Rothes.

NOTES   Speyburn started up in the last week of December 1897. Doors and windows still had not been fitted to the still house and, as a severe snowstorm was sweeping the district, employees had to work in overcoats. Just one butt of spirit was bonded with 1897 on its head.

WATER   The Granty (or Birchfield) Burn.

Age 10 years   **Strength** 40% abv

Sweetness   8   Peatiness   2   Availability   7

Colour Very pale straw with lemon highlights **Nose** Fresh, clean and aromatic with a rich lemony fruitiness, medium-bodied and quite lightly peated **Flavour** Fresh, clean, rich and medium-sweet; quite full-bodied **Finish** Long and sweet with a touch of spice **Notes** Inver House bottling

Distillation 1971   **Strength** 40% abv

Sweetness 8   Peatiness 5   Availability 4

Colour Rich peaty, amber with good gold highlights **Nose** Sweet, fruity and slightly spirity **Flavour** Medium-sweet, quite light and smooth **Finish** Mellow, of reasonable length with oak on the end **Notes** Gordon & MacPhail bottling

Age 15 years   **Distillation** 1975   **Strength** 60.1% abv

Sweetness 7   Peatiness 5   Availability 4

Colour Straw with pale gold highlights **Nose** Medium-sweet and fresh with a touch of greenness, light, nutty and biscuity **Flavour** Medium-sweet with a good dollop of creamy fresh-ness, fresh, clean, smooth and round **Finish** Sweet, fresh and creamy with an edge of greenness and good length **Notes** Wm Cadenhead bottling

KINGUSSIE, INVERNESS-SHIRE EST. 1990

The malt from the new Speyside distillery is bottled as Drumguish by its owners. Speyside was built opposite the former distillery of the same name (1895-1911) on land purchased by owners, the Christie family, in 1956 together with stretches of the Spey and Tromie rivers. In the previous year they had formed the Speyside Distillery & Bonding Co. The driving force behind the company, whisky blender George Christie, gradually built the new distillery, starting in 1962 and finally completing the work in 1987. The first spirit ran from the distillery's two stills on 12 December 1990.

LOCATION At the confluence of the Tromie and Spey rivers.

NOTES The distillery is said to have a maximum capacity of 200,000 gallons a year, although it is planned to produce just 50,000 to 100,000 a year, all of which is intended for the company's own use. The company produces a blended whisky called *Speyside* and a vatted malt, *Glentromie*. The first of the new single malt takes its name, *Drumguish*, from that of its precise location. George Christie lives in the house previously owned by G. McPherson Grant who, as well as building the original Speyside distillery, also built Tomatin and Newtonmore. Only Tomatin of this original trio today exists.

WATER A spring on the neighbouring Gaick Deer estate.

Age 3 years **Strength** 40% abv

Sweetness 5 Peatiness 7 Availability 4

Colour Pale-mid amber with old gold highlights **Nose** Young, quite mashy, soft and medium-sweet, quite fresh with a slight menthol character, gently peated with a slight earthy touch **Flavour** Medium-dry, minty with good body and a firm, but gentle dark earthy smokiness **Finish** Of good length, almost dry with a good peaty character **Notes** Drumguish Distillery Company bottling

SPRINGBANK

AGED **21** YEARS

AGED **21** YEARS

CAMPBELTOWN

Scotch **SINGLE MALT** Whisky

PRODUCT OF SCOTLAND
Distilled by J. & A. MITCHELL & CO. LTD.
Springbank Distillery · Campbeltown · Scotland

70cl

46%vol

CAMPBELTOWN, ARGYLL EST. 1828

Said to have been originally licensed to the Reid family. It was acquired by John and William Mitchell in 1837 and run by various members of the family until 1897 when the present owning company, J & A Mitchell & Company was incorporated. The fact that Springbank has three stills has encouraged debate as to whether the whisky is triple distilled. In fact, none of Springbank is triple distilled

LOCATION The distillery is in the centre of the town.

NOTES The family owners of Springbank are direct descendants of the illicit distillers who established the once-numerous Campbeltown distilleries, and the present managing director is the great-great-great-grandson of its founder. The Campbeltown area once boasted around 30 legal distilleries, but the years of Depression after the First World War and prohibition in America almost brought about the total demise of Campbeltown whisky. Springbank is now one of only two survivors and the only one open at the time of writing (July, 1997). Fortunately Springbank now continues to go from strength to strength, its reputation and renown being second to none. It is the only distillery where everything from malting through to bottling is carried out on the premises for all of the distillery's own production.

WATER Crosshill Loch.

SPRINGBANK

Age 9 years **Strength** 61.2% abv

Sweetness 5 Peatiness 6 Availability 4

Colour Very pale watery straw with pale mint green highlights **Nose** Young, spirity, mashy, quite full-bodied with a dark peatiness and almost dry **Flavour** Almost dry, but with a developing richness and a dark smokiness, good body, a lanolin smoothness and mashy **Finish** Spicy, elegantly smoky with a salty tail and a sweetness to the edge **Notes** Wm Cadenhead botlling

Age 12 years **Strength** 57% abv

Sweetness 5 Peatiness 6 Availability 3

Colour Deep amber with bronze highlights **Nose** Quite full-bodied, with a slightly tarry rope character, a note of lightly charred oak and a rich peatiness **Flavour** Big-bodied with good richness and quite chewy vanilla tannins, medium-dry with kindly peatiness **Finish** Long and gently chewy with a salty tang on the tail **Notes** Bottled as *Springbank 100° Proof* by J&A Mitchell

Age 15 years **Strength** 46% abv

Sweetness 7 Peatiness 5 Availability 6

Colour Light mid-amber (honey-coloured) with lemony highlights **Nose** Medium weight, rich, oily oak with a touch of greenness, quite lightly peated **Flavour** Clean, smooth, medium-dry with good creamy oak and a touch of sweetness and greenness **Finish** Long and smooth with a touch of tannin and hints of richness and saltiness on the tail **Notes** J & A Mitchell botlling

Age 21 years **Strength** 46% abv

Sweetness 8 Peatiness 5 Availability 5

Colour Deep amber **Nose** Definite fruity notes, stickily sweet in their richness, also floral notes and a suggestion of coconut and medicinal cloves **Flavour** Silkily smooth, full-bodied and creamy with a salty tang **Finish** Very fine, long, dark and oaky **Notes** J & A Mitchell botlling

Age 25 years **Strength** 46% abv

Sweetness 7 Peatiness 6 Availability 2

Colour Full, peaty amber with bronze highlights **Nose** Rich, ripe, sweet and full-bodied, smoky with a touch of ozone and oak **Flavour** Full, round, smoky and medium-sweet with oaky tannins and a salty tang **Finish** Long, smoky-oak and tangy with a touch of spiciness **Notes** J & A Mitchell botlling

Age 30 years **Strength** 46% abv

Sweetness 8 Peatiness 6 Availability 2

Colour Full amber with old gold highlights **Nose** Full and rich, almost raisiny with a touch of liquorice, almost tarry and medium-dry **Flavour** Sweet, and rich with a good peaty character, flavour of bitter chocolate and a salty tang **Finish** Long and tangy with good sweetness **Notes** J & A Mitchell bottling

Age 18 years **Distillation** 1975 **Strength** 43% abv

Sweetness 7 Peatiness 4 Availability 1

Colour Pale amber with pale yellow highlights **Nose** Quite full-bodied, rich and medium-sweet underpinned by peat and with a hint of green coffee **Flavour** Fresh, green, rich, round and medium-sweet, almost grapey with a vanilla note **Finish** Long, salty, lingering and gently smoky **Notes** *The Ultimate Collection* bottled for Van Wees of Holland from cask no 3596 distilled 17 December 1975

Age 17 years **Distillation** 1975 **Strength** 55.8% abv

Sweetness 7 Peatiness 4 Availability 1

Colour Mid-amber with gold highlights **Nose** Dry, fresh, smoky and rich, quite full-bodied with a good richness at the back **Flavour** Big-bodied, medium-sweet and rich with gentle tannins and delicately peated **Finish** Tangy and rich with good length and a touch of spice **Notes** Signatory bottling from cask nos. 3592/3, distilled 17 December 1975

Age 28 years **Distillation** 1965 **Strength** 53.2% abv

Sweetness 7 Peatiness 5 Availability 2

Colour Full amber with old gold highlights **Nose** Full, warm, nutty (hazelnuts), medium-sweet with a fruitcake richness and a green peatiness at the back, a lanolin oaky unctuousness and a slight medicinal touch **Flavour** Medium-dry, very rich, quite big-bodied with chewy tannins, good body and quite delicately peated **Finish** Powerful with good richness - even a sweetness at the end - and a salty tang on the tail **Notes** Adelphi Distillery bottling; bottled 1993

"STRATHISLA"
PURE HIGHLAND MALT
SCOTCH WHISKY
THE OLDEST DISTILLERY IN THE HIGHLANDS

AGED **12** YEARS

70 cl ℮   DISTILLED AND BOTTLED BY CHIVAS BROTHERS LTD
STRATHISLA DISTILLERY, KEITH, AB55 3BS, SCOTLAND   43% vol

KEITH, BANFFSHIRE EST. 1786

Built in 1786 as Milltown (Keith was the centre of the Scottish linen industry) and later known as Milton, Strathisla was originally the name of the make and subsequently also became that of the distillery. It was converted into a flour mill in 1838. After reconversion to distilling, the distillery was twice badly damaged in the 1870s: first by fire in 1876 and three years later by an explosion. Extensive modernisation took place after these events and again in 1965, when the distillery was enlarged from two to four stills. It is today owned by Chivas Brothers Ltd, a subsidiary of The Seagram Company of Canada.

LOCATION Half a mile from the centre of Keith.

NOTES On 15 June 1993 Strathisla received an unexpected visitor from Louisville, Kentucky; a young black and white cat fell asleep among some Bourbon barrels in a container awaiting shipment to Scotland. On opening the container some four weeks later, the cat staggered out, weak from hunger and drunk from the Bourbon fumes in the enclosed space. After six months' quarantine, the cat, for obvious reasons called Dizzy, is now employed by Chivas Bros. as a "mouser".

WATER The Broomhill Spring. The reservoir which holds the distillery's water supply is said to be visited nightly by the "water kelpies" which could account for its special flavour.

Age 8 years   **Strength** 40% abv

Sweetness 8   Peatiness 3   Availability 2

Colour Amber with good gold highlights **Nose** Fruity, spirity and sweet with a lanolin oiliness **Flavour** Spicy, quite smooth and medium-sweet with a touch of oak **Finish** Good body, although perhaps a little short because of its youth **Notes** Gordon & MacPhail bottling

Age 12 years   **Strength** 43% abv

Sweetness 5   Peatiness 5   Availability 6

Colour Mid-amber with yellow/gold highlights **Nose** Quite big and round, a dark hazelnut character with good richness at the back, just a hint of sweetness and a delicate burnt peaty character **Flavour** Medium-dry with a smoky nuttiness and a touch of dark, oaky tannins with a nice green edge **Finish** Quite long, hazelnut and smoky **Notes** Seagram bottling

Age 18 years   **Distillation** 1974   **Strength** 57.8% abv

Sweetness 6   Peatiness 7   Availability 3

Colour Amber with old gold highlights **Nose** Full-bodied with a dark nuttiness and medium-dry oaky vanilla **Flavour** Smoky with a dark nuttiness, medium-sweet with gentle oaky tannins and a slight astringency **Finish** Long, creamy & smoky with a background of sweetness **Notes** Gordon & MacPhail bottling, distilled 23 March1974

Age 21 years   **Strength** 40% abv

Sweetness 8   Peatiness 4   Availability 4

Colour Amber with bright copper highlights **Nose** Medium-sweet and malty, lightly peated and oaky **Flavour** Medium-dry, oaky and spicy and creamy **Finish** Long and spicy with hints of bitter chocolate **Notes** Gordon & MacPhail bottling

Distillation 1989   **Strength** 60% abv

Sweetness 7   Peatiness 4   Availability 2

Colour Straw with pale gold highlights **Nose** Medium-sweet and quite full-bodied with a young spiritiness, quite delicate peatiness and a slight hint of toffee richness **Flavour** Medium-sweet and smooth with a gentle peatiness **Finish** Long, fresh, clean and quite sweet **Notes** Clydesdale Original bottling from cask no. 9408

By Appointment to H.M. King George V

Strathmill

FINE OLD
SCOTCH WHISKY

STRENGTH—30 under proof by distillation when bottled
MEASURE —Six bottles or twelve half-bottles contain approximately one gallon

Bottled & Guaranteed by **W & A Gilbey** Ltd.
STRATHMILL DISTILLERY, KEITH.
Price **12/6** (One Penny refunded on return of bottle)
Includes **8/5**½ Government Tax

KEITH, BANFFSHIRE EST. 1891

Originally a corn and flour mill, it was converted in 1891 as Glenisla-Glenlivet. Acquired by W & A Gilbey in 1895, when it was renamed Strathmill. Became part of IDV in 1962 and now absorbed into Grand Metropolitan. Four stills.

LOCATION Just off the B9014 from Keith to Dufftown.

NOTES Very rare as a single malt, most of the make goes into the J&B blend. The above label has not been used for over thirty years.

WATER A spring at the distillery.

Age 12 years   **Strength** 55.5% abv

Sweetness 6   Peatiness 3   Availability 0

Colour Very pale watery with watery green highlights **Nose** Light and cereally, lightly smoky with a touch of perfume and a delicate nuttiness **Flavour** Medium-sweet, smooth and quite round with good body **Finish** Long and spicy with a pleasant leafy greenness **Notes** A cask sample kindly supplied by J&B Scotland Ltd, who also supplied the above label from their archives. The whisky is not now available bottled by J&B.

Age 11 years   **Distillation** 1980   **Strength** 60.6% abv

Sweetness 7   Peatiness 3   Availability 4

Colour Pale straw with lemon highlights **Nose** Fresh, young, mashy vegetal greenness with an edge of richness, medium-sweet and lightly peated **Flavour** Cereally, corn flake-like, medium-sweet with soft tannins, smooth and quite round **Finish** Good sweetness, quite good length, clean with a mashy vegetal character and a green edge to the tail **Notes** Wm Cadenhead bottling

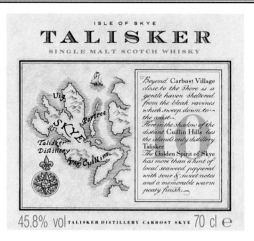

45.8% vol | TALISKER DISTILLERY CARBOST SKYE | 70 cl ℮

CARBOST, ISLE OF SKYE EST. 1830

The distillery was originally sited at Snizort, to the north of the island, but was closed and mysteriously moved. The current buildings were founded by Hugh and Kenneth MacAskill in 1830. Rebuilt 1880-87 and further extended in 1900. Merged into Dailuaine-Talisker Distilleries Ltd in 1898, under which name it still trades although absorbed fully into DCL in 1925. Rebuilt again 1960-62 after the still house was destroyed by fire on 22 November 1960. Operated by UMGD. Five stills.

LOCATION Situated in a gentle bowl which forms a lonely, very sheltered glen on the west coast of Skye.

NOTES The only distillery on the island of Skye, it took its name from a farm about six miles distant. The make was triple distilled until 1928. One of United Distillers' *Classic Malts* portfolio.

WATER A burn on the slopes of Cnoc nan Speireag (Hawk Hill), cooling water comes from the Carbost Burn.

Age 10 years	**Strength** 45.8% abv	
Sweetness 1	**Peatiness** 10	**Availability** 8

Colour Straw with gold highlights **Nose** Pungent, peaty with a burnt heather character and hints of ozone **Flavour** Peaty, dry, spicy and quite creamy **Finish** Smoky, spicy, smooth, almost salty at the end **Notes** United Distillers bottling

Age 8 years   **Strength** 57.8% abv

Sweetness 3   Peatiness 10   Availability 0

Colour Full amber with green highlights **Nose** Pungent, full and peaty, but soft **Flavour** Pungent, dry, spicy and full-bodied with a lot of smokiness **Finish** Long with a burst of flavour on swallowing **Notes** DCL (pre-Guinness) bottling

Age 14 years   **Distillation** 1979   **Strength** 64.3% abv

Sweetness 2   Peatiness 9   Availability 2

Colour Straw with gold/yellow highlights and just a tinge of green **Nose** Quite big and pungently smoky with a medicinal burnt oak character and a slight touch of richness **Flavour** Big, powerful with quite gentle pungency, earthily oaky and quite soft richness **Finish** Long, smoky with a touch of fresh greenness and pungent with a salty tang **Notes** Wm Cadenhead bottling

Age 38 years   **Distillation** 1955   **Strength** 53.6% abv

Sweetness 2   Peatiness 9   Availability 1

Colour Deep amber with bronze highlights **Nose** Deep, dark, nutty and woody with a medicinal character and just an edge of richness **Flavour** Big, dark and tannic, quite pungent with an almost burnt peaty character and a touch of richness **Finish** Long, tannic, chewy and pungent. **Notes** Gordon & MacPhail bottling; cask nos. 1257, 1310 & 1311, distilled 12 and 28 May 1955

DISTILLED

≋ *1955* ≋

CASK

≋ 53.6% ≋
VOL

NATURAL HIGH STRENGTH

SINGLE MALT
SCOTCH WHISKY
TALISKER

PROPRIETORS JOHN WALKER & SONS LTD
SPECIALLY SELECTED, PRODUCED AND BOTTLED BY
GORDON & MACPHAIL
ELGIN · SCOTLAND
PRODUCT OF SCOTLAND

NATURAL
CASK
STRENGTH
1955
53.6%
VOL
70cl

CASK No.
1310, 1311
1257
DISTILLED
28/5/55
12/5/55
BOTTLED
October 1993

KNOCKANDO, MORAY   EST. 1897

Built by the Tamdhu Distillery Company Ltd which was owned by a consortium of blenders. Owned by Highland Distilleries Company since 1898. Closed from 1927 to 1947, but extended in 1972 from two to four stills and again to six stills in 1975. A feature is Tamdhu's Saladin Maltings which have been largely rebuilt.

LOCATION   Sited on the banks of the River Spey south of the B9102 between Knockando and Archiestown.

NOTES   The old railway station at Knockando has been converted into a visitor centre for Tamdhu. Tamdhu does not have the traditional pagoda heads atop its kilns, having instead a short, square concrete chimney. The Visitors' Centre was closed at the time of writing, summer 1997, and it is not known if it will be reopened.

WATER   A spring under the distillery

Age No age statement	**Strength** 40% abv	
Sweetness 7	**Peatiness 4**	**Availability 8**

Colour Straw/amber with yellow highlights **Nose** Medium-bodied, fruity and a touch floral, medium-sweet with a greenness **Flavour** Medium-sweet, quite light, mashy, biscuity and quite smooth **Finish** Quite short; spirity and sweet **Notes** Highland Distillers bottling

Age 19 years	**Distillation** 1978	**Strength** 54.9% abv
Sweetness 7	**Peatiness 4**	**Availability 1**

Colour Pale straw with lemon/yellow highlights. **Nose** Quite full and open with floral and cereal notes, a touch of vanilla, medium-sweet and creamy with a touch of lanolin and a definite aroma of shortbread. **Flavour** Soft, velvety smooth, round and medium-sweet, it has a delicate touch of peat with a syrupy texture. **Finish** Long and quite delicate. **Notes** Scotch Malt Whisky Society bottling from cask no. 3966

TOMNAVOULIN, BANFFSHIRE EST. 1966

Built by the Tamnavulin-Glenlivet Distillery Company, a subsidiary of Invergordon Distillers and now owned by JBB (Greater Europe) plc. A very modern distillery, it can be operated by just a handful of technicians. Mothballed early in 1995.

LOCATION On the B9008 at the village of Tomnavoulin.

NOTES The only distillery actually positioned on the River Livet, from which the cooling waters are drawn. Tomnavoulin from the Gaelic means "mill on the hill" and an old carding mill which stands at the riverside just below the distillery has been converted into a very attractive visitor centre, which is still open. The mill machinery has been preserved inside. Equally pleasant are the grassy banks of the river which have been turned into a picnic area.

WATER Subterranean springs at Easterton in the local hills.

Age 12 years   **Strength** 40% abv

Sweetness 7 Peatiness 4 Availability 3

Colour Mid-straw with pale lemon highlights **Nose** A dark nuttiness and a gentle peaty character, medium-sweet with a rich, charred oak note **Flavour** Dark and medium-dry with nice weight and a good dollop of peat at the back **Finish** Smooth, long and nutty with a rich, oaky tail **Notes** JBB Brands bottling

Age 18 years   **Strength** 46% abv

Sweetness 8 Peatiness 3 Availability 1

Colour Very dark, teak coloured **Nose** Nutty, quite spirity, light and medium-sweet **Flavour** Smooth, oaky, quite velvety and nutty **Finish** Smooth and spirity, quite long with a dry end **Notes** Wm Cadenhead bottling

HIGHLAND
SINGLE MALT
SCOTCH WHISKY

The *Cromarty Firth* is one of the few places in
the British Isles inhabited by *PORPOISE*. They
can be seen quite regularly. *swimming*
close to the shore *less* than a *mile* from

TEANINICH

distillery. Founded in 1817 in the *Ross-shire*
town of ALNESS, the *distillery* is now one
of the largest in *Scotland*. TEANINICH
is an assertive *single MALT WHISKY*
with a *spicy, smoky, satisfying* taste.

AGED **10** YEARS

43% vol

Distilled & Bottled in SCOTLAND
TEANINICH DISTILLERY,
Alness, Ross-shire, Scotland

70 cl

ALNESS, ROSS-SHIRE   EST. 1817

Founded by Captain Hugh Munro. Sold to SMD in 1933. When SMD took over, there were four stills, two of which were described as being very small. When production restarted after The Second World War, the two smaller stills were removed. Capacity was increased from two to four larger stills in 1962 and to ten when an entirely new distillation unit named "A side" began production in 1970. The milling, mashing and fermentation part of the old distillery, "B side", was rebuilt 1973. Now owned by United Distillers.

LOCATION   Sited to the south of the A9 on the western outskirts of Alness and on the west bank of the River Alness, three-quarters of a mile from its outflow into the Cromarty Firth.

NOTES   Alfred Barnard recorded in 1887 that Teaninich was the only distillery north of Inverness to be "lighted by electricity". In 1925 both malting floors were of solid clay. "A side" is in production, but "B side" was mothballed in the mid-1980s.

WATER   The Dairywell Spring.

Age 10 years   **Strength** 43% abv

Sweetness	7	Peatiness	5	Availability	6

Colour Pale straw with yellow highlights and a tinge of lemon **Nose** Fresh and quite light with a good green peatiness, medium-sweet with an appley character **Flavour** Medium-dry, gently smoky, smooth and round **Finish** Clean and fresh with a sweet tail **Notes** United Distillers bottling

Age 18 years   **Distillation** 1975   **Strength** 43% abv

Sweetness 7   Peatiness 5   Availability 1

Colour Straw/pale amber with pale lemon highlights **Nose** Fresh, green, quite cerealy and clean, medium-sweet and quite full-bodied **Flavour** Fresh and clean with an earthy smokiness, medium to full-bodied and medium-sweet with a touch of richness **Finish** Clean, quite long with an almost perfumed smokiness **Notes** Master of Malt bottling; cask no. 13988, distilled 12 November 1975

Age 17 years   **Distillation** 1975   **Strength** 43% abv

Sweetness 9   Peatiness 3   Availability 1

Colour Quite pale straw with lemon highlights **Nose** Quite full-bodied, spirity and fresh, almost salty with fruity and floral notes **Flavour** Quite sweet, round, spicy, full-bodied, rich and delicately peated with a nutty character **Finish** Long, sweet and slightly smoky **Notes** Master of Malt bottling from cask no. 13984

Age 21 years   **Strength** 57.2% abv

Sweetness 6   Peatiness 6   Availability 1

Colour Straw with pale yellow highlights **Nose** Medium-bodied, medium-sweet with a slight burnt stick peatiness and an edge of richness **Flavour** Medium-dry, with good body and weight of peat **Finish** Long and quite darkly smoky, albeit gently **Notes** James MacArthur bottling

In
Celebration
500 Years
of
Scotch Whisky
1494 - 1994
TEANINICH
HIGHLAND SINGLE MALT
AGED 21 YEARS
70cl   JAMES MACARTHUR & CO. LTD.
EDINBURGH   57.2%vol

TOBERMORY, ISLE OF MULL EST. 1798

Established by local merchant John Sinclair. Owned from 1890 to 1916 by John Hopkins & Son & Co., when taken over by DCL. Silent from 1930 to 1972 when revived as the Ledaig Distillery (Tobermory) Ltd. This company went into receivership in 1975 and the business was acquired in 1978 by the Kirkleavington Property Co. of Cleckheaton. Tobermory was in production between 1979 and 1981, before closing again until 1989. It was purchased in 1993 by Burn Stewart Distillers for £600,000 plus £200,000 for stock. Four stills.

LOCATION Situated at the head of Tobermory Bay.

NOTES The only distillery on Mull. Because the distillery was closed for several years, very little Tobermory single malt has been produced until recently, all distilled between 1972 and 1975 and 1979 and 1981. Tobermory is now becoming more readily available, however. The older bottlings of Tobermory that are available have been bottled as Ledaig. Owner Burn Stewart has decided to use only unpeated barley in the production of Tobermory, although a few mashes will be produced each year using peated barley. These will be reserved for whiskies marketed under the name Ledaig. Independent bottlings are also under the distillery name of Ledaig.

WATER A small private loch close by the Mishnish Lochs.

TOBERMORY
Age No age statement   **Strength** 40% abv
Sweetness 4   Peatiness 6   Availability 6

Colour Straw/amber with bright gold highlights **Nose** Quite full-bodied, medium-dry with an edge of richness, a touch of liquorice to the smokiness, a fresh, green hedgerow note and a mashy character **Flavour** Quite rich, clean and round with a slight coffee tang **Finish** Fresh, clean, quite long and rich with a slight tangy touch and liquorice on the tail **Notes** Burn Stewart bottling as Tobermory

LEDAIG
SINGLE MALT
FROM
THE ISLE OF MULL

1974
Vintage

This rare old single malt whisky
was distilled at the Ledaig Distillery
on the Isle of Mull by
Ledaig Distillers (Tobermory) Ltd.

PRODUCE OF SCOTLAND

70cl   43%Vol

LEDAIG
Age 18 years   **Distillation** 1974   **Strength** 43% abv
Sweetness 2   Peatiness 8   Availability 2

Colour Medium-pale straw with lemony/gold highlights **Nose** Medium-bodied, woody with a slight greenness and smokiness at the back and an almost Christmas cake yeasty character **Flavour** Medium-bodied, oaky with a slight greenness and good richness at the back **Finish** Of good length with a green smoky tail **Notes** Ledaig Distillers (Tobermory) bottling

LEDAIG
Age 21 years   **Distillation** 1974   **Strength** 60% abv
Sweetness 3   Peatiness 6   Availability 0

Colour Very pale straw with pale yellow highlights **Nose** Fresh, clean, quite delicately peated, a slight floral note and a touch of citrus/sherbet **Flavour** Clean, medium-dry, quite rich, fresh with a citrus character **Finish** Fresh, of quite good length with a slight coffee tang **Notes** Blackadder international bottling

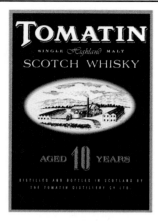

TOMATIN, INVERNESS-SHIRE EST. 1897

Founded by the Tomatin Spey District Distillery Co. Ltd. Extended from two to four stills in 1956, to six in 1958, to ten in 1961, to 11 in 1964 and finally to 23 in 1974.

LOCATION   Sited on the west of the A9 at the village of Tomatin, 12 miles south of Inverness. At 1,028 ft above sea level, it is one of Scotland's highest distilleries.

NOTES   The first Scottish distillery to be owned by a Japanese company, when purchased by the Takara and Okura Consortium following its then owner's liquidation in 1985. It has the potential for the greatest output (more than 12 million litres of alcohol) of all the malt distilleries. From the Gaelic, Tomatin means "the hill of the bushes".

WATER   Allt-na-Frithe (a local burn).

Age 10 years   **Strength** 43% abv

Sweetness 6   Peatiness 5   Availability 5

Colour Honey with straw/gold highlights **Nose** Light, slightly sweet, a little spirity, malty and leafy **Flavour** Light, sweet, malty and peaty with a hint of pepperiness **Finish** Smooth, slightly spicy and grapey **Notes** Tomatin Distillers bottling

Age 13 years   **Distillation** 1976   **Strength** 60.5% abv

Sweetness 6   Peatiness 5   Availability 1

Colour Pale amber with gold highlights **Nose** Medium weight with a hint of green hedgerows, fresh, light oak notes, medium-sweet with a light smokiness at the back **Flavour** Medium-sweet, clean, tangy and lightly smoky **Finish** Quite sweet and spicy with good length **Notes** Wm Cadenhead bottling

NEAR TOMINTOUL, BANFFSHIRE EST. 1964

A modern distillery, production began only in 1965 and it was not until 1972 that the make began to appear in bottle. Built by Tomintoul Distillery Ltd and bought by Scottish Universal Investment Trust (part of Lonrho) in 1973. Managed by Whyte & Mackay, which was itself bought from Lonrho by Brent Walker in February 1989 and subsequently sold to American Brands Inc. the following year. Doubled from two to four stills in 1974. Now managed by JBB (Greater Europe) plc.

LOCATION Situated in the valley of the River Avon on the B9136 off the A939 Grantown-on-Spey to Tomintoul road.

NOTES Tomintoul is the highest village in the Scottish Highlands, although the distillery itself, being outside the village, is not quite as high above sea level as Dalwhinnie. Tomintoul is regularly cut off by snow in winter.

WATER The Ballantruan Spring.

Age 12 years **Strength** 43% abv

Sweetness	7	Peatiness	3	Availability	4

Colour Peaty straw with gold highlights **Nose** Medium-sweet, rich and slightly spirity with vanilla and fruity, almost orangey, notes **Flavour** Medium-sweet, lightish, slightly peppery and with an oaky touch **Finish** A little spirity, although smooth and the oaky vanilla lingers **Notes** Whyte & Mackay bottling

Age 17 years **Strength** 43% abv

Sweetness	9	Peatiness	4	Availability	1

Colour Pale amber/straw with yellow highlights **Nose** Rich, sweet and nutty and delicately peated **Flavour** Sweet and rich with quite good body and a gentle peatiness **Finish** Clean, quite long and rich with a delicately smoky tail **Notes** Blackadder International bottling

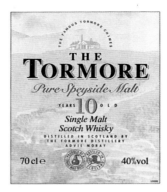

THE
TORMORE
Pure Speyside Malt

YEARS **10** OLD

Single Malt
Scotch Whisky

DISTILLED IN SCOTLAND BY
THE TORMORE DISTILLERY
ADVIE MORAY

70 cl e   40%vol

ADVIE, GRANTOWN-ON-SPEY, MORAY   EST. 1958

Built 1958-60 by Long John Distillers Ltd. Now part of Allied Domecq and operated by Allied Distillers Ltd. Doubled from four to eight stills in 1972.

LOCATION South of the A95 between Grantown-on-Spey and the Bridge of Avon.

NOTES The first new Highland malt distillery buildings to be constructed in the 20th century. The novelist (and former exciseman) Neil M. Gunn was invited by Lord Bracken to search for a suitable site for this new distillery. The expedition is described in "An Affair of Whisky", published in *New Saltire* (Dec. 1962). Glen Keith, established the previous year, used the buildings of a former mill. Tormore distillery and associated buildings are of a most striking design, the work of Professor Sir Albert Richardson, a past President of the Royal Academy.

WATER The Achvochkie Burn.

Age 10 years   **Strength** 40% abv

Sweetness 8   Peatiness 3   Availability 6

Colour Pale golden **Nose** Light and quite delicate with a strange dryness which is sometimes described as flintiness **Flavour** Slightly sweet, of medium weight and slightly spirity **Finish** Fine, distinguished and long **Notes** Caledonian Distillers bottling

TULLIBARDINE

Fine / Rare

Tullibardine

SMOOTH & MELLOW

**SINGLE
HIGHLAND MALT**
Rare Scotch Whisky

Tullibardine Distillery nestles at the foot of the Ochil Hills in Perthshire,
where the Highlands of Scotland begin.
These hills are renowned for the crystal purity
of their spring water. The Distillery draws its water from
the spring which originally fed the first
public brewery in Scotland during the 12th century.
Tullibardine Single Malt whisky has a smooth and mellow taste
with a fruity flavour.

BLACKFORD, PERTHSHIRE EST. 1949

There was a previous distillery of the same name near Blackford which was established in 1798, although its exact location is not known. The new distillery was the work of Delme Evans, who also designed Jura and Glenallachie. Owned by Invergordon Distillers since 1971, and Whyte & Mackay since 1993. Rebuilt 1973-74 and enlarged from two to four stills. Mothballed January 1995. Now managed by JBB (Greater Europe) plc.

LOCATION North of the new A9 on the south-western outskirts of the village of Blackford, four miles south of Auchterarder.

NOTES On the site of an ancient brewery, the distillery takes its name from the nearby Tullibardine Moor, home of Gleneagles Hotel and golf courses. This area has always been famed for its water: Highland Spring and Gleneagles mineral waters are both from Blackford. Tradition has it that the fair Queen Helen of Scotland was drowned at a ford on the Allan Water (the local river), hence the name Blackford.

WATER The Danny Burn.

Age 10 years   **Strength** 40% abv
Sweetness 3   Peatiness 6   Availability 5

Colour Straw with golden-green highlights **Nose** Quite full, soft, malty and earthy **Flavour** Quite dry and spicy with a richness and roundness, quite smooth **Finish** Peppery, warm and quite long with a slight bitterness at the end **Notes** Invergordon bottling

JAPAN

Matured Quality
100% MALT WHISKY
貯蔵 **15** 年
Floral & Velvety,
The masterpiece born of the
selected finest malts

JAPANESE MALT WHISKY DISTILLING   EST. 1924

The history of whisky distilling in Japan has very Scottish roots. In 1918, Settsu Shuzou, a spirit producer, made plans to start distilling whisky. Deciding that the best way to learn the art of distilling was to send a representative of the company to Scotland to study Scottish whisky production techniques, he sent Masataka Taketsuru, who also studied Applied Chemistry at Glasgow University. When he returned to Japan in 1921 (with a Scottish wife), he found the country was in the depths of a recession and Settsu could no longer finance the project. Kotobukiya (now Suntory) appointed him to develop a distillery for that company and the Yamazaki distillery in Osaka started production in 1924. Taketsuru managed Yamazaki until he left to establish his own company (Nikka), and distillery, at Hokkaido. Today there are seven major working distilleries in Japan, and at least two others, one of which, the Mars Whisky Shinshu Factory at Kamiina Nagano, produces a single malt, *Komagatake.* The success of Scotch Whisky in Japan and other world markets has encouraged Japanese drinks companies to produce Japanese whisky with the characteristics of Scotch.

Y A M A Z A K I   Built at the foot of Mt. Tennou near Osaka in 1923 by Shinjiro Torii, founder of Suntory. The water supply in this area is famed for its purity. There are 12 stills producing a wide range of styles of whisky; direct-fired gas heating is used, as is steam-heating. Owned by Suntory.

H O K K A I D O   Founded in 1934 close to the sea at the neck of the Shakotan peninsula by Masataka Taketsuru with one pot still - he could not afford a second. The second distillation was carried out in the one still which was washed out between distillations. Taketsuru felt that the humidity and water supply here were similar to Scotland and the buildings have a very Scottish appearance. There is a peat moor nearby and four of the six stills are direct-heated by coal.

K A R U I Z A W A   Built in 1955 by winemaker Daikoku Budoushu to the west of Karuizawa, Nagano, at the foot of Mt. Asama, an active volcano, in an area popular as a summer resort. The distillery has four stills and the warehouses are ivy-clad, which keeps summer temperatures down. Only Sherry casks are used for maturation. Bottles of "Karuizawa" malt contain 90% malt whisky from Karuizawa distillery and 10% malt whisky from another Mercian-owned distillery in Yamanashi. Owned and run by the Mercian Company.

S E N D A I   In order to produce different styles to those produced at Hokkaido, Nikka built a new distillery at Sendai, Miyagi in 1969. It has 8 stills, all of which are steam-heated. The distillery is located in a mountain area, between the Rivers Nikkawa and Hirose.

G O T E M B A   Founded in 1972 at Shizuoka by Kirin Seagram, a joint venture between the Kirin Beer Co. & Seagram. Its make is also only used for blending. Located in an ancient forest at the foot of Mt. Fiji, the buildings also house a grain distillery and blending and bottling plant.

HAKUSHU   Built, in 1973, by Suntory in a beautiful forest at Yamanashi at the southern end of the Japanese Alps, to the west of Mt. Fuji. Hakushu has 24 stills. Suntory has established a bird reserve which is open to the public. There is also a fascinating whisky museum on the site. Hakushu malt is used only for blending.

HAKUSHU HIGASHI   This second Hakushu distillery was built in 1981 to supplement the output of the original Hakushu, but with different styles. There are 12 gas-fired stills. Hakushu Higashi produces the bottled "Hakushu" malt.

JAPAN

KARUIZAWA
Age 15 years **Strength** 40% abv

Sweetness 6 Peatiness 7

Colour Mid-amber with old gold highlights **Nose** Quite full-bodied and medium-sweet with a touch of richness and an almost minty note, a slightly perfumed peaty character and a little touch of apple **Flavour** Medium-sweet and of good body with smooth vanilla and a dark, tarry peaty flavour **Finish** Long, smoky, elegant and complex **Notes** Mercian Co. bottling

Age 17 years **Strength** 40% abv

Sweetness 7 Peatiness 3

Colour Amber with bronze highlights. **Nose** Dark, nutty, medium-sweet, round and quite full-bodied with a smooth vanilla note, delicately peated. **Flavour** Medium-sweet, round, nutty and with good body and lightly peated **Finish** A lingering sweetness and very gently chewy with an ethereal smokiness on the end **Notes** Mercian Co. bottling

Age 13 years **Distillation** 1981 **Strength** 58% abv

Sweetness 3 Peatiness 7

Colour Quite a deep amber with bronze highlights **Nose** Full-bodied and medium-dry with a darkly peaty charcoal aroma and a hint of rubberised fabric **Flavour** Big-bodied and medium-dry with a dark, peaty smokiness, a good broad edge of richness and slightly chewy tannins **Finish** Very long, quite smooth and complex with notes of smoky liquorice and quite rich vanilla **Notes** A single malt from Karuizawa Distillery

MIYAGIKYO
Age 12 years **Strength** 43% abv

Sweetness 3 Peatiness 3

Colour Mid-amber with gold highlights **Nose** Of good body with a vegetal aroma, medium-dry, quite lean with a green touch and lightly peated **Flavour** Dry, good body, quite smooth with a bubble gum flavour **Finish** Long, clean, bubble gummy, gently peated **Notes** Nikka bottling from Sendai Distillery

YOICHI
Age 12 years **Strength** 43% abv

Sweetness 2 Peatiness 6

Colour Amber with gold highlights **Nose** Light, medium-dry, closed -giving very little- a slight greenness and a touch of dirty oak **Flavour** Dry, medium-bodied and quite oakily tannic with a smokily-toasted peaty character **Finish** Of reasonable length with a slight greenness and notes of tea **Notes** Nikka bottling

SHIRAKAWA

Age 27 years **Strength** 55% abv

Sweetness 6 Peatiness 4

Colour Amber with gold highlights **Nose** Full, quite round and medium-sweet, rich, malty and nutty with a hint of toffee **Flavour** Medium-sweet, quite full-bodied, rich with slightly chewy tannins and a good, quite creamy weight of peat at the back of the palate **Finish** Long, smooth and pleasantly smoky **Notes** Shirakawa distillery is owned by Takara Shuzou

YAMAZAKI

Age 10 years **Strength** 40% abv

Sweetness 7 Peatiness 3

Colour Pale amber with yellow highlights **Nose** Quite light with an appley, sweet vanilla-oaky nuttiness, medium-dry and delicately peated **Flavour** Medium-sweet, smooth, soft and delicately peated **Finish** Good length, quite delicate and smooth with a sweet oaky character **Notes** Suntory bottling

Age 12 years **Strength** 43% abv

Sweetness 2 Peatiness 5

Colour Pale amber with gold highlights **Nose** Medium-sweet, of medium weight with good richness, a touch of toffee and tablet with a hint of apples and rich liquorice **Flavour** Dry, of medium weight, medium peatiness and a tea character **Finish** Very dry, with really quite a tannic dryness, quite delicate, but short **Notes** Suntory bottling

Age 18 years **Strength** 43% abv

Sweetness 4 Peatiness 6

Colour Amber with old gold highlights **Nose** Medium-dry and rich with an almost riesling-like petrol aroma, good body and delicately peated **Flavour** Medium-dry and rich with good body and gentle, but firm, peat **Finish** Long and quite flavoursome with a touch of chewy tannin **Notes** Suntory bottling

HAKUSHU

Age 12 years **Strength** 43% abv

Sweetness 5 Peatiness 1

Colour Pale amber with yellow/gold highlights **Nose** Fresh, clean and medium-sweet with quite good body and a buttery shortbread aroma with a hint of liquorice, very lightly peated **Flavour** Medium-dry and fresh with good body, a touch of richness and a round maltiness **Finish** Long, medium-sweet and smooth with a slightly perfumed tail **Notes** A single malt from the Hakushu Higashi distillery

WILLOWBANK, DUNEDIN EST. 1968

The large number of Scots among the early settlers to New Zealand meant that a thriving distilling industry soon developed, only for it to be crushed by punitive duty rates in 1875. In 1968, Wilson's, a subsidiary of Seagram, opened a distillery on the site of the old Willowbank distillery in Dunedin. The distillery has only one pot still which is used for both stages of the distillation. The whisky produced is sold as Lammerlaw, taking its name from the hills, the Lammerlaw Ranges, from which the distillery's water supply, Deep Creek, runs through peat and moss.

LOCATION   At Dunedin on New Zealand's South Island.

NOTES   New Zealand has a strong historical link with Scotland, many of the original settlers having come from "God's own country". Dunedin (the Gaelic for Edinburgh) was one of the first landing points for these settlers in 1848. Not surprisingly, these early settlers brought their distillation methods with them.

WATER   Deep Creek.

Age 10 years **Strength** 43% abv

Sweetness 6 Peatiness 1 Availability 2

Colour Pale amber with gold highlights **Nose** Fresh, clean, medium-bodied and medium-dry with a hint of rich liquorice, a slightly green touch and a floral note **Flavour** Medium-sweet and smooth with good body, a touch of liquorice, very gentle smokiness and quite a lush texture **Finish** Long and clean with a note of fennel on the tail **Notes** A single malt from Wilson Distillers in New Zealand

THE BENNACHIE
Age 10 years   **Strength** 43% abv

Sweetness 6   Peatiness 5   Availability 2

Colour Mid amber with gold highlights. **Nose** Medium-bodied, quite delicately peated with a green edge and medium-dry with a slight hint of chewy toffee. **Flavour** Medium-sweet, with good body and flavours of creamy-smooth toffee vanilla, quite gently peated. **Finish** Long, medium-sweet and smooth with delicate peat on the tail. **Notes** A vatted malt from Bennachie Scotch Whisky Company Ltd.

BLACK RIBBON
Age No age statement   **Strength** 40% abv

Sweetness 7   Peatiness 7   Availability 0

Colour Mid-Amber with yellow and gold/green highlights **Nose** Medium-bodied, gently smoky with hints of apple and coffee and an edge of sweetness **Flavour** Quite full-bodied and round, smoky, oily smooth and medium-sweet, quite rich with hints of coffee and toffee and with a slight greenness at the end **Finish** Full with a hint of spice, a gentle greenness and a dark smokiness **Notes** A vatted malt, vatted in Scotland and bottled in Sweden by Vin & Sprit. Available only in Sweden

BLAIRMHOR
Age 8 years **Strength** 40% abv

Sweetness 4   Peatiness 7   Availability 3

Colour Pale amber with pale straw highlights **Nose** Clean with a full, dark, almost charred peatiness, full-bodied, almost dry and with a slight dark richness **Flavour** Medium-dry, round and smooth with a good firm dollop of smoky peatiness **Finish** Long and chewy with notes of smoke and vanilla **Notes** A vatted malt from R. Carmichael & Sons Ltd.

EILEANDOUR
Age 10 years **Strength** 40% abv

Sweetness 7 Peatiness 3 Availability 2

Colour Amber with gold highlights **Nose** Rich and medium-sweet with a honeyed toffee character, delicately peated and of good body **Flavour** Fresh, smooth, quite soft and medium-sweet with a delicate peatiness and of good weight **Finish** Long, rich, clean and quite elegant **Notes** A vatted malt from Isle of Arran Distillers

GLENCOE
Age 8 years **Strength** 57% abv

Sweetness 8 Peatiness 4 Availability 6

Colour Bright mid-amber with lemony gold highlights **Nose** Malty, spirity with an apple character, quite full-bodied, medium-dry with a touch of peat **Flavour** Medium-dry, round and smooth, appley with good body **Finish** Sweet and of good length **Notes** R N Macdonald bottling

OLD ELGIN
Age 8 years **Strength** 40% abv

Sweetness 7 Peatiness 6 Availability 4

Colour Mid-amber with gold highlights **Nose** Medium to full-bodied, medium-dry and smoky with a touch of greenness and dark, appley fruit **Flavour** Rich, medium-sweet, quite full-bodied and peppery, fresh, round and smooth **Finish** Fresh, medium-sweet and clean **Notes** Bottled by Gordon & MacPhail

POIT DHUBH

Age 12 years **Strength** 40% abv

Sweetness 6 Peatiness 4 Availability 4

Colour Amber with good yellow highlights **Nose** Medium-sweet, slightly green and quite rich **Flavour** Smooth with a touch of dryness, lightly peated and quite elegant, although light **Finish** Long, smoky and slightly perfumed **Notes** Bottled by Praban na Linne

POIT DHUBH GREEN LABEL

Age 12 years **Strength** 46% abv

Sweetness 7 Peatiness 7 Availability 3

Colour Light amber with gold highlights **Nose** Medium-bodied with good body, firm dark smokiness, a touch of liquorice, a slight rich green touch of citrus **Flavour** Quite full-bodied, medium-sweet and rich with a good backbone of peatiness **Finish** Long, smooth and smoky **Notes** Bottled without chill-filtration by Praban na Linne

POIT DHUBH
Age 21 years **Strength** 43% abv

Sweetness 5 Peatiness 4 Availability 3

Colour Mid-amber with old gold highlights **Nose** A rich, almost fruity note, medium-sweet, quite restrained and delicate, gently peated with a soft toffee/vanilla note **Flavour** Medium-dry and of good body with a nutty peatiness, slightly chewy and smooth with a soft vanilla flavour **Finish** Long, tangy and complex with a final elegance **Notes** An unchillfiltered vatted malt from Praban-na-Linne

PRIDE OF ISLAY
Age 12 years **Strength** 40% abv

Sweetness 1 Peatiness 10 Availability 4

Colour Mid-amber with yellowy gold highlights **Nose** Full-bodied and smoky with a rich, chocolatey nuttiness **Flavour** Big and smoky, quite pungent and bone dry with a slight edge of richness **Finish** Full, long and smoky with a slight tang of bitter chocolate **Notes** Bottled by Gordon & MacPhail

YEARS **12** OLD

PRIDE of the LOWLANDS
Malt
SCOTCH WHISKY

DISTILLED IN THE LOWLANDS

PRODUCED & BOTTLED IN SCOTLAND

70 cl **GORDON & MACPHAIL** ELGIN, SCOTLAND 40% vol

PRIDE OF THE LOWLANDS
Age 12 years **Strength** 40% abv

Sweetness 3 Peatiness 2 Availability 4

Colour Amber with yellowy gold highlights **Nose** Medium weight, fresh, oily-rich and medium-dry with a slight unripe grapey character **Flavour** Smooth and medium-dry with a touch of coffee and good richness; medium weight **Finish** Quite long and fresh with the tang of coffee on the tail **Notes** Bottled by Gordon & MacPhail

PRIDE OF ORKNEY
Age 12 years   **Strength** 40% abv

Sweetness 2 Peatiness 5 Availability 4

Colour Light to mid-amber with gold highlights **Nose** Quite light and rich with dried fruit characters and hints of honey **Flavour** Off-dry, smooth, lightly smoky and malty **Finish** Clean with a refreshing greenness **Notes** Bottled by Gordon & MacPhail

PRIDE OF STRATHSPEY
Age 12 years   **Strength** 40% abv

Sweetness 8 Peatiness 3 Availability 4

Colour Amber with gold highlights **Nose** Medium-sweet with a touch of creamy oiliness, rich oak and a hint of nuttiness **Flavour** Medium-sweet, quite full-bodied, smooth and round with a hazelnut character **Finish** Long and nutty with a dry edge and nice oaky tannins **Notes** Bottled by Gordon & MacPhail

SHEEP DIP
Age 8 years   **Strength** 40% abv

Sweetness 3 Peatiness 6 Availability 5

Colour Pale amber with good yellow highlights **Nose** Dry, softly peated and slightly green **Flavour** Dry, but with a nice richness, spicy, a good peatiness, round and medium-bodied **Finish** Of medium length and with a gentle smokiness **Notes** Sheep Dip is said to have become popular with farmers because invoices for "Sheep Dip" could easily be lost in their accounts if they kept a few sheep!

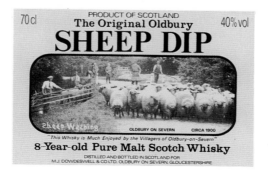

SPEYSIDE
Age 8 years **Strength** 40% abv
Sweetness 8 Peatiness 3 Availability 3

Colour Straw with good yellowy green highlights **Nose** Fresh, spirity, mealy and malty **Flavour** Sweet, smooth, round and soft **Finish** Malty, spicy and quite long **Notes** Bottled by the Speyside Distillery Company

TAMBOWIE
Age 8 years **Strength** 40% abv
Sweetness 8 Peatiness 3 Availability 2

Colour Mid-amber with gold highlights **Nose** Fresh and medium-dry with good body and touches of toffee and oaky vanilla **Flavour** Medium-sweet with a touch of richness, of good body and lightly peated with a smooth vanilla flavour **Finish** Long, clean and quite sweet **Notes** A vatted malt from the Vintage Malt Whisky Co. named after a distillery which used to exist in the Glasgow suburb of Bearsden

BLAIRFINDY

Age 20 years **Distillation** 1976 **Strength** 51.8% abv

Sweetness 8　Peatiness 4　Availability 2

Colour Amber with bright gold highlights **Nose** Full-bodied, medium-sweet and quite intensely hazelnutty with a slight green edge and a touch of coffee/toffee **Flavour** Big-bodied, rich, sweet and round with a smooth, unctuous toffee-like character and a gentle, green peatiness **Finish** Long, sweet, smooth and elegant **Notes** A single malt from Blackadder International

FINLAGGAN

Age 12 years　43% abv

Sweetness 2　Peatiness 8　Availability 2

Colour Pale amber with yellow/gold highlights **Nose** Quite dry, fresh and slightly perfumed with a burnt heather roots peatiness, good body with a little hint of ozone **Flavour** Almost dry and smoky with good body **Finish** Full, long and smoky with a fine edge of richness **Notes** A single Islay malt from the Vintage Malt Whisky Co. named after the ancient stronghold of the Lord of the Isles.

GLEN EASON

Age 10 years　**Strength** 40% abv

Sweetness 3　Peatiness 7　Availability 2

Colour Full amber with old gold highlights **Nose** Fresh and medium-dry with a slightly green edge to the almost sooty peatiness and with the cerealy aroma of a maltings floor **Flavour** Quite full-bodied, medium-dry, smooth and with a good, firm peatiness **Finish** Long and gently smoky with just a hint of sweetness on the end **Notes** A single malt from Isle of Arran Distillers

INDEPENDENT BOTTLINGS

MACPHAIL'S MALT
Age 10 years   **Strength** 40% abv

Sweetness 6   Peatiness 6   Availability 4

Colour Mid-amber with old gold highlights **Nose** Quite light, fresh, dark and smoky, medium-dry **Flavour** Medium-dry with good body, an earthy peatiness and a touch of spiciness **Finish** Fresh, quite smoky and long-lasting with a touch of oak **Notes** Single malt bottling under Gordon & MacPhail's own label

MACPHAIL'S 106
Age No age statement   **Strength** 60.5% abv

Sweetness 7   Peatiness 6   Availability 4

Colour Amber with old gold highlights **Nose** Quite full-bodied and medium-dry with a slight earthy peatiness, a rich lanolin note and a fresh greenness **Flavour** Full-bodied, medium-sweet, rich, round and smooth with a slight green peatiness, good body and gentle, chewy tannins **Finish** Long and complex with a nice, slightly green nuttiness and pleasantly chewy **Notes** Single malt under Gordon & MacPhail's own label

MAR LODGE
Age 12 years   **Strength** 43% abv

Sweetness 7   Peatiness 3   Availability 1

Colour Quite pale straw with amber highlights **Nose** Medium-bodied, floral with a leafiness and rich nuttiness and unctuous oily oak **Flavour** Medium-sweet, quite rich, round and smooth with good body **Finish** Quite lingering and pleasantly sweet **Notes** Bottled by Invergordon Distillers Ltd

LOCH INDAAL
Distillation 1983   **Strength** 43% abv

Sweetness 2   Peatiness 8   Availability 2

Colour Pale straw with bright yellow highlights **Nose** A light creamy peatiness and fresh with a slight mashy cereal character **Flavour** Smooth with a creamy smokiness, quite good body and almost dry **Finish** Long and gently earthily smoky **Notes** A single malt bottled by Blackadder International

THE OLD MAN OF HOY
Age No age statement **Strength** 43% abv

Sweetness 6 Peatiness 4 Availability 3

Colour Mid-amber with old gold highlights **Nose** Medium-bodied, malty and medium-sweet with a slight herbaceous character and a rich, honeyed edge **Flavour** Medium-bodied and quite fresh with a slightly rich greenness and a sweet edge **Finish** Long, medium-sweet and rich, a touch tangy with a slight nuttiness on the end **Notes** A single Orcadian malt

TANTALLAN
Age 10 years **Strength** 40% abv

Sweetness 7 Peatiness 6 Availability 2

Colour Very pale straw with pale lemon highlights **Nose** Fresh, clean and medium-dry with a gentle floral note and a slightly green peaty character **Flavour** Medium-sweet, big-bodied and powerful, round, smooth and clean with a slightly chewy peatiness **Finish** Long and clean with a green, spicy freshness **Notes** A single malt from the Vintage Malt Whisky Co.

VINTAGE SINGLE ISLAY MALT
Age No age statement   **Strength** 40% abv

Sweetness 1   Peatiness 9   Availability 1

Colour Quite deep amber with old gold highlights **Nose** Big-bodied, slightly pungent and dry with a charred smoky character and almost a perfumed note **Flavour** Dry, full-bodied, smooth and very smoky **Finish** Long and dry with a fragrant peatiness **Notes** A single Islay malt from the Vintage Malt Whisky Co.

OAK B RANDY CASK
Distillation 1970   **Strength** 40% abv

Sweetness 6   Peatiness 3   Availability 1

Colour Pale amber with yellow/gold highlights **Nose** Quite lightweight, medium-dry with a green fruity character, malty and spirity with a hint of acetone **Flavour** Medium-sweet with an oaky dryness, smooth and soft **Finish** Quite long with a cough linctus character and lightly smoky **Notes** A single Speyside malt matured in a brandy cask and bottled by Gordon & MacPhail

OAK BRANDY CASK
Distillation 1963   **Strength** 40% abv

Sweetness 5   Peatiness 3   Availability 1

Colour Amber with gold highlights **Nose** Medium-sweet and medium-bodied with a hint of smokiness and a rich, honeyed character **Flavour** Medium-dry, soft, quite light and fresh with a touch of richness **Finish** Quite long with a dry finish and a touch of honey on the tail **Notes** A single Speyside malt matured in a brandy cask and bottled by Gordon & MacPhail

OAK PORT CASK
Distillation 1970   **Strength** 40% abv

Sweetness 5   Peatiness 5   Availability 1

Colour Amber with gold highlights **Nose** Medium-sweet, quite rich with a ripe Christmas cake fruitiness and a slight touch of perfume on the tail **Flavour** Medium-dry and quite round with a demerara sugar character, lightly smoky, dark and nutty **Finish** Long, quite dry and chewy **Notes** A single Speyside malt matured in a port cask. Bottled by Gordon & MacPhail in 1993